The Vanishing Jungle

by the same author

PORTRAIT OF A WILDERNESS
PORTRAIT OF A RIVER
PORTRAIT OF A DESERT
THE HAWFINCH

A FIELD GUIDE TO THE BIRDS OF BRITAIN AND EUROPE
with Roger Peterson and P. A. D. Hollom

Guy Mountfort

THE VANISHING JUNGLE

THE STORY OF THE WORLD WILDLIFE FUND
EXPEDITIONS TO PAKISTAN

Illustrated by
ERIC HOSKING

Foreword by
H.R.H. THE PRINCE OF THE NETHERLANDS,
G.C.B., G.C.V.O., G.B.E.

Collins
ST JAMES'S PLACE LONDON 1969

To our friends and collaborators in Pakistan
whose concern for their
country's rich natural heritage
was our constant inspiration

Contents

Illustrations

Line illustrations by Penelope Gillespie

Foreword

By H.R.H. The Prince of the Netherlands, G.C.B., G.C.V.O., G.B.E.

Those who travel in Asia to-day cannot fail to be impressed by the evidence of the destructive impact of man's technology on his environment. In the struggle to keep pace with the ever increasing need for more and more agricultural land, greater yields per acre and more hydroelectrical development, not only is the face of the continent changing, but in many countries the whole complex of interrelated communities of natural vegetation and wildlife is threatened.

With every year that passes, man's capacity to master his biosphere increases. His earth-moving and forest-destroying machinery grow steadily larger and more powerful and his industrial effluents more widely destructive. Though few of us are yet willing to admit it, man himself is now an increasingly threatened species, caught between the millstones of over-population and the self-imposed debasement of the quality of human life. The brilliance of his technology has confused his priorities and blinded his ability to plan his future by scientific appraisal of his unbridled powers over his surroundings.

In the western world, where so little now remains unchanged by man, we have become accustomed to these problems, because we have grown up with them. The scale of their impact on the vast green wilderness of Asia is as yet much smaller. Nevertheless, powerfully stimulated by technical and financial aid from more highly developed areas, the Asian scene is changing with dramatic speed and with the same disastrous results. Already one sees the same pitiful consequences of the massive misuse of arsenical, DDT and organo-phosphorus chemicals to control agricultural pests; the same replacement of rich natural forests by sterile monocultures of commercial trees; the same inevitable disappearance of wildlife; and the same creation of new social problems by the loss of recreational areas to make way for the expansion of over-crowded cities.

In *The Vanishing Jungle* Guy Mountfort portrays vividly what has happened to the once abundant wildlife of Pakistan and provides the first authoritative account of its present status. He also gives a lavishly documented example of the kind of work in which the World Wildlife Fund is engaged in its struggle to save endangered animals and their habitats from extermination. Eric Hosking's superb photographs add greatly to the value of the book. Those who support the World Wildlife Fund and thereby enable it to introduce effective conservation, such as is now flourishing in Pakistan as a result of the efforts of Guy Mountfort and his colleagues, will share the sense of solid achievement which this volume provides.

The author analyses the consequences of man's recent influence on nature throughout the varied habitats of Pakistan, from the high western Himalayas to the tropical jungles of the Chittagong Hill Tracts. It is a fascinating if sometimes depressing story. It has, however, a happy ending. The recommendations arising from the two exploratory expeditions, which Guy Mountfort led at the invitation of President Ayub Khan, produced far-reaching results. Not least of these was the establishment of two important national parks and a number of wildlife reserves. New legislation has been introduced to protect endangered animal species and model programmes of conservation and public education launched. There is now good prospect that many of the animals which had been brought to the verge of extinction in Pakistan will be saved. These vigorous measures being taken by the Central Government are of much more than local importance and fully deserve our applause.

As one of the International Trustees of the World Wildlife Fund, Guy Mountfort played a leading part in saving the Coto Doñana in Southern Spain and later in creating the Azraq Desert National Park in Jordan. By their work in Pakistan he and the members of his expeditions have now made another notable contribution to the cause of conservation, in a particularly vulnerable area.

The Prince of the Netherlands,
President of the World Wildlife Fund.

Author's Preface

Pakistan, a nation of 126 million people, is surprisingly little known in the western hemisphere and at present it enjoys only a negligible share of the world's tourist trade. Yet its places of historic interest and its archæological treasures are legion and facilities for seeing them at least as good as in most other countries. Moreover, its scenery is spectacular and within its boundaries are some of the largest and most beautiful mountains, rivers, deserts and forests in the world. All this deserves to be better known; but to anyone even mildly interested in wildlife, the claims of Pakistan for priority are overwhelming.

Because of its unique geography, straddling the wings of a subcontinent, the two halves of the country embrace a quite extraordinary range of climates and vegetation, from the sub-tropical dry regions and thorn forests of West Pakistan, to the high tropical evergreen and deciduous forests and tidal jungles of East Pakistan. Its mammals, reptiles and plants are bewildering in their infinite variety. Of birds alone it has nearly one thousand different species. These are essentially birds of the Oriental tropics, with a heavy influx of seasonal migrants. The great majority of the endemic species have Indo-Chinese affinities, followed in equal parts by smaller numbers from the Palaearctic and Ethiopian zoogeographical regions.

At the time of my first acquaintance with the country, some twenty-five years ago, the numbers as well as the variety of animals were everywhere impressive. The Sind Desert teemed with Chinkara Gazelles and Blackbuck and with various bustards and sandgrouse. Crocodiles, storks and pelicans could always be seen along the banks of the great rivers. There were flocks of several kinds of big-horned mountain sheep and goats in all the major ranges. Elephants, tigers, four or five smaller species of cats and many deer were plentiful in the vast jungles of Sylhet and the Chittagong Hill Tracts. The whole of what is now called Pakistan was, in fact, a naturalist's paradise.

Since that time, as in every other country, the wildlife and wilderness areas have suffered severe losses. Virgin forests are disappearing; swamps have been drained and rivers dammed; agriculture, roads, railways, airports and new towns have gobbled up thousands of square miles of countryside; and the hunting, trapping and poisoning of wild animals have increased beyond all reckoning.

The exact extent of the losses was unknown, but by 1965 there was widespread uneasiness, particularly among sportsmen in Pakistan, that game animals including birds were increasingly difficult to find. The World Wildlife Fund and its technical advisers, the International Union for the Conservation of Nature, were becoming desperate for information; but at that time no appropriate scientific body or wildlife society existed in Pakistan to provide it. Although many books had been written about the wildlife of India up to the time of the Second World War, these were now badly out of date so far as the status of species was concerned. No post-war study had been made in Pakistan and no books devoted to the wildlife of that country yet existed, apart from a few dealing broadly with the whole subcontinent. It was at this point that my expeditions were planned, with the object of establishing the facts.

The credit for the idea that my team should be invited to Pakistan is due to Naser-ud-Deen Khan and Christopher Savage, to both of whom I am greatly indebted. The former is a prominent industrialist who has a deep concern for the wildlife of his country. Christopher Savage represents the International Wildfowl Research Bureau and the International Council for Bird Preservation in Pakistan. I had known him long before he took up an engineering appointment in that country, where in his spare time he quickly became the leading authority on the ducks and geese of the subcontinent.

The studies of the wildlife problems of Jordan, which had been made by my team in 1963 and 1965, had aroused considerable interest in other countries, including Pakistan. When King Hussein made his now famous broadcast announcing the creation of the Azraq Desert National Park and other conservation measures which we had recommended, this lent support to the notion that we should be invited to conduct similar studies in Pakistan. The proposal was immediately endorsed by the International Trustees of the World Wildlife Fund.

Two expeditions were made, in 1966 and 1967. They were respectively the eighth and ninth we had organised for similar purposes and they were certainly the most ambitious. Apart from the journey to Pakistan, they involved a total of some 15,000 miles of travel, chiefly in very wild country. In the course of these explorations we compiled notes on 99 different mammal species, 423 species of birds and 45 species of reptiles. In addition to assessing the status of wildlife and habitats, we had to ascertain the reasons why populations had declined and how best to protect and if possible restore what remained. This required studies of the direct and indirect influences of human activities and of the country's overall plans for land use in relation to agriculture, commercial forestry and other factors affecting the survival of wildlife. We then had to plan a programme of conservation for a country which hitherto had been interested in animals chiefly in terms of hunting, and in land and forests mainly in terms of agriculture and commercial values. We were not, of course, concerned merely with saving endangered animal species from extinction. Conservation, in its modern sense, means the application of wise principles of co-existence between man and nature; it also means planning for the maintenance of the quality of the human environment.

Our tasks could not have been accomplished had it not been for the personal interest of President Ayub Khan in our work. Under his direction every facility we needed was provided and we had the great benefit of discussing our progress with him during both expeditions. He encouraged us to be bold in our recommendations and indeed half measures would have been useless in the face of the problems which had to be solved.

We found that the losses of wildlife and primary vegetation were much greater than had been feared. Some animal species had disappeared altogether and many others were nearing extinction. In West Pakistan the spread of villages into the semi-desert and savannah areas, followed by over-grazing by large flocks of goats and camels, had destroyed the biological capital of huge tracts of land. In East Pakistan the jungles were rapidly being cleared for conversion to commercial plantations or agriculture. Even areas ostensibly reserved for wildlife were in some instances being whittled away by tree plantations, shifting cultivation on a slash-and-burn basis, or by flooding for hydro-electric schemes. Other reserves were subjected to constant poaching and none was staffed by men trained in the management of wildlife. Illicit hunting was on a massive scale, especially in the mountainous areas. A thriving export in the skins of wild animals, and particularly of all the cats and crocodilians, had caused gigantic losses.

The recommendations which we made to the Central Government were far-reaching. They included the formation of a Government Committee to deal with wildlife problems, changes in the administrative structure affecting conservation, a ban on the export of skins of wild animals, changes in the hunting regulations, the introduction of training in wildlife management at certain universities, and the creation of two large national parks and eight wildlife reserves in the most critical areas.

Our proposals were accepted with an extraordinary degree of goodwill by everyone concerned and I must here pay high tribute to the spirit of complete co-operation with which they were discussed. It was, I think, generally recognised from our reports that a situation approaching crisis proportions had arisen, not by neglect so much as by the lack of the specialised knowledge which the conservation of wildlife demands. Once in possession of the facts, action was immediately taken. To-day the rich natural heritage of Pakistan is on the road to survival and the Government fully deserves the added lustre which this will bring to its prestige at home and abroad.

Two aspects of this book call for explanation. A critic,

reviewing one of my books about an earlier expedition, com-
plained that I had neglected the description of personalities
and the personal adventures involved in our work. Another remarked that my description of the wildlife of the country was
biased towards birds. Taking the first point, my belief is that
readers are more interested in the country and its wildlife than
in the individuals studying them, or in their occasional hardships. Nevertheless, in giving my own impressions of our travels
I fear I inevitably do less than justice to the very big part played
by my colleagues. I must therefore make it clear at the outset
that the successful outcome of our work was entirely dependent
on their individual skills. As to the second criticism, there is a
practical reason why birds, as distinct from other animals,
receive so much attention and this also explains the numerical
superiority of ornithologists in the composition of my team. On
previous expeditions we had developed a technique of using
birds as 'ecological indicators.' Birds are the most easily observed form of wildlife. With experience it is possible broadly to
categorise the type of country and vegetation through which
one is passing by the species of birds which are seen. For a study
group as essentially mobile as ours, this proved to be a very
useful and speedy guide to the classification of habitats. However, I have tried to avoid technicalities of this kind in the
narrative.

The number of people who helped us in Pakistan was so
great that it is unfortunately impossible to name them all here.
Some of them are mentioned in the book. I must, however,
express our thanks to those to whom we were most particularly
indebted. Air Marshal Asghar Khan, then Chief Administrator
of Civil Aviation and Tourism, comes first to mind. His close

personal interest in our work, his invaluable guidance in dealing with Government matters and his generosity in providing everything we needed, were an inspiration to all of us. We are deeply indebted to Air Commodore B. K. Dass, who bore the brunt of the detailed planning in Pakistan for both expeditions and treated all our problems with the utmost kindness. Equal thanks are due to the dynamic Mr Masud Mahmood, at that time Director General of the Department of Tourism, whose passion for efficiency resulted in flawless arrangements being made for us to explore even the remotest regions of Pakistan. We were indebted to His Highness the Amir of Bahawalpur and the late Nawab of Kalabagh for entertaining us regally at their palaces, and to Mr S. H. Haidar, Commissioner of the Bahawalpur Division, for arranging a special exhibition of the crafts of Cholistan in our honour. We also thank Lieutenant-General J. H. Marden and Colonel Angus Hume for joining us in the field and giving us the benefit of their extensive knowledge of the wildlife of their regions.

By arrangement with the Central Government, we had the pleasure of being accompanied on both expeditions by Mr M. S. U. Siddiqi, Director of the Department of Zoological Survey. As a professional zoologist and as an interpreter of the customs and natural history of his country he rendered valuable service to us all. Dr Rahman Beg, of the Institute of Forests at Peshawar, and Mr Z. B. Mirza, Curator of the Natural History Museum at Lahore, each spent a week with us during the second expedition, the former while we were at Gilgit and the latter in the Indus Delta. Their help in these areas was greatly appreciated and we enjoyed their company. I must also pay a special tribute to Mr G. M. M. E. Karim, Deputy Director of the Department of Tourism, who was attached full time to both expeditions. He cheerfully submitted to our arduous routine and often worked far into the night to keep us supplied with food, guides, transportation and the hundred and one other things we needed. Without his help and that of his assistant Hemayat-ud-Din Khan much valuable time would have been lost.

The Department of Forests and its District Officers, who now play the leading role in the new conservation programme, gave us unstinted assistance in all regions. We particularly thank Mr Amir Ahmed Khan, Secretary of Agriculture, Mr M. I. R. Khan, Director of the Institute of Forests, and Mr Nooruddin Ahmad, Chief Conservator of Forests in East Pakistan, for their very generous co-operation.

Six members of our team were from England, taking part for varying periods in one or both expeditions. These were Eric Hosking, George Shannon, Dr Duncan Poore, Lord Fermoy, James Hancock and John Buxton. From Pakistan we recruited Christopher Savage, Tom Roberts and Jerry Wood-Anderson. All are outstanding naturalists, specialising in one or several of the tasks in which we were involved. This book can give little impression either of the extent or of the value of the contributions each of them made. I fear that at times the demands I made of them were outrageous and I want to express my thanks and unbounded admiration for their enthusiasm.

I am especially indebted to Eric Hosking, who, as on all our previous expeditions, directed our photographic work. Modern field studies depend heavily on photography as an essential supporting element to observation. All of us carried cameras and

Eric helped us with unfailing generosity. His skill is so well known that it scarcely needs elaboration. The examples of his work in this book, selected from the thousands of pictures he took in Pakistan, show the wide range of his expertise. Whether he is making a snapshot of a running deer at twilight, or the portrait of a flying bird at high noon, the unmistakable stamp of the Hosking quality is apparent. His contribution did not end with the expeditions; for three months after we returned he was hard at work in his darkroom processing our films.

Nowadays many people are interested in the technicalities of photography. I therefore asked Eric Hosking to write a brief description of the photographic problems we found in Pakistan and of the equipment we used, so that readers wishing to try their hands at taking pictures of wildlife in that country may benefit from our experience. These notes will be found at Appendix 'D.'

George Shannon, too, had been a vital member of all our previous expeditions. In Pakistan he served a triple role as cinematographer, ornithologist and medical officer. He has an ability, rare among wildlife photographers, to study and record the behaviour of his subject while at the same time concentrating on the technicalities of filming. He and John Buxton produced between them a fascinating documentary film, with superb sound recordings of the wildlife by Edmund Fermoy.

The part played by Duncan Poore also deserves special acknowledgment. Both during and after the expeditions he gave me the full benefit of his wisdom and experience as Director General of the Nature Conservancy in preparing our recommendations to the Pakistan Government. We also depended heavily on him as our vegetation ecologist.

Jimmy Hancock and Jerry Wood-Anderson took part in the first expedition, the former as an ornithologist who already had wide experience in Asia, the latter, who lives in Pakistan, providing a wealth of knowledge of the local mammals and reptiles.

Both Christopher Savage and Tom Roberts were deeply involved in planning the expeditions. In spite of their business responsibilities they found time to make prodigious contributions to our work in the field. Tom is one of the best all-round naturalists I have ever known and Christopher's special knowledge of wildfowl and wetlands ecology was essential to our work. I gratefully acknowledge the constructive help they both gave me in reading the manuscript of this book.

Last but by no means least I thank my wife, who not only patiently put up with being left to face the worst of two English winters while I was enjoying the sunshine in Pakistan, but assisted me greatly with the typing, editing and proof-reading of this book.

The cost of our travel, food and accommodation during the expeditions was borne by the Government of Pakistan. Grants towards the remaining expenses of both expeditions were made through the World Wildlife Fund by the Volkart Brothers Foundation, the Smithsonian Institution, Burmah Shell Ltd., and a generous donor who wishes to remain anonymous. The cost of making the film of the expeditions was the subject of a grant from Anglia Television Ltd. I acknowledge this financial assistance with gratitude.

GUY MOUNTFORT

Plovers Meadow,
Blackboys,
Sussex.

I

The First Expedition

We landed at Karachi, the federal capital of Pakistan, just after
midnight on 21 October. There were five of us—Duncan Poore,
Eric Hosking, George Shannon, Jimmy Hancock and myself.
On the tarmac we were greeted by Christopher Savage and our
Pakistani hosts, led by Mr Karim and Mr Siddiqi. It was a hot,
clear night and in spite of the late hour the thermometer at the
airport still registered 85°F.

When we presently entered the brightly illuminated city I
was struck by the contrast with my last visit, which had been in
1944 when I was on my way to join the 12th Army in Burma. My
recollection was of ill-paved streets lined with a jumble of ram-
shackle, open-fronted shops. The air had been heavy with a
mixture of yellow dust blown off the Sind Desert and the
inescapable odour of the East—a sickly brew of spices, sweat and
cow dung. There had been little traffic in the streets apart from
military vehicles, the inevitable *tongas* pulled by half-starved
horses and a few creaking wagons being drawn at snail's pace
from the docks by camels. Karachi was now a flourishing
modern metropolis, with wide boulevards, blazing neon lights
and as much automobile traffic as could be found in any
western city of comparable size. The hordes of crippled beggars
had disappeared and the only smells were exhaust fumes and

the heady scent of the flowering frangipani trees in the residential areas. The ultra-modern hotel to which we were driven scarcely conformed to the Spartan standards we normally maintained on our expeditions; our hosts, however, seemed determined to pamper us and we all slept soundly.

One thing at least had not changed. When I awoke next morning, the first sound I heard was the long, peevish squealing of a Black Kite. My balcony gave a wide view over the city and on almost every roof-top sat the familiar scavenger of the East. Locally called the Pariah Kite, this bird acts as an efficient disposer of all street refuse and as such enjoys a considerable measure of public esteem. An immensely successful species, it has a range extending throughout most of Europe, Africa and Asia to Japan and the northern half of Australia. Though now able to find food only in the docks and refuse dumps of modern Karachi, the Black Kites continue to nest on the roof tops (plate 2b).

Our first study area was to be Cholistan, in the Bahawalpur Division. An aircraft had been put at our disposal and we were soon flying high over the featureless Sind Desert, on the first leg of our explorations. We were to land at Multan airfield, about sixty miles from the town of Bahawalpur, which lies on the left bank of the Sutlej River 450 miles from Karachi. Everyone was eager to begin serious work.

Looking down on the desert, I reflected that the huge basin of the Indus and its tributaries had once been fertile land cradling one of the earliest civilisations in the world. Here, it was once believed, had lived the 'godless, lawless and noseless barbarians of hostile speech, who inhabited fortified cities and possessed herds of cattle.' This description of the original inhabitants of

Pakistan had been emphatically disproved in the 1920s by the excavation of the ancient cities of Moenjodaro and Harappa. The ruins of Moenjodaro lay somewhere in the dusty haze to our left, on the bank of the Indus. Harappa was far to the north-east on a tributary, the Ravi River. Archæologists had now discovered that the civilisation of these two Bronze Age cities had been far from primitive: it had possessed a high standard of art and craftsmanship. Although its pictographic alphabet has not yet been deciphered, it is clear that by 2250 BC, long before the Indo-Aryans arrived in the Indus Valley, the Harappa Civilisation, as it is called, was already flourishing. Agriculture was its mainstay and trade with Iran and Mesopotamia was carried out by barter. The cities, which have been well preserved by the hot, dry climate, were constructed of burnt brick, with an elaborate system of brick-lined drains. The architecture was modest but practical, the houses being solidly constructed and well equipped with baths. The seals, painted pottery and figurines of the period, which depict local animals such as the Two-horned Rhinoceros, Indian Elephant and Tiger, provide clear evidence that the climate of the Indus Valley at that time must have been moist, with plentiful vegetation, or these animals could not have survived.

It is not known what brought this interesting civilisation to an end around 1800 BC. The total absence of warlike weapons in the excavations, which were otherwise rich in artefacts, suggests that neighbouring tribes may have been tempted to sack the defenceless cities; or perhaps the gradual change to an arid climate was the downfall of a peaceable people dependent on agriculture. Meanwhile, the glories of Moenjodaro and Harappa certainly deserve to be embraced in the National

Parks system which we hoped to see established in Pakistan. In Jordan, our inclusion of Petra and the Crusader castles within the National Parks which we had helped to create had been extremely valuable in attracting tourists and in no way interfered with the conservation of wildlife, which had been our primary objective.

When in 326 BC Alexander the Great bridged the Indus and marched through the area now known as Cholistan, it is believed to have been a still fairly fertile region. In those days the now dry Saraswati and Ghaggar rivers may still have contained water, though the fate of Cholistan had already been sealed as early as the last interglacial period, when the gradual transition from a cool, moist climate to a hot and arid one is thought to have begun. Certainly it was not until about AD 1000 that real desert conditions prevailed and the small remnant human population was forced by the desiccation of the land to adopt a nomadic existence. Since then the steady encroachment of sand carried by the prevailing monsoon winds from south to north has destroyed more and more of the remaining vegetation, blocked the rivers and covered huge areas of once fertile soil. Bad agricultural practices during the last century and particularly the destruction of indigenous trees to make way for crops, has accelerated the incursion of sand from the banks of the Indus. Much of the present devastation of the land appears to be due to over-grazing and burning, which, combined with earlier malpractices and faulty irrigation, have led to the formation of surface salts and extensive hardpans. Over-drainage, rather than irrigation, has totally destroyed soil productivity in many regions.

To-day the climate of Cholistan is atrocious for most of the year; the annual rainfall, which occurs spasmodically from mid-June to September, varies from 3.7 inches to an infrequent maximum of 7 inches. Daily maximum temperatures during the hot period from April to June vary from 109° to 125°F and suffocatingly hot winds and dust storms sometimes blow for weeks on end. Most of the land is at sea level and there is a desperate scarcity of water, as the monsoon clouds usually pass over the region without letting rain fall. The little water which is available below ground lies anything up to 300 feet deep. A scattering of wells and rain-water pools, known locally as *tobas*, sustains the population for part of the year; but when these have dried out and the grazing is exhausted, the people are forced to drive their cattle, camels, sheep and goats to the richly fertile irrigated land in the north of the Bahawalpur Division. To the east and south lie the inhospitable Indian deserts of Bikanir and Jaissalmir; to the north-west is the great Hakra Depression.

Although so great a part of Cholistan's 13,000 square miles now consists of arid sand dunes and concrete-hard clay flats, there is a network of abandoned canals running through potentially good soils which, if fed with surplus water from the Sutlej River, could bring agricultural prosperity to the land. This has been done with great success by the Sutlej Valley Project farther north. One day this dream will come true and the patient Rajput and Jat peasants of Cholistan, who endure their hardships with typical Muslim resignation, will cease their thousand years of nomadic wanderings.

Any region as large as Cholistan, inhabited by only three persons per square mile, is interesting to naturalists who are accustomed to England's population density of 865 per square mile. A low pressure of human enterprise on the land usually means that the local wildlife has a fair chance of survival. I could remember flying low over the Cholistan desert during the Second World War and seeing large herds of Blackbuck and Chinkara Gazelle, to say nothing of the dense flocks of sand-grouse which took off to right and left of the aircraft. The list of desert creatures inhabiting the country was an impressively long and varied one. As I ate the sandwich lunch which our thoughtful hosts had provided, I felt impatient to reach our destination and learn what Cholistan had in store for us now.

We were met at Multan by Lieutenant-General J. H. Marden, a close friend of the Amir of Bahawalpur at whose palace we were later to be guests.

Christopher Savage had already told us something of the history of the remarkable soldier who greeted us. He looked no more than middle-aged, though he had long since passed his seventieth birthday. After a distinguished career in the Indian Army, during which time he was three times wounded in action, he had stayed on through the worst horrors of the bloody holocaust which accompanied Partition, playing a leading part in the eventual restoration of law and order in the Bahawalpur region. Now fully occupied as administrator of the Amir's estates, he continued to extract the maximum out of life, which had recently included riding forty miles on a camel in a single day. A brisk gallop every morning before breakfast, a full day's work and six sets of tennis twice a week was his recipe for keeping fit. Rarely have I seen a man who so obviously thrived on it.

We had to call first on the Commissioner of Bahawalpur Division. As we drove through the dusty countryside the

General talked about the economic and political problems of Pakistan. The transition from British rule and the power of the native princes to the new order had taken place over such a relatively short period that the difficulties had been almost insurmountable. Yet throughout the tumultuous years of change the civil administration had continued to function and equilibrium had eventually been regained. The bitter struggles which had surrounded the birth of the nation were gradually receding into history. Meanwhile, the economic problems, the demands of a rapidly expanding population and anxieties over the intentions of neighbouring States tended to distract attention from the solid achievements of the new Republic. These were undeniable, though seldom publicised abroad.

When the Land-Rovers entered the drive of the Commissioner's residence I was quite unprepared for what awaited us. I stepped out to the accompaniment of loud trumpeting by two magnificently decorated elephants which had been made by their *mahouts* to kneel and sound this shrill greeting. A small boy in tribal garb then advanced and hung around our necks the traditional garlands of greeting, gaudy affairs of shiny sequins and tinsel with colourful medallions which hung almost to our knees. Thus decorated, we advanced down a red carpet to meet the Commissioner, Mr S. H. Haidar and his wife, who led us to a beflagged marquee. At the entrance we were showered with pink rose petals by a group of bearded and turbanned retainers.

Inside the tent was an exhibition of the crafts of Cholistan, which the Commissioner had arranged for our benefit. Here, neatly identified, were colourful rugs, embroidery, richly decorated camel harness and samples of the local wool and cotton for which Cholistan is famous. We were offered a local delicacy known as *makri*, which turned out to be roasted locusts, and *kohi*, the native Cholistan bread, which was excellent.

Along one side of the tent was a row of trestle tables, on which were exhibited in large glass jars about a dozen different live snakes and lizards of the region. We were seriously informed that one of the lizards, the brightly marked but completely inoffensive Leopard Gecko, was so deadly that not only its bite but its breath could kill a man instantly. When Eric Hosking presently insisted on photographing the little creature in the hand, the expressions on the faces of the bystanders was one of undisguised consternation (plate 3*a*).

In a land where fatalities from snake-bites are commonplace, it is understandable that superstition about the powers of reptiles should persist. These were reflected in picturesque manner in a typed leaflet which had been prepared for us. Unfortunately, the snakes and lizards were identified only by their native names and we were not yet sufficiently familiar with many of them to establish their scientific identities. Some of them probably referred to the different colour phases of the Cobra, each of which was locally regarded as a distinct species.

The *khanni* lizard, we were informed, does not reproduce its kind by copulation, but is born of a snake. Another lizard, the *gilai*, if seen by a woman at the churn, will cause the quantity of butter to increase. The *wains* snake, on the other hand, steals milk by climbing up a buffalo's leg and sucking its udder (a custom once attributed in England to the Nightjar, or Goat-sucker, as it used to be called). The deadly *ghor-dang* is a snake which moves so swiftly that it can chase and bite a galloping horse; while the *kulsar* has the power of conveying its poison to its human assailant merely by biting his stick, which instantly disintegrates. Perhaps the most elaborate legend concerned the *sah-pivna*. This snake, according to the leaflet, never bites in daylight, even when handled; at night, however, it 'crawls in a sleeper's breast and kills him with its breath, striking him with its tail before making off.' As an additional refinement it 're- moves all sticks from the bedside, lest its victim awakens and pursues it.' The *damuken* was described as 'a snake with a head at each end.' This evidently referred either to the Sand Boa, or to one of the harmless skinks, or legless lizards, which have heads, bodies and tails of equal thickness and contour. To the casual observer, one end looks much the same as the other.

Fortified by this local folk-lore, we emerged to the still sunlit lawn, where a snake charmer squatted by a jar containing a large Black Cobra. Removing the lid, he began to swing a piece of white cloth back and forth. The snake reared up, with hood expanded, intent on the moving cloth, at which it struck from time to time (plate 3*b*). There was none of the customary musical accompaniment which is supposed to soothe the cobra. When the performance was over, a similarly large Krait was produced and 'charmed.' This is one of the deadliest snakes in Asia. Whether the poison fangs had been removed, or the venom had just been milked from the snakes, I did not learn, but the spectacle was impressive.

We were then invited to inspect a full-grown Caracal, a tawny, lynx-like carnivore which, though scarce, is still fairly widely distributed in Baluchistan and the Thar Desert region (plate 20). It snarled and spat at us malevolently from its cage and I wished so fine an animal had not been trapped. Next to it, also caged, was a sad-looking blue-grey Nilgai. These are rather strangely proportioned animals closely related to the true antelopes. They are as large as a horse, high at the withers and low at the rump (page 31). In spite of their size they can run extremely fast in rough country. Their heads are relatively small, with very short but sturdy horns. The bulls are dark blue-grey (hence the synonym 'Blue Bull') and the cows tawny. Both sexes have short, bristly manes and strikingly marked black and white hocks. The adult bull has a prominent tuft of black hair below a white throat-patch. The superficial resemblance of the Nilgai to domestic cattle has been its salvation in India, where it is usually regarded as sacred; but even in Pakistan few sportsmen now consider it to be a game animal. Indeed it is so ungainly that it does not *look* worth hunting. Its undoing in Pakistan was its fondness for foraging in cultivated areas and it has now become rare in a wild state.

Beside the Nilgai's cage was a pair of dainty Chinkara Gazelles (plate 11), which eyed us timidly, nostrils quivering and needle-fine legs braced. The final exhibit was a splendid specimen of a male Blackbuck, which, judging by the way it charged the bars of its cage, had not been in captivity for long. Once a familiar sight in the deserts of West Pakistan, the beautifully proportioned, spiral-horned Blackbuck has suffered a relentless persecution which has brought it very near to extinction (page 95). It is already rare in India. Probably the best chance of survival for the species lies in the huge herds which roam the prairies of Texas, where a few introduced Blackbuck have now multiplied to at least 5,000.

It was already dusk when the final and most colourful spectacle was presented. Six of the famous dancing camels of Cholistan were ridden on to the lawn. For elegance and sleek grooming they far outclassed the finest animals we had seen in

Arabia. To the accompaniment of drums and bagpipes and with their riders sitting behind their humps instead of in front, they slow-marched, danced, trotted and pirouetted in perfect time with the music. As a demonstration of dressage by animals justly famed for vile and intractable tempers it was very impressive; it would have brought the house down at any Royal Tournament (page 167).

The Commissioner responded to our enthusiasm by offering to have the performance repeated in daylight if we cared to return another day, so that we could film it. We accepted with gratitude, not knowing then that our second visit would be something of a social calamity, as I shall relate in the next chapter.

Nilgai

2

The Cholistan Desert

With headlights ablaze we left the Commissioner's residence
and headed for the desert and Fort Abbas, where we were to
spend the night. Our guide said he knew of a short-cut which
would get us there in time for dinner. I am always sceptical
about short-cuts in the desert, but as he sounded so confident I
said nothing. An hour later, when it became obvious that we
were hopelessly lost among high sand dunes, I wished I had
made him stay on the highway.

I called a halt, flashing our headlights to assemble the other
vehicles which were wandering about seeking to escape the soft
sand among the dunes. After taking a bearing from the stars
and examining a map, I found that we had been heading in
almost the opposite direction from Fort Abbas. This time, I said,
the vehicles would keep together and only the leading car would
navigate. I headed for a canal shown on the map and once this
was reached we made better progress. Nevertheless it was
2.30 a.m. before we arrived at our destination, by which time we
were all not only very tired but bright yellow from head to foot
after five and a half hours in stifling desert dust.

Local officials greeted us at the rest-house with an excellent
meal and we were in bed by three-thirty. On our first day in
Pakistan we had been up and about for a stretch of twenty
hours.

Next morning we had our first taste of the rich bird life of Cholistan. There were birds everywhere around the rest-house. A Tawny Eagle (plate 1) and several Egyptian Vultures sailed overhead. Pond Herons and several species of kingfishers were feeding along the canal. Emerald-green Rose-ringed Parakeets were squabbling noisily in the trees and Mynas, Drongos and Red-vented Bulbuls were flitting around the garden. All these could be seen from the doorway, where shortly afterwards George Shannon spotted the nest of a White-throated Munia in a climbing rose bush.

After the pounding which our Land-Rovers had given our equipment during the night, George was anxious to test his cinema cameras on these subjects. Jimmy Hancock, who has a special knowledge of the Asiatic herons, volunteered to stay with him and do some work on the Pond Herons (plate 58). The rest of us loaded the vehicles and set out for the desert, with the little military outpost of Churi Wala as a rendezvous for lunch.

On our way we passed through the picturesque old town of Fort Abbas, its crumbling battlements and ancient white mosque looking almost too romantic to be true. Once out in the open desert, our tally of bird species mounted rapidly. The various wheatears, shrikes, warblers and larks were particularly numerous and often confusing. In this bleached waste all the small birds tended to have the same sandy coloration as their surroundings and to skulk in the scanty shade provided by the stunted vegetation.

The birds of prey, however, were busy hunting at this hour, boldly maintaining their lookout perches on the tops of the scattered acacias and allowing our vehicles to approach within a few yards. One of these, a particularly fine specimen of a

Laggar, permitted me to photograph it as it launched into flight from a dead tree. All the fierce beauty of a flying falcon was captured in that instant (plate 5). The Laggar, or Lanner as it is called in some countries, is related to the Peregrine, from which it is distinguished by a paler appearance, a sandy crown, a much narrower moustachial stripe and spotted, instead of barred, underparts. The Laggar *Falco biarmicus jugger* is resident in both West and East Pakistan and most of India. The range of the species extends from southern Europe through Africa as far east as China. Two other races, the Saker *F. b. cherrug* and the Shanghar *F. b. milvipes*, occur as winter migrants in West Pakistan and the northern regions of India. As three races of the Peregrine also occur in Pakistan, and two of these breed there, we had to examine every large falcon with particular care to distinguish them.

We were most anxious to see the Houbara Bustards which at this time of year should have been plentiful. They are migrants to Pakistan, usually arriving in October, when every *shikari* turns out to shoot a *Taloor*, as they are called locally. Presently we sighted one among the dunes and were able to circle it fairly closely in the Land-Rovers. After the manner of its kind it was reluctant to fly, walking with powerful strides and head erect, like a tawny turkey, from one patch of stunted thorn to another. We hoped it might crouch and remain immobile, allowing us to walk right up to it, as Houbaras sometimes do. Instead, it displayed momentarily, spreading the feathers of its long striped neck in a sudden flash of black and white and then flew majestically away. It was the only one we saw in Pakistan.

As a family, all the bustard species are particularly vulnerable to human predators, wherever they occur. Only those which live in the well-protected National Parks of Africa are thriving. Shooting, the mechanisation of farming and the progressive destruction of their natural habitats have reduced the remainder to small remnants of their former populations. The Great Bustard, exterminated as a breeding species in England by the 1830s, soon disappeared also from France, Denmark, Sweden and Greece and to-day survives only on the plains of central Europe and the Iberian peninsula. Small numbers still occur in Morocco and Asia Minor and in parts of Asia as far east as the Amur Valley. The Little Bustard, which still occurs in Pakistan, is also disappearing from many regions where only twenty years ago it was plentiful. The Houbara, which replaces the Great Bustard in the desert regions along the south of its range, is now fairly numerous only in parts of Syria. In Jordan, once one of its chief strongholds, we found it had been almost exterminated by about 1960.[1] All the literature up to the time of the Second World War referred to the Houbara as common in the deserts of West Pakistan, where we were now to discover that it was rapidly disappearing. Only a mere handful of Great Indian Bustards, perhaps the most spectacular member of the family, exists in the western parts of India, where its final extinction is expected within a very few years. It used to be seen, and shot, in Sind every year until just before our visit. But unless strict protection on an international scale can be provided for the bustards, few of the present world total of twenty-two species are likely to remain by the end of this century.

Long after our expedition I heard from Christopher Savage

[1] See *Portrait of a Desert* by Guy Mountfort. Collins, London.

that seven Great Indian Bustards were seen near Bhawalnagar in 1967. From March until August 1968 seventeen remained in the region and an astonishingly large flock of twenty-two was found by General Marden to the west of Fort Derawar in December of that year. Fortunately by then Pakistan's new conservation campaign was in full swing and the birds were closely guarded.

We left the lonely Houbara in peace and made our way to the little desert outpost at Churi Wala, where the platoon of soldiers guarding it made us very welcome. It was a desolate and scorching locality, with low dunes and bare mudflats extending to the false horizon beneath a watery mirage. Here and there the monotony was broken by an occasional tree of *Prosopis spicigera* or *Capparis aphylla,* or a gnarled *Zizyphus nummularia* whose thorns had been closely browsed by camels. We were not far from the Indian frontier and the men were still basking in the success of Pakistan's army against the numerically superior forces it had faced in this sector. We were very thirsty after our first spell in the open desert and glad to accept the succulent melons and oranges which were offered us. The soldiers obligingly dragged their *charpoys* out from their sleeping quarters into the shade of the building and we lay on them at ease while our picnic lunch was being unpacked. We shared our food with them and, with only slight misgivings, drank the cold but tawny water from their well. Brown-necked Ravens, Crested Larks and Collared Doves were in attendance, eager for fallen crumbs.

1 The Tawny Eagle is a typical bird of the drier regions of Pakistan. Sluggish in habit, it lives chiefly on carrion, but also robs other raptores of the prey they have caught.

We went in search of Blackbuck and Chinkara Gazelles after lunch. We succeeded in finding both species, though only a single Blackbuck and three Chinkara which raced away the moment we appeared. It was almost inconceivable to me that these animals which had once been so common in West Pakistan were now such rarities. Their virtual disappearance throughout the subcontinent has undoubtedly been one of the major factors in the probable extinction of the Asiatic Cheetah, which used to prey chiefly on these two species and on the now almost equally rare Chital, or Axis Deer.

Our later studies showed that the Blackbuck, which is the only representative of the true antelopes in the subcontinent and the most beautiful species of its genus, is in fact very near to extinction as a wild animal in both Pakistan and India. Just how easily it could have been saved had reserves been created is shown by the Maharaja of Baroda, who has kept a strictly protected herd on his estate in Gujarat and now has more than five hundred of them in semi-captivity. The Chinkara, which has been as ruthlessly hunted in Pakistan as the Blackbuck, now survives in any appreciable numbers only in the border region between Baluchistan and Iran. A few stragglers remain in Bahawalpur and in the foothills of the Kirthar Range and Salt Range.

During our journey we came across a family party of chestnut-red mongooses gambolling up and down the dunes. They belonged to the erythristic race of the Indian Grey Mongoose *Herpestes edwardsi ferrugineus*. Like otters and monkeys,

2 *Above* The White-eyed Buzzard is often shot by those believing it kills game birds; it feeds on harmful rodents and locusts. *Below* The Black Kite is the familiar scavenger in towns and villages.

mongooses are always ready to take time off for play and they make charming pets.

The six species of mongoose found in the Indo-Pakistan sub-continent are probably all descended from a common progenitor of the African genus *Herpestes*. Four are typical animals of the forested foothills. The Grey Mongoose *H. edwardsi* (page 192) and the Small Indian Mongoose *H. auropunctatus*, both of which are common in Pakistan, show considerable adaptability in environmental tolerance. Some races occupy completely arid desert, others quite high mountains, tropical jungles or cultivated areas close to human habitation. The western desert races are the smallest, size increasing towards the south-east of the range of the species.

Though quite small, mongooses readily and with apparent gusto attack much larger animals, their sheer ferocity and un-hesitating boldness usually giving them a *Blitzkrieg* victory. Nevertheless, in spite of their occasional attacks on the hen-run, they are of immense benefit to man, killing unlimited numbers of poisonous snakes, scorpions and rodents which would quickly assume plague proportions in the subcontinent without the pressure of this predation. Mongooses are not, of course, immune to snake poisons, though they can resist bites which would kill many other animals. Their dense fur, which is erected like a bottle-brush when engaging a snake, combined with their extreme rapidity of movement in combat, normally suffices to protect them from being bitten. A duel between a mongoose and a large cobra used to be a familiar attraction during village festivities; though the result was a foregone conclusion, the spectacle always aroused the kind of insensate enthusiasm which is associated with bull-fighting.

In the desert we noticed many fresh tracks and droppings of Striped Hyenas. This animal has a wide distribution in the open country and foothills of West Pakistan. Although generally regarded as sinister and unlovely, it is a very interesting creature. It has shaggy, greyish fur, with transverse stripes on the body and legs and a thick dorsal crest. Its head is massive, with powerful bone-crushing jaws. The fore-legs are strong and well adapted to digging; but the hindquarters are weak and drooping and the hind-legs short and knock-kneed, which give it an ungainly appearance. However, the Hyena is very well proportioned to its particular mode of life, which is that of a scavenger of carcasses left by others and not that of a hunter. Unlike the Spotted or the Brown Hyenas of Africa, the Striped Hyena is seldom seen by day, preferring to dispose at night of the bones left by vultures after their daylight feasts, or carcasses buried by the large carnivores.

Although the jaws of no other animal can match the tremendous crushing power of a Hyena's, it swallows large portions of bone uncrushed and its characteristic round droppings are composed almost entirely of bone fragments. The Hyena has little chance of escape if chased by a pack of dogs, as its ambling gait is too slow. It therefore usually stands fast under attack and often defends itself courageously. Its reputation for cowardice is unfounded. Occasionally during its nocturnal scavenging around villages it attacks domestic animals, killing several in quick succession if it is in the mood. There are records of it killing children and even adult humans, though this is exceptional. Its weird, chattering cry (the Hyena's laugh) has a ghoulish quality when heard in the dead of night, as we heard it later, and its habit of disinterring human graves adds to its unpopularity. Nevertheless, both in India and in the Middle East, superstitions about the mystical properties obtained by eating certain parts of a Hyena's body persist, both as curative medicine and as a means of absorbing the animal's great strength and courage.

On our journey we also came across tracks of Jackals and Foxes and hundreds of burrows of various desert rodents such as Gerbils, or Antelope Rats, and Jirds, which live in small colonies (plate 41*b*). Several species of these beautiful little animals are common in Cholistan, as are the Metads, or Soft-furred Field Rats. The Gerbils and Jirds have very long tails and behave like Jerboas by jumping with extreme rapidity instead of running, which is the normal method of progress by the rat-like Metads. (It is a pity that so much confusion exists over the English vernacular names of so many of the species in the subfamilies of Gerbillinae and Murinae to which these little animals belong. Many of them have at least two and some three synonyms; however, to avoid confusion, the scientific names of those we identified are given in Appendix 'A' of this book.)

It was very evident to us that the populations of micro-rodents in the desert were very large, in spite of the constant predation to which they were subjected by Mongooses, Weasels, Jackals, Desert Cats, birds of prey and various snakes. We could imagine the catastrophic losses which agriculture around the villages would suffer if the predators were destroyed. Yet we were to find throughout our travels that all of them, and particularly the birds of prey, were constantly being shot as 'vermin.'

I had expected to come across some of the 4–5 foot Desert Monitor lizards, which used to be such a picturesque feature in the deserts of West Pakistan; but like so many other animals they had been nearly exterminated by the skin traders. In 1966 no fewer than 65,000 'lizard' skins were exported from Pakistan and most of these were monitor skins. However, Jerry Wood-Anderson later showed us captive specimens of the Yellow Desert Monitor and the Tricolour Caspian Monitor (plate 14*b*) and we saw three other species—the Ocellated, the Grey and the Ruddy Snub-nosed—in the course of our explorations elsewhere.

Before reaching Fort Abbas we stopped to examine a noisy party of Imperial Sandgrouse (plate 4*b*) and half a dozen self-confident Indian Coursers; the latter were in pairs and behaving as though they might be nesting. These rounded off a thoroughly exciting day.

Meanwhile, George and Jimmy had also been busy. In addition to filming the Pond Herons, White-breasted King-fishers and beautiful little Five-striped Palm Squirrels around the rest-house (plate 57*b*), they had added a long list of new birds to our list. After only two working days in Pakistan we had between us already seen a hundred different species.

Our usual practice on expeditions is to write the diary of our observations every evening, no matter how fatigued we may be, though I had waived this rule on the previous exceptional night. Only by subjecting every record to close scrutiny by all members on the day it is made, can real accuracy be assured. Doubtful records have little chance of survival under the cross-examination to which they are all submitted and deletions are always accepted with good grace. We gave each locality a code letter. Every species of bird, mammal or reptile had a separate page in the diary and the locality codes were inserted against each observation, with the date. By the end of the expedition the diary was to contain about 350 quarto pages of notes.

We were busy with the diary that night and I was writing it while we dined. Eric and George were overhauling their cameras and Duncan Poore was preparing detailed descriptions of the vegetation through which we had passed during the day. Looking round the disordered table, I reflected that we were settling down excellently to our familiar routine. The only difference this time was that we were dining off the Amir's beautifully monographed china and an expensive damask tablecloth, instead of out of tin plates on a bare trestle table.

At that juncture a servant entered with a bowl of fruit— papayas, loquats, custard apples, sweet lemons and the delicious little green bananas of East Pakistan. Simultaneously the two remaining members of the expedition, Tom Roberts and Jerry Wood-Anderson, arrived.

None of us except Christopher Savage had met them before, but I soon realised how great a contribution they were likely to make. Both had long and detailed knowledge of the wildlife of Pakistan and, what was equally important to me, both were meticulous and careful observers who readily accepted our rather strict methods of work.

As I was anxious to do as much field work as possible before moving on to Dera Nawab Sahib, I arranged that we should leave before sunrise. In a hot climate, more wildlife can be seen at dawn than at any other time of day and we were accustomed to taking advantage of this. Only the soaring birds such as the vultures, eagles and buzzards were sluggish at dawn, waiting for the hot thermals to rise and give them the buoyancy they needed before they could ride on motionless wings high over the desert.

Progress next morning, however, was slow. We were away before sunrise, to the accompaniment of a diminutive Spotted Owlet's quiet chuckling from a hidden perch in the garden; but there were so many new species of birds and lesser animals to be seen along the canal that it was broad daylight before we had gone many miles.

White-breasted Kingfishers, resplendent in chocolate-brown and iridescent blue, with huge scarlet bills, were cackling like Australian Kookaburras from vantage points beside the water. Their relatives the Pied Kingfishers, strikingly barred and spotted with black and white, were equally numerous. Green Bee-eaters skimmed gracefully over the water, their long central tail feathers making them look rather like miniature parakeets. Many Red-wattled Lapwings frequented the canal banks (plate 24b). A Golden-backed Woodpecker and a noisy party of Rose-coloured Starlings were seen and a Grey Partridge betrayed her brood of recently fledged young to us by her nervous and persistent 'qu-ink' call. (This was an exceptionally late brood, as the Grey Partridge normally nests in May, though we also found late broods during our second expedition.) Again and again the Land-Rovers were halted to examine the numerous birds of prey—Tawny Eagle, Spotted Eagle, Bonelli's Eagle, Laggar Falcon, White-backed Vulture, Marsh Harrier, Kestrel —and still the list grew. White-eyed Buzzards were particularly common (plate 2a). In the rank undergrowth in the ditches were family parties of Jungle Babblers, locally called Sat Bhai, meaning 'Seven Sisters,' because of their habit of travelling in groups of about half a dozen.

Our chief study area that day was Lal Suhanra, one of the very few wetland areas in Cholistan. Christopher Savage felt that it deserved to be turned into a protected reserve, because of the great variety of wildlife which it attracted. When we had examined it we had no hesitation in agreeing with him. The varied vegetation which flourished along the canals provided food and shelter to an unusually high concentration of bird species, while some eight square miles of swamp with shallow Lotus pools surrounded by beds of *Typha* reeds provided water for all the animals of the surrounding desert. Along the north side ran the Desert Branch Canal, with a little-used roadway linking Bahawalpur to Bhawalnagar. North to south lay the Bahawal Canal and in the south the Hakra Canal. These would provide admirable boundaries. If a sufficiently large tract of desert to the east could be included for the protection of Black-buck and Chinkara, the site would be ideal—a combined wetlands and desert reserve. Moreover, there was an attractive little rest-house in a picturesque setting only seven miles from the main canal, which could be the headquarters for organised studies and the management of the reserve. We decided to recommend this plan to the Pakistan Government. Work had already begun on the new reserve by the time this book went to press and it had been adopted for financial support by the Netherlands National Appeal of the World Wildlife Fund.

Most of the pools at Lal Suhanra were occupied by stately Great White Egrets and by Little Egrets with characteristic black legs and yellow feet, which made them look as though

3 *Above* Peasants in Cholistan believe the harmless Leopard Gecko can kill a man with its breath. *Below* A snake charmer 'charming' a Black Cobra by waving a cloth in front of it.

they wore yellow socks (plate 4a). River Terns and Little Cormorants were there in considerable numbers and we saw several Darters, swimming with only their slender heads and necks above water, reminding us of their popular name of 'Snake Birds' (plate 42a). Moorhens and stout Purple Gallinules clucked and hooted among the projecting Lotus seed pods, where Pheasant-tailed Jacanas walked precariously on the floating, dish-shaped leaves, high-stepping on their grotesquely long toes and raising their wings like butterflies to maintain their balance.

All the 'Lily Trotters,' as the Jacanas are often called, are spectacular birds, but none surpasses the Pheasant-tailed for elegance. Its plumage is a neat combination of chocolate-brown and white, with a golden-yellow patch down the back of the neck. Its bill is blue and its tail, as its name implies, is long, narrow and down-curved. This remarkable tail is shed after the breeding season and no other Jacana assumes such a distinctive nuptial plumage. Like the Pond Heron, its wings appear dramatically snow-white when it flies. Only its call, a maniacal, high-pitched laugh, is inelegant. Later in East Pakistan we saw its relative, the Bronze-winged Jacana; at a distance its stubby shape and glossy black plumage gave a superficial resemblance to a Moorhen, but closer inspection revealed a short chestnut-red tail and a bold white stripe running back from the eyes. Its blue-green legs and ridiculously long toes looked even bigger than those of the Pheasant-tailed Jacana. The exact systematic position of the Jacanas is still obscure. The seven

4 *Above* Great White Egrets, Little Egrets and Little Cormorants at Lal Suhanra, an important marsh on the edge of the desert. *Below* We often saw Imperial Sandgrouse in the Cholistan desert.

species found in south-east Asia, Indonesia, Australia, tropical America, Africa and Madagascar are at present divided into six different genera.

Along the canal road the tall trees of *Saccharum bengalensis* produced a number of interesting birds. Here we saw our first Crow Pheasants, rather heavy, black birds with long graduated tails and conspicuous orange wings. A pair of crimson-eyed Koels was shrieking noisily and we had a good view of them, the male in glistening black with a green bill and the female closely speckled in brown and white. These parasitic birds usually lay their eggs in the occupied nests of House Crows and Jungle Crows and as many as thirteen Koel eggs have been found in the nest of a single unlucky host.

A pair of Indian Rollers was feeding young in a tree-hollow by the roadside. These beautiful creatures had bands of iridescent light and dark blue on their wings, lilac breasts and rufous backs. The male, perturbed by our inspection, indulged in a sudden display, rocketing up into the air and descending in a series of wild gyrations and zig-zags, to the accompaniment of raucous screeching. The female ignored us and went on battering a luckless lizard to death before carrying it to the nest-hole.

By one of the pools I caught sight of a remarkable member of the flycatcher family, a tiny silvery-white bird with a black, crested head and an astonishingly long white tail fluttering behind it like a ribbon. This was the first and only Paradise Flycatcher observed during the whole expedition. As the species is migratory in this part of Pakistan we were fortunate in finding it so late in the year. The Paradise Flycatcher's nest, which I had seen in Burma, is an exquisite little cup plastered with silvery spiderwebs, usually in the crotch of a bare twig;

when the parent is incubating, its stiffly crested head and long, drooping tail on either side of the little nest make an entrancing picture.

Time pressed. We had arranged to go back and film the dancing camels at the Commissioner's residence before meeting the Amir at his palace and had many miles to go. We left the canal road and took a narrow track through a large area of tree plantations, stopping only once to examine a Pallas's Fishing Eagle, in whose powerful talons was a five-pound fish. We were making good progress through difficult country when our guide let his attention wander and his vehicle slid off the soft shoulder of the track. It came to a halt tilted sideways at 45 degrees, supported only by a sapling tree; the wheels spun and the angle of the vehicle increased until we were in imminent danger of rolling down into the valley (plate 9). Branches were placed under the wheels and the baggage was unloaded; but when the engine was restarted, the car merely slid farther down the sandy slope. Eventually I decided that it would have to be abandoned until a rescue truck could be sent to winch it out. Meanwhile, by sitting on each other's knees, we could just manage to cram into Tom Roberts's Land-Rover, leaving all our baggage in the derelict car. In great discomfort we continued our journey and once we reached the Bahawalpur highway, drove as fast as the overladen Land-Rover would go.

An hour and a half late for our appointment, we reached our destination. By not so much as a raised eyebrow did the Commissioner show displeasure or surprise; instead, he waved aside apologies and invited us to take refreshments. The dancing camels were then put through their paces for us again on the lawn and the spectacle made a valuable addition to our film.

We then drove to the Sadiqgarh Palace, where the gateway was guarded by mounted sentries in the colourful uniform of the Amir's bodyguard. Beyond stood the ornate palace, gleaming white like a huge and elaborate wedding cake. The black standard of the Amir flew above the central dome. In front of the palace a wide formal garden blazed with Bougainvillæas, Hibiscus and Canna Lilies, surrounding a reflecting pool on which tame White Pelicans and Bar-headed Geese were swimming. Around the tall palm trees beside the palace and over the palace roof Large Indian Parakeets with scarlet bills swooped in graceful flight. The scene had an almost fairy-tale quality, a sudden glimpse of the bygone age of the great Rajas (plate 9a).

We explained our lateness and dusty attire to the Amir, who accepted our apologies with good grace, quickly disarming us by saying that he had expected us to look like naturalists rather than visiting diplomats.

His Highness the Amir is a descendant of the Abbasid Caliphs, a branch of whose history we had studied in Jordan, and the ancestral throne of the Abbasids is still preserved in the palace. The dynasty broke with the Afghans before the end of the eighteenth century and in 1947 the princely state acceded to the new republic of Pakistan. Its territory has now become three districts within the new Bahawalpur Division.

Our host was obviously familiar with the status of the animal life of the region. He offered to let us photograph his tame pelicans on the ornamental pond if we were unable to find any wild ones. It was fortunate that we accepted his offer, as we found none until our very last day in Pakistan. The once numerous White and Spot-billed Pelicans which used to provide such a spectacle over the rivers and *jheels* of Pakistan had been almost exterminated, on the grounds that they ate too many fish. Plans for a factory on the Indus River to extract oil from their carcasses had to be abandoned when it became clear that there were none left to kill. Pelicans are voracious feeders and as such are heavily persecuted in many countries, bounties often being paid for their destruction; but public opinion is at last beginning to come to their rescue. Pelicans are admired for their spectacular flight and picturesque behaviour by almost all except those who make their living by fishing. We had been instrumental in saving the White and Dalmatian Pelicans which breed on the Danube in Bulgaria.[1] The Russian and Rumanian governments now protect these species where they breed in their countries and I was anxious that the few winter migrants which still visited Pakistan should survive. The Amir encouraged me to take the matter up with the government, which I was able to do at the conclusion of the expedition.

After lunch the Amir invited us to visit his museum. The family collection of early illustrated manuscripts of the Koran is one of the largest in the world, and there was a fine hall full of medieval weapons, armour, uniforms and head-dresses which had belonged to the Amir's ancestors. In a gallery I noticed photographs of King George V and Queen Mary reviewing the Amir's household cavalry. Perhaps the most fascinating exhibit was an immense Venetian glass four-poster bed, which had made the last part of its long journey to the palace by barge and ox-drawn transport. Beside it were a number of solid silver elephant *howdahs*, used by visiting royalty.

[1] See *Portrait of a River* by Guy Mountfort. Hutchinson, London.

We slept that night in splendid luxury. The photographers were soon busy next morning taking pictures of the Amir's birds which he used for falconry, a fine Goshawk and a couple of Red-capped Falcons *Falco perigrinus babylonicus*, which are one of the local races of the Peregrine. We also examined a group of very wild Chinkara Gazelles in an enclosure behind the palace (plate 11). The Amir has since offered this valuable herd of eighteen animals as a breeding stock for the new reserve which is being created at Fort Abbas.

An all too hasty visit was made to General Marden's delightful house on the estate, where we had the pleasure of meeting his wife, and as we drove from the enclosure the whole guard turned out to present arms, with flashing sabres and bayonets in a manner which would have done credit to Buckingham Palace.

With the General as our guide, we headed for Fort Derawar, which still stands on its high mound, massive and majestic, commanding the caravan route across the desert. Successive restorations have not marred its austere contours, though the Abbasid village sheltering beneath its flank is now no more than a cluster of roofless mud shells. Half a mile away gleamed the beautiful white domes and minarets of the tombs of the Amir's ancestors, with a large ornamental pool surrounded by feathery date palms. This was the only patch of relieving colour in a vast expanse of tawny and featureless desert which, within living memory and before it had been stripped of its timber, had been pleasantly green savannah, dotted with trees.

We drove up the steep approach road through the immense gateway of the fortress and into a courtyard, set thirty feet below the battlemented walls. Here two battalions of troops

could have manœuvred with room to spare. In the centre was
a collection of ancient cannons, pyramids of cannon balls,
chain-shot and wicked looking spiked projectiles which had
once been fired by catapult. From one of the great bastion
towers we obtained a sweeping view of the desert approaches.
Deep below us were vaulted cellars with ventilators going up to
ground level on all sides. Like the Jerboas of the desert, the
defenders of the fortress could pass the heat of day in complete
subterranean comfort, while besiegers had to endure the sizzling
torture of the shadeless plain. A huge well, lined with ancient
and now crumbling bricks, completed the resources of the
garrison. It was easy to understand why Fort Derawar had
played so important a part in the history of the region.

Leaving the desert we moved to more verdant country, with
bright green fields of sugar cane, cotton and rape. The roads
here were carpeted with the yellow fallen blossoms from avenues
of *Acacia arabica* and the ditches were lined with the tall, waving
white plumes of *Saccharum bengalensis* grasses. Near the primitive
village of Firoza the fields were flooded and thousands of
waders were feeding eagerly. Black-winged Stilts favoured the
water nearest the road and we stopped to photograph them as
they picked their way delicately through the shallows on their
astonishingly long, cherry-red legs.

We lunched at the Nur Afshan rest-house, where a flock of
hungry Black Kites over the kitchen midden enabled us to take
some flight pictures. Then we resumed our journey to the royal
hunting lodge at Jhajjia Abbasian, where we were to spend the
night. The country roads were appallingly dusty and although
we kept our cameras and binoculars covered in plastic bags, an
abrasive flour-like film soon coated everything we possessed.

On the way, we came across a village wedding party. The guests were arriving in gaily decorated ox-wagons, or on camels carrying voluminous basket-work panniers crammed to bursting with women and children in festive attire. The bridegroom, surrounded by friends, was celebrating at the roadside and shyly agreed that so colourful a spectacle should be included in our film. His face was hidden behind scarlet and gold streamers hanging from his brow and dozens of rupee notes had been pinned to his white *kameez* by well-wishers. This was a poor farming community and a rupee represented hours of back-breaking toil. We thanked him for permitting us to interrupt the celebrations, which, judging by the noisy enthusiasm of some of the guests, was going to be quite a big social occasion in the village.

General Marden rejoined us for dinner at the hunting lodge· Six silver vases of roses were on the table and by every napkin a posy of orange Lantana and pink rose-buds carefully arranged. We felt these somewhat lavish for a stag party and wished our far-away wives had been dining with us.

Next day we visited two important wetland areas, the Gagri and Tatar *jheels* on the hunting estate. The indefatigable General had arranged for the mule tracks to these localities to be repaired, so that our Land-Rovers could negotiate them.

The *jheels* were fed by water from canals when there was any surplus, and, although they formed a valuable asset to the shooting, the soil was too permeable to retain water for very long in the dry season. We therefore felt that their value to any

5 *Above* Grace and freedom are epitomised by this portrait of a Laggar Falcon. *Below* The Brahminy Kite frequents rivers, marshes and coasts, often following ships to pick up garbage.

wildlife conservation plan would be limited. Gagri was rather disappointing, but the Tatar *jheel* harboured a considerable variety of wildfowl. Pheasant-tailed Jacanas were particularly numerous on the big expanse of Lotus vegetation which dominated the open water. In the broad reed-beds were Mallard, Teal and various herons, while flocks of Green Bee-eaters posed artistically on isolated reeds, or circled gracefully over the Oleander bushes along the shores (plate 6*b*).

Two rather ancient punts were waiting for us, surrounded by about twenty villagers, all anxious to act as boatmen. The General had insisted on trying out the punts before our arrival and one of them had sunk 80 yards from shore, giving him a ducking. They had since been re-caulked and we were soon safely afloat. After the dusty journey of the previous day it was very restful gliding slowly over the still water, with the Lotus pads hissing gently against the broad punts.

We mounted our cameras and basked in the hot sunshine, taking pictures of the many interesting dragonfly nymphs and spiders which frequented the floating vegetation. So passive a procedure did not suit the active spirit of the General, however, and he soon took his punt back to the shore to organise a party of beaters, so that we might see more ducks. Before long a hideous din broke out as the beaters began circling the *jheel*, beating gongs and thrashing the reed-beds with unconstrained enthusiasm. Flights of startled Mallard and Teal and innumerable Coots were soon on the wing.

It was our first opportunity to examine a large area of Lotus.

6 *Above* The noisy Rose-ringed Parakeet is equally at home in towns or country; its flocks cause much damage to crops and orchards. *Below* Green Bee-eaters resting on a fishing pole.

This very beautiful plant behaves rather like the notorious Water Hyacinth and, once established, rapidly spreads its powerful growth from shore to shore. In summer its dark pink blossoms above the vivid green leaves are enchantingly beautiful; these are followed by massive seed pods which provide a rich source of food to aquatic birds. These seeds and the long fleshy roots of the Lotus are also eaten by the human inhabitants of the marshlands. In this respect the Lotus has a certain value, whereas the exquisite Water Hyacinth, the arch invader of the waterways of the tropics, can lay no claim to virtue but its beauty. Research is, however, being conducted into the possibility of using it for fodder and in China it is already being fed successfully to pigs.

That evening we were invited to watch a troupe of local acrobats performing on the lawn of the rest-house. The star turn was a boy of six, who not only supported the combined weight of his burly father and brother on his arched body, but later dived repeatedly through a two-foot hoop fringed with sharp knives. When he fumbled a trick his father gave him a savage kick which sent him sprawling; the high standard of the rest of the performance evidently owed its perfection to the fear of punishment rather than the hope of reward.

The General accompanied us to the railway station at Khanpur and when the Lahore express arrived he inspected our accommodation to make sure everything was in good order. The train was gathering speed and half-way out of the station before he was satisfied and then, with our hearts in our mouths, we saw him leap casually off the carriage steps as nimbly as a school-boy. We waved vigorously until the trim, soldierly figure of our extraordinary septuagenarian friend was hidden from view.

3

The Wildlife of West Punjab

There was still an hour before sunrise when our train reached Renala Khurd and we assembled our thirty-two pieces of baggage on the dimly lit platform. We were now in West Punjab and the night was unexpectedly chilly. We climbed into the Land-Rovers which had been sent to meet us and drove in the pre-dawn darkness through wooded country, which presently opened out into an area of dry mudflats dotted with bushes. The dominant natural vegetation of West Punjab is classified as tropical thorn forest, but little of this now remains.

In the distance we could make out a wide sheet of water. This was the *jheel* of Kharrar, in Sahiwal District. The sun was about to break the horizon as we drove towards the water and almost immediately we noticed two shadowy forms crossing the waste ahead of us. Our binoculars showed them to be a very fine pair of tawny Desert Wolves, returning to their lair after a night's hunting. They came from the direction of a distant farm and doubtless had been raiding the sheep or goats. Wolves are now rather rare animals in most parts of West Pakistan; but in 1855 they were so numerous that 600 peasant children were reported to have been killed by them in the Lahore and Sialkot districts alone.

The Wolves made a good start to our observations; but when we reached the shore of the *jheel* another exciting spectacle awaited us. Spread out across the water was a superb galaxy of wildfowl, among which the gleaming pink of a group of Flamingoes was conspicuous.

Kharrar *jheel* normally has about four square miles of open water. For the past twenty years or more it has been fed from springs and is therefore well waterlogged. Although the salinity of the water is increasing, the many springs around its periphery are of fresh water, so that a good variety of different biotypes is maintained and the margins are richly productive of varied food (or eutrophic, as the biologists would say) for the huge numbers of ducks and waders which frequent it during the migratory seasons.

We settled down to counting the wildfowl. Christopher Savage, who has spent many years studying ducks, is very expert in assessing numbers and when we had cross-checked each other's figures we felt inclined to accept his calculations where they varied from our own. Here is the list we compiled:

Pochard	350	Flamingo	14	Spotted Redshank	1
Gadwall	42	Little Grebe	4	Common Sandpiper	2
Pintail	15	Coot	400	Wood Sandpiper	10
Teal	350	Avocet	10	Green Sandpiper	75
Shoveler	25	Black-winged Stilt	2,000	Kentish Plover	10
Ferruginous Duck	12	Greenshank	10	Little Stint	1,000
Ruddy Shelduck	1	Redshank	40		

This seemed a goodly list, though Christopher grumbled that we were too early to see big numbers. He had seen as many as 15,000 ducks on the *jheel* one winter's day.

The small flock of Flamingoes contained several immature birds and one obvious young one, which suggested that during the summer breeding had taken place somewhere in the region. We later came across 47 old nests of Flamingoes on one of the mudflats, each carefully built up like a hollow mud crown. We could not tell whether they had contained young, but Flamingoes have a poor record of breeding success and frequently build nests which come to grief by flooding, drought, predation, or other causes.

We had been invited to breakfast by Colonel J. H. Taylor at the Renala stud farm. The estate, when we reached it, reminded me of the famous stud farms of Kentucky, with its neatly fenced paddocks and avenues of fine trees. After a typically English breakfast Colonel Taylor, looking every inch the county squire, drove us round the property in a smartly turned-out gig drawn by a spanking bay.

The estate was founded in 1913 by the late Major D. H. Vanrenen, who brought 8,000 acres of jungle under cultivation. Since then few classic races have not been won by the Renala blood-line. A number of horses were brought out for our inspection. Like the impeccably ordered estate they were in superb condition. We talked to some of the grooms and were impressed by their obvious pride in their work; they were all shareholders in the private company which managed the enterprise. Before leaving, we snatched the opportunity to take some pictures of the many Rose-ringed Parakeets which were nesting in the Acacia and Shisham trees by the stables (plate 6).

Our next stop, at the Chhanga Manga forest reserve, was also interesting. It is an irrigated plantation of some 12,000 acres 44 miles south of Lahore. The area was once the haunt of two bloodthirsty brigands named Chhanga and Manga, who were so successful that their hide-out became known as Rakh Chhanga Manga. With the eventual demise of the brigands and the coming of irrigation an experimental plantation was created, chiefly to provide fuel for the railway locomotives. By 1871 9,000 acres were planted and soon afterwards the Chhanga Manga area was declared a Reserved Forest, which has since been enlarged. Its importance after Partition was greatly increased by the fact that Pakistan inherited only 3.6 per cent of land under forest. West Pakistan is in fact extremely short of trees for timber and firewood, let alone shelter for animals. All the extensive bamboo thickets and other protective vegetation which used to shelter Tigers, Asiatic Lions and Rhinoceroses in the valley of the Indus disappeared more than a hundred years ago. To-day desert prevails and 76 per cent of the land-mass of West Pakistan is subject to serious erosion.

One of the most valuable trees in the Chhanga Manga reserve is the Mulberry. It is the mainstay of the sports goods industry in Pakistan, besides supporting the basket-making industry and providing food for silk-worm farms. It colonised the plantations partly by seed carried on the canal waters, but chiefly by seed in the droppings of migrant Rose-coloured Starlings, or Rosy Pastors, as they are sometimes called. These birds are very numerous in the Punjab in the spring and are passionately fond of the fruit. The other chief tree species in the reserve are Shisham *Dalbergia sissoo*, Bakain *Melia azdarach*, Simbal *Salamlia malabarica* and Palma Christi *Ricinus communis,* all of which have important commercial uses, the last-mentioned being the source of castor oil.

We were, of course, particularly anxious to know what wildlife was to be found in the reserve and gladly accepted an invitation to tour the plantations by means of the miniature railway which, at 7mph, enabled us to see most of the area. There was a good variety of birds, but unfortunately the little steam locomotive was so infernally noisy that any larger animals in the vicinity disappeared long before we could see them. We were told, however, that there were a few Blackbuck, Nilgai and introduced Chital, or Axis Deer, in the forest. There were certainly some in the little zoo which had been created for the education of visitors. Nilgai were once so numerous here that great *battues* were organised to exterminate them. By 1938 it was estimated that the population had declined to about 1,000. During the Second World War, when the reserve was used as an army training area, most of these were killed, as indeed they were in the rest of Pakistan. No shooting is now permitted in the reserve, except for Jackal, Wild Boar and Porcupine, which are regarded as harmful pests. The Wild Boar in West Pakistan benefits greatly from the fact that it is a highly repugnant animal to Muslims and is therefore not hunted. In many agricultural areas its increasing numbers are a great problem and the army has had to be called in to organise large-scale shoots.

On reflection I felt that the reserve, which attracted large numbers of visitors from Lahore and elsewhere, served an admirable purpose for recreation and education. But the disturbance caused by the noisy little railway and the comings and goings of a labour force of more than 1,000 engaged in forestry and other tasks ruled it out as a satisfactory game reserve. Its economic value was obvious and it was a pity that in a region so desperately needing a fully protected area for all forms of wildlife, it could only partly fulfil this purpose.

We headed northwards for Lahore and as we approached the city the traffic increased in volume. A peculiarity of Pakistan is its freelance country bus service. Most of the vehicles seem of considerable age and are usually crammed to overflowing, often with passengers clinging to the steps and always with a mountain of baggage on the roof. With their native genius for decoration, the owners paint every inch of the buses, including the windscreens, with intricate and colourful designs, or hang them with tassels or plastic flowers. The riders of bicycle rickshaws share this pleasant habit, and decorate their little vehicles similarly too. Both country bus-drivers and rickshaw riders career along with gay and terrifying abandon: on the forty-odd miles to Lahore we passed two wrecked buses, one of which was upside down in a field, one wrecked rickshaw, one recently killed donkey and four dogs which had been run over. As an indication of the customary overcrowding of vehicles in Pakistan, I quote a recent newspaper report of a traffic accident: 'Three of the occupants of the taxi were killed outright; the *seven other passengers* all suffered broken arms or legs.' The italics are mine.

We met Christopher and his pretty wife on the terrace of Faletti's Hotel, which I had not seen since the war. It still had a vaguely romantic atmosphere, with its shady arcade of little shops where you can buy anything from an imitation Parker pen to a genuine Afghan flint-lock. Rooms had been reserved for us so that we could change and take a shower before catching the Mari Indus express westward to Kalabagh.

We had time for a drink on the hotel terrace as the sun went down, to a deafening chorus of croaking and chattering from a host of House Crows and Mynas roosting in the trees. House Crows swarm in every city in West Pakistan, nesting wherever a convenient site can be found. One of them chose to build on a

7 *Top left, Hibiscus schizopetalus* growing in the jungle: *top right* Common Tiger butterfly: *centre* Mantis on Frangipani flower: *below* Carpenter Bee on flowers of Sodom Apple *Calotropis procera.*

pole carrying high-voltage wires in Karachi, opposite a cinema. After the scavenging manner of its kind, the crow added a long piece of wire to its nest. This short-circuited the cables and electrified the pole, so that when a man came out of the cinema and relieved himself against the pole he was instantly electrocuted. The moral in this story was not lost to the public health authorities.

A bottle of Scotch whisky costs more than £10 in Pakistan, so we drank slowly. Representatives of the local radio station then arrived with a tape recorder and I was asked to make a twenty-minute recording about the expedition. This was a trifle disconcerting, with people passing by every few minutes, but as I was anxious to spread the gospel of conservation in Pakistan I crammed as much as I could into the time.

When we boarded our railway carriage that evening we noticed an engraved plate which gave its date of construction as 1916. It had undoubtedly been a de luxe vehicle in its day, and though after fifty years it was now much dilapidated, we were looking forward to a good night's rest and the bedding was spotless. As soon as the train was in motion, however, our carriage, being rather short and at the end of the train, began to swing from side to side like the tail of a whip, with a loud and ominous clanking. It was impossible to sit still, much less write the diary legibly. Few of us slept at all that night.

We breakfasted during a halt at Kundian and the train then headed north across a sandy plain towards the mountains of Waziristan, with the Indus on our left. Finally we reached

8 *Above* A full-grown male Punjab Urial. *Below* The photographers had a narrow escape when these two Gayal bulls charged them on a jungle trail in the Chittagong Hill Tracts.

Mari Indus and after a short journey by road arrived at the guest-house of the Nawab of Kalabagh.

Malik Amir Mohammad Khan, the Nawab of Kalabagh, was a big man and rather impressive, with a dignified walrus moustache and flowing white robes. He had been Governor of West Pakistan for six and a half years, having retired only recently. During his term of office he had wielded great influence and was said to have been stern and autocratic. I expected this to be reflected in his manner, but his greeting was charming and we were all captivated by his quiet sincerity and concern for our comfort.

'I am neither prince nor politician now,' he assured us, 'but just a plain farmer.' His devotion to farming was no mere affectation but, as we learned later, the result of intimate personal experience with agriculture in a harsh desert region. He had learned the hard way that the desert could be made to yield good crops if one was prepared to use unorthodox methods. We found it interesting that a man who could trace his ancestry through an unbroken line of 950 years of martial Awan noblemen should turn with such obvious pleasure to this peaceable pursuit.

The guest-house was on the bank of the Indus and had a long terrace overlooking the river which, although 800 miles from the sea, was still nearly half a mile wide. Behind the building was a formal garden giving on to an orchard which attracted a large variety of birds. Among them we noticed the Indian Honey Buzzard *Pernis ptilorhynchus ruficollis*, which here was at the western extremity of its range (plate 19*a*).

On one side of the garden was the Nawab's walled palace and on the other a gigantic Banyan tree, whose pendent roots had enabled it to spread over nearly half an acre. Our guest-house, known as the Bor Bungla, was named after this huge tree, which is locally called a *Bor*. Several other *Bors* grew nearby and gave rise to the name Kalabagh, meaning a black (or perhaps dark or shady) garden.

Sentries armed with rifles and submachine-guns guarded the entrances to the palace and patrolled the terrace where we had drinks. We were told that when we made excursions into the wilder parts of the estate, which extended for many miles into the mountains of the Salt Range, armed guards would accompany us. I was horrified by this notion, but when I inquired whether it was really necessary, the Nawab reminded me that we were now near the territories of hill tribesmen who were not averse to taking a pot-shot at strangers, or kidnapping them for ransom. Indeed only recently they had ambushed and captured six of his men, which had obliged him to take severe reprisals; but as a matter of fact the Pathan guards who later accompanied us proved to be such superb game scouts and such excellent fellows that we were only too glad of their company.

While we were settling into our new quarters there was an amusing incident. Our array of various cameras, tripods, telephoto lenses and other equipment was temporarily spread all over the veranda and this caused intense interest among the men-servants who, judging by their excited comments, had never seen such extraordinary things before. Admittedly Eric Hosking's huge 400mm lens mounted on a shoulder brace and pistol grip does look rather like a new kind of machine-gun. To escape the congestion on the veranda, George Shannon had sat himself under a shady tree in the garden, to watch birds through his binoculars, while shaving himself with a battery-operated razor in the other hand. This combined operation

quickly attracted the attention of one of the elderly Awan
servants, who contrived again and again to walk past, each time
drawing closer. Finally, unable to contain himself and fascinated
by the mysterious buzzing of the razor, he tiptoed silently on
bare feet behind George and cautiously leaned over his shoulder
to examine it. George, suddenly aware of the bearded and
turbanned apparition six inches from his ear, lowered his
binoculars and bestowed a beaming smile on the intruder, who
fled in confusion.

We made a short excursion that day to examine Nammal
jheel, at the foot of the Salt Range. It was an attractive lake
which mirrored the jagged, lilac and gold foothills. As we
approached, the placid water was suddenly churned into spray
as 3,000 Coots pattered along the surface and took wing, with
a noise like the thunder of an express train. Several hundred
Little Grebes which had been among the Coots dived momentarily and then resumed feeding. The only other birds of interest
were a few Brown-headed Gulls, a species not previously recorded in the Salt Range area (plate 43*a*).

The Nawab and his son Malik Asad Khan, whose gaiety was
a source of constant pleasure to us, came to dine with us that
evening and we plied them with questions about the Salt Range
country which we were to explore during the next three days.

The Salt Range proper forms a roughly 'S' shaped southern
boundary to the high plateau which extends southward from the
sub-Himalayas through the Rawalpindi, Jhelum and Attock
districts. Beginning near the Indus at Kalabagh, the mountains
run south-west and then east, parallel with the Jhelum River,
finally bending south as far as Jalalpur, giving a total length of
about 120 miles to the range. It is precipitous along its southern

edge, but on the northern side it slopes more gradually to the plateau. Its highest peak, Sakesar, is just short of 5,000 feet above sea level. The mountains are deeply eroded and almost devoid of vegetation, except for the northern slopes and the deep ravines. They contain rich deposits of gypsum and a little coal. The valleys below are fertile and the soil washed from the mountains has been carefully terraced to hold whatever water flows down. There are four sizeable *jheels* in the valleys, one of which, Nammal, we had already visited. The region on the south side of the range is probably the hottest in the subcontinent during the summer months.

In this wild and inhospitable country, which was so full of interest to us as naturalists, one man had laboriously compiled notes over a period of thirty years from 1918 onwards, concern- the birds which he had observed there. This great English ornithologist, H. W. Waite, was a guest at our dinner party that night in Kalabagh. Advanced in years and no longer able to trudge the rugged Salt Range trails, he lived in scholarly retire- ment in a house on the Nawab's estate.[1] He warned us that many of the 250 bird species which he had recorded as common thirty years ago had now become rare, or no longer appeared in the Salt Range, because of increased cultivation and the pressure of shooting and trapping. From him we first learned of the apparently widespread custom among local tribes of bring- ing down migrating Cranes and Demoiselle Cranes by slinging lead weights or stones on long ropes into the flocks. Both these species, as well as Spot-billed and White Pelicans, were con- sidered good to eat by the local population.

---

[1] Alas, he died the following year.

While the birds of the Salt Range were important to us, it was the mountain sheep, the Punjab Urial, which we were most anxious to study. After dinner Malik Asad Khan produced for us the mounted head of the largest ram shot in the Salt Range. The massive, wrinkled horns, set close together and curving in a circular sweep, measured 36 inches and were certainly impressive in girth and length.

The Punjab Urial *Ovis orientalis punjabiensis* is a very distinctive race of a once plentiful species. The ram is a most handsome animal, reddish-golden in colour, with white on the insides of the legs and a dark 'saddle.' From its throat and chin hangs a striking ruff of long black hair (plates 8*a* and 11*a*). The agility of the Urial in climbing precipitous rocks often rivals that of the Ibex and this, combined with its extreme wariness, has inevitably led to it being regarded as a favourite sporting trophy by the mountaineering hunter. The Urial has now disappeared from most of the mountains of Pakistan. The unique and now isolated Punjab race survives only by grace of the protection it receives on the Nawab's estate in the Salt Range. A much greyer race, known as the Shapu *P. o. vignei*, occurs in Gilgit (plate 32) The Afghan race *P. o. blanfordi* is still reasonably plentiful and extends southward through Baluchistan and along the Kirthar Range to Iran. The last mentioned race has horns which tend to spiral outwards.

While permitting the occasional shooting of the older rams, in order to maintain the virility of the race, the Nawab had placed a very strict limit on the number which could be taken. In consequence the population in the Salt Range is thriving. We eagerly accepted his invitation to see if we could photograph these rare creatures, with the aid of his stalkers.

So, at 4.30 next morning by the light of a still brilliant moon, we set out for the mountains, our plan being to climb before sunrise to good vantage points from which the stalkers thought the Urial would best be seen. Having already examined the steep rocks at long range through binoculars from the plain, I imagined we should have a pretty stiff climb.

We clattered over the long iron bridge spanning the Indus, startling the armed sentries, who were unaccustomed to seeing traffic at such an hour, and drove for a while through cultivated country interspersed with dense thickets of sweet-smelling trees. The villages were still asleep, but at one point our head-lights picked out a ghostly string of loaded camels plodding silently along the road, with the shrouded herdsman oblivious to the world on the back of the leading animal. Presently we left the highway and began to climb into the foothills by a rough track. The moon was now setting, but the animals of the night were still afoot. A fox darted through the beam of the headlights and several hares with large rounded ears were also picked out, gleaming suddenly golden before they vanished into the darkness. Jerry Wood-Anderson, who was sitting next to me, said they were the desert race of the Indian Hare *Lepus nigricollis dayanus*, which in the nominate race in southern India has a dark patch on the nape of the neck. Jackals, Desert Cats and Jungle Cats are their chief enemies; they are said frequently to hide from them by day in the burrows of Porcupines.

At a little building on the shoulder of a deep ravine the Land-Rovers came to a halt and Malik Asad Khan, who was accompanying us as far as the mountains, introduced us to a group of lean and hawk-nosed hill tribesmen who were to be our guides and stalkers. Most of them carried service rifles and wore bandoliers of cartridge cases over their dark green garments. They were Kuttak Pathans, speaking a Pushtu dialect. According to local custom the beards and waxed moustaches of the older men were dyed orange with henna. We shouldered our rucksacks and gave some of the heavy gear to the tribesmen to carry and, dividing into two groups, started to climb a narrow and very rocky trail up the mountain.

After half a mile the track disappeared and we began to climb in earnest up loose shale and steep ravines. The light was beginning to increase and the sweaters which had seemed necessary when we set out were soon discarded. Before long I was perspiring profusely and short of breath, striving to keep up with our guide who, encumbered with a heavy rifle and a loaded rucksack, nevertheless treated the climb as though walking on level ground. I had made the mistake of mounting my heavy, foot-long telephoto lens on my camera, which I carried at the ready, leaving only one hand free for holding on to rocks and bushes as I climbed. This was soon my undoing and I fell heavily when a rock slipped. I grabbed at a bush to prevent myself from sliding into a gully. Inevitably at this altitude the bush was of *Zizyphus* and several long thorns were driven into my skin, one painfully below my thumbnail. The guide quickly came to my aid and insisted on taking the load from my shoulders, which he added to his own.

When we had climbed about 2,000 feet we came to a sheltered ledge, perhaps fifteen paces long by six wide. The guide pointed to a number of circular, bare patches on the ground,

9 *Above* The Sadiqgarh Palace, where the Amir of Bahawalpur entertained members of the first expedition. *Below* We sometimes had difficulty in negotiating tracks intended for ox-carts rather than motor vehicles.

KALABAGH WILDLIFE RESERVE

This reserve was created by the Nawab of Kalabagh
in collaboration with the World Wildlife Fund. All
animals within its boundaries are strictly protected.

پناہ گاہ برائے جنگلی جانور کالا باغ

each a yard wide and surrounded by a ring of droppings. This was obviously the favourite dormitory of a flock of Urial. Some of the droppings were fresh. Above and below the ledge the rocks were almost vertical, providing excellent protection from a surprise attack by a Leopard or a Wolf, which, apart from man, were the only predators the Urial had to fear in these mountains.

The final part of our climb was the hardest and in places extremely steep. I made the last few yards in a state of complete exhaustion and Eric and I lay for a few minutes on the rocky summit to regain our breath. Our guide, whose age, I judged, probably exceeded sixty years, was not even out of breath and grinned at us sympathetically. Or was it sardonically?

The sun was now rising and the view from our vantage point was magnificent. The valley far below was still shrouded in indigo darkness, but the chain of jagged peaks around us was suddenly gleaming with golden brilliance against an amethyst sky. Dawn is my favourite hour of the day and I had watched the sun rise on a similarly wild scene in many countries through-out the world. What magic is held in these few moments be-tween night and day, when the animals of the darkness return from their hunting and the birds burst into the dawn chorus!

> *Full many a glorious morning have I seen*
> *Flatter the mountain-tops with sovereign eye,*
> *Kissing with golden face the meadows green,*
> *Gilding pale streams with heavenly alchemy.*

Eric said, 'My light meter is still registering nearly zero, but we

10 A ranger of the Kalabagh Wildlife Reserve. Punjab Urial mountain sheep are protected in this reserve created for them by the Nawab of Kalabagh. The Panda on the notice is the symbol of the World Wildlife Fund.

should be able to take some pictures pretty soon if there are any Urial about.' Brought back to reality, I gestured to the guide that we were ready to continue. He was scanning the mountains closely and indicated that we should now proceed with caution and in silence. Following his example we crept on all fours along a fissure in the rocks and took up a position where we were able to command a fair view of the next ridge, while remaining hidden.

Suddenly the guide whispered '*Choop-choop*' excitedly and put his finger to his lips. We gathered that this meant 'quiet' and held our breath. He had heard the tell-tale rattle of stones, which indicated that something was approaching. A few seconds later he pointed cautiously and there, silhouetted against the brightening sky, stood a magnificently-horned Urial ram and seven ewes, heads high and ears alertly forward. They were about 250 feet from where we crouched and our camera shutters clicked simultaneously. Though the light was still poor, we had obtained our first pictures. The Urial were suspicious and soon disappeared from view. I was just turning to congratulate the guide when I heard an agonised whisper from Eric, 'To your right—to your right!' Barely fifty feet from us and previously hidden by the big rocks among which we lay, was a group of ewes, which bounded away down the gorge as I turned. They had seen my movement. Eric had been unable to swing his big lens on them from his cramped position.

After some more careful stalking among the peaks we succeeded in obtaining several more pictures of the shy mountain sheep and saw in total about seventy of them, usually at too great a distance for photography. The most exciting moment had undoubtedly been the first encounter; but an almost

equally thrilling incident was hearing a big ram call suddenly—
a wild, reverberating sound more like a roar than a bleat, which
echoed grandly among the high peaks. I reflected that during
the rutting season the crash of the head-on collision between the
mighty horns of the duelling rams would also echo here like
gun shots, a memorable sound I had last heard while watching
American Bighorn Sheep in the Rocky Mountains.

As the sun climbed to its zenith the heat became almost un-
bearable and the rocks burning hot to the touch. The Urial had
all retreated to the highest peaks, where from time to time we
caught sight of them watching us intently, safe in the knowledge
that they and not we were masters of the Salt Range. We decided
it was time to give up the attempt and have lunch. There being
no shade, we selected a flat-topped crag and quietly roasted
while we ate our sandwiches. The sky above us was now a hard,
ultramarine blue and the scene around us quivering in the
radiated heat haze. Nothing, not even the lizards, moved in the
huge sweep of broken rocks beneath us. Yet, far below, we could
hear the voices of a party of Grey Tits and Bulbuls feeding in
the bushes growing along a stream bed.

Lunch finished and our water bottles empty, we began the
long descent, choosing a route which enabled us to slide whenever possible down the scree slopes. We made instinctively for
the green zig-zag of vegetation marking the course of the stream
and presently found that among the deeply worn rocks a trickle
of clear water was running. In one place a small pool had formed
in a hollow and we plunged our burning arms and faces in it.
The stream bed led us to the bottom of the valley, where we
then had to climb a long slope back to the guard hut where
we had left the vehicles. As we toiled up the rocky track in the

full blaze of the sun, I found I could think of nothing but the joys of drinking the clear, cold water which we would find there.

When we reached the hut and had quenched our thirst, we removed our boots and lay for half an hour on the *charpoys* in the cool sleeping-quarters. The thick mud walls and tiny window gave complete insulation from the heat outside. We would have been asleep within five minutes had we not previously seen the remainder of our party toiling up the mountainside a mile behind us when we arrived. When we detected their approach we went out with beakers of water, to tantalise them as they scrambled panting up the last few yards. They, too, had observed many Urial, but having traversed the long valleys had also compiled an impressive list of birds which we had not seen, including our first records of the local race of the White-cheeked Bulbul *Picnonotus leucogenys humei*, which occurs only in the Salt Range, as well as Red-breasted Flycatchers and a flock of brilliantly coloured Short-billed Minivets, which descend from the Himalayas to the Punjab in the winter. The blue-black and scarlet males of the last-mentioned species feeding in a stunted pine had provided George Shannon's party with an unforgettable spectacle. The unmistakable sound of a head-on collision between two duelling Urial rams had rounded off their day.

Jerry Wood-Anderson, who was for ever picking up snakes and other small animals and stuffing them into canvas bags for later examination, now produced his finds. He had already shown us an attractive snake, which he identified as a lizard-eating Cliff Racer *Coluber rhodorhachis*. Next came half a dozen enormous yellow Scorpions, twice the size of those we had seen in Jordan; he was collecting them for a hospital in Paris which specialised in antitoxins. Eric soon had one of the dangerous creatures out of the collecting jar for photography and we placed a cigarette beside it in order to show its size (plate 12*b*). It was finally manœuvred into position with a twig, after repeatedly seeking shade beneath the instep of Jerry's boot. Finally a delightful Hedgehog was produced and was also photographed as it trotted back and forth in the courtyard. This was Brandt's Lesser Gypsy Hedgehog *Paraechinus hypomelas blanfordi*, a particularly engaging species with an eager expression, long ears and contrasting black quills and white underparts (plate 12*a*).

Tom Roberts, too, had had a good day and we had benefited greatly from his knowledge of the smaller and less easily identified birds. None of us from England was familiar with the butterflies of Pakistan and here again he was extremely useful in identifying them for us. Even so late in the year there were many colourful species to be seen, the most frequent in the Salt Range being the Salmon Arab, the Pioneer and the White-edged Rock Brown.

Our first day in the Salt Range had been very rewarding and as we drove back to Kalabagh we were determined to do the area justice. Our efforts to photograph the Urial had been only partially successful and none of us felt we had obtained a really good picture. It was impossible for George to stalk them in such country while carrying a heavy movie camera. The obvious solution was to install him on a good vantage point and then try to drive the Urial within photographic range. At dinner that night we put this suggestion to the Nawab, who immediately promised to organise a drive with the aid of his mountaineer guards and the local villagers. This would be on our last day in the area. Meanwhile, he had arranged that we should be taken to the Masan plateau next morning, for a display of falconry and coursing, followed by a picnic lunch at one of his farms. This suited us admirably, as it would enable us to see something of the wildlife of the plateau and in a cultivated area.

In the course of dinner that night we were introduced to an unusual local delicacy, a sweet made with rice, pumpkin, nuts and fruit sauce, on which had been placed the thinnest imaginable pieces of metal foil, or 'silver paper.' I presumed this was merely for decorative effect until I noticed that our host was eating it with apparent relish. When I inquired what it was made of, he replied that it was high grade silver, which had been beaten to this very fine state between pieces of chamois leather. 'Go on—try it! *Warraq* is very good for you,' he said. I ate it and felt no ill effects. The cooking at Kalabagh was of a Lucullan standard and we were told that there was a different sweet for every day of the month. We were all by now extremely fit from so much exercise and fresh air, but if we had stayed very long with the hospitable Nawab we should have put on a lot of weight.

We arrived at the Masan plateau at about seven next morning. The air was like wine in the early sunlight and the distant jagged peaks of the Salt Range stood out sharply above the golden plain in varying shades of blue, with deep purple shadows in the erosion channels. Here and there on the plain were steeply outcropping yellow sandstone bluffs.

A large crowd of picturesquely dressed beaters awaited us. Among them were the falconers, one of whom was on horseback an impressively dignified and turbanned figure with a fine Goshawk on his wrist (plate 13). Falconers the world over have a language of their own in talking about their birds and the

Pakistani devotees are no exception. To them the 'Long-wing' or falcon is the '*Sia chashme*,' meaning black-eye; the 'Short-wing' or hawk is called a '*Ghulab chashme*,' or rosy-eye. In West Pakistan the Goshawk is the favourite hawk and the Laggar the favourite falcon, though Peregrines, Sakers and Red-capped Falcons are also used, some of them being imported from other countries.

The dog handlers were there, each with a handsome greyhound whose feet had been dyed with henna, which made it look as though it was wearing orange boots. The dogs were keenly aware of the occasion and eager for the chase. When everyone had come forward to greet Malik Asad Khan, we moved off in line abreast across the plain, with the falcons in the centre and the dogs on the wings.

I do not happen to enjoy the so-called blood sports of any kind, particularly when the contest is loaded against the victim. On this occasion, however, the odds favoured the quarry. In the space of three hours many Grey Partridges were flushed, but the Goshawks failed to strike them. Hares also were plentiful and were frequently chased in spectacular manner by the greyhounds; but all except two escaped, chiefly by their greater speed in ascending the little hills which were dotted about the plain and then going to cover on the other side.

Disappointed by the poor results, the beaters lost interest and the hunt gradually disintegrated. The Land-Rovers were brought up and the Nawab himself also arrived. At that juncture Tom spotted an eagle in the distance, pouncing on a hare. It then alighted on a rocky outcrop and several of us drove over to examine it with our binoculars. It was a beautifully marked Bonelli's Eagle and was eating the hare. We were well pleased to have seen it and, without thought of the consequence, reported what we had seen when we rejoined the group assembled around the Nawab's vehicle. We had forgotten the incident when, twenty minutes later, one of the hunters with us, who had stayed behind, was seen approaching with a dead Bonelli's Eagle dangling from either hand. He had shot the pair while they were finishing eating the hare. All the members of my group were shocked by this senseless killing of rare birds; but in a country where all birds with hooked beaks were regarded as harmful vermin, irrespective of their feeding habits, the hunter obviously thought he was only doing his duty. It was, in a way, a salutary reminder to me that the task of saving the wildlife of Pakistan depended first and foremost on education and propaganda, rather than on enforced legislation.

The picnic at the Nawab's farm in the Jubba area was a very pleasant event. After lounging in the shade of the trees on the edge of an orange orchard, drinking large quantities of fresh lemon squash, we sat cross-legged around an impressive display of food set out on the ground on a white tablecloth.

While we feasted, the Nawab, looking very patrician in our midst, told us how the farm had been created and how he had converted a desert region into a highly productive enterprise. The water here came not from wells but from seepage and every drop was made to work to the full. Behind us was a 'Persian Wheel,' a primitive but highly efficient contrivance consisting of a horizontally mounted wooden wheel, to which was harnessed a blindfolded ox, which trudged patiently round and round the

11 *Above* A young male Punjab Urial, photographed after a difficult climb in the Salt Range. *Below* Once common in West Pakistan, the Chinkara Gazelle is now nearing extinction.

enclosure. The wheel had creaking wooden gears driving a chain of earthenware buckets mounted on long wires, which brought up water from below ground and emptied it into an irrigation channel. The channel fed a network of narrow ditches running out among emerald-green crops, which contrasted vividly with the bleached desert beyond. Maize and corn cropped heavily here and two crops of good potatoes were raised every year. More surprisingly in such a climate, cattle were also farmed successfully. The Nawab had introduced from north-west Sind a small, short-legged, but immensely hardy race called *lohanis*, which provided meat, milk, hides and bone fertiliser, as well as being used for ploughing. They were disease-free and 'fed well on next to nothing.' To illustrate the hardiness of these animals, which resemble miniature zebus with a high hump and are less elegant than the local Salt Range *dhannis*, he told the story of a *lohani* cow in calf which had stepped on a leopard trap. The powerful jaws of the trap all but severed her leg. The limb was amputated and a wooden leg substituted and, in spite of the shock, the cow not only recovered but gave birth to her calf without aborting. For men and beasts it is a tough life in the rugged Salt Range country and no place for weaklings.

All the Awans we had seen in various parts of the Nawab's estate had a notably military bearing and the salutes they gave us were strictly according to the British Army drill manual. It was explained to us that without exception they were ex-servicemen who, because of their long warlike tradition, en-

12 *Above* Brandt's Lesser Gypsy Hedgehog, the most attractive of the various species found in Pakistan. *Below* The impressive size of the Scorpions of the Salt Range is shown by comparison with the cigarette.

joyed nothing better than active service. They had all volunteered to rejoin the colours when India attacked the frontier
and the farm had been kept in operation by old men who were
no longer able to disguise their age. All tenants on the farm were
shareholders. A small part of their wages was paid in supple-
mentary food in order to overcome a tendency to hoard money
instead of feeding their families adequately, and there was a
system of inspection to ensure that a healthy diet was maintained. The taking of anti-malaria pills and typhus injections
was also compulsory, so that sickness had been greatly reduced
in the area. The men certainly looked strong and healthy and
were obviously devoted to the Nawab and his son.

We drove back to Kalabagh by way of the Jinnah head-
works, where there was a wide barrage and a very beautiful
blue *jheel* which again reflected the mountains in spectacular
pink and lilac. Along one side was an extensive bed of tall green
Typha reeds and *Tamarix* bushes, where many terns and various
kingfishers were feeding, while along the road embankment an
avenue of venerable *Acacia arabica* trees were in the full glory
of their yellow blossom. A group of stately Great White Egrets
stalked the shallows, each bird faithfully reflected in the still
water. Blue-tailed Bee-eaters and Large Pied Wagtails (which
are much bigger and more dramatically marked than their
European counterparts) were also feeding along the sandy shore.

That night Christopher Savage had to return to Lahore on
business and we gave him a good send-off. He had already
made a great contribution to our work and I was glad that we
were to see him again before the expedition ended.

Our filming of the Punjab Urial next day was a complete
success. Eric, George and I took up a position on a small peak

in the centre of a wide valley soon after sunrise, while the remainder of our group made a wide detour into the mountains. Our Pathan guides, by now fully conversant with our photographic techniques and thoroughly enjoying the prospect of accompanying us again, gave us a big welcome. I was assured that their greeting '*Astara masha*' ('May you never be tired') was traditional and no reflection on our previous physical performance, so we made the appropriate response '*Qhara masha*,' which I gathered meant 'The same to you.'

Two parties of beaters ascended the far side of the ridge behind us and an hour later slowly drove several groups of Urial in our direction. Although most of them kept to the steeper slopes beyond the range of our cameras, a few came fairly close and George obtained a brief sequence of a fine ram and several ewes which could not have been more admirable. He also filmed large family parties running with extraordinary agility across the face of an almost perpendicular cliff.

When we did the diary that night we found that our total of bird species seen in West Pakistan had already reached the 200 mark. It was not a bad figure for ten days' work at a time of year when many migrant species were absent, and bearing in mind that most of our observations had been made in desert regions.

After dinner we had had a long talk with the Nawab and his son about the future of the Punjab Urial. It seemed obvious to us that such a concentration of a rare species in an ideal and already well protected habitat had immense value to Pakistan. The Nawab had told us there were probably about five hundred Urial on his property and we knew that elsewhere in Pakistan this very distinctive race had now disappeared. Who could tell what the future had in store for this remnant flock? So many animal species had already been lost to Pakistan that the need to turn the area into an inviolate and perpetual sanctuary had impressed itself on all of us. Very tentatively I had proposed this to the Nawab and pointed out that in view of the international importance which was attached to the survival of the Punjab Urial, the World Wildlife Fund had a particular interest in it. To our delight he had agreed immediately and thus had come into being the first World Wildlife Fund reserve in Pakistan. To-day, a notice-board in Urdu and English, bearing the Panda symbol of the Fund, stands at the entrance to the Kalabagh Reserve, proclaiming the protection of one of Pakistan's rarest animals (plate 10).

I must insert a sad footnote to this chapter. During our expedition the following year, when we were working in the Sunderbans jungle in East Pakistan, we heard on the radio that the Nawab of Kalabagh had been shot under circumstances which even today remain obscure. It seemed inconceivable to us that such an apparently gentle and charming man should die in a shooting affray. He was succeeded by his eldest son, Malik Muzaffer Khan.

4

From West to East Pakistan

On the first of November we left Kalabagh, having risen at three-thirty and driven out of the compound an hour later. Although it was still dark, Malik Asad Khan, as gay as ever, was there to see us off. We had covered sixty miles by sunrise.

As our Land-Rovers sped across the desert and began to enter the cultivated regions, the rising sun turned the grey landscape suddenly into vivid colours, etching the wind-made ripples in the dunes with strong shadows and turning the mean hovels of the little villages into things of momentary beauty. We passed Nammal *jheel*, which lay steely blue below the reflection of the gilded mountains and was again carpeted with thousands of ducks and waders. Then across the Nikki bridge, where a grossly overladen donkey had collapsed and was being beaten to its feet, and, turning eastward, we drove straight into the eye of the sun. The villages were stirring now and long lines of labourers were making their way out into the fields of millet and corn, accompanied by graceful women carrying large earthenware water jars on their heads. Packs of Indian, or Chestnut-bellied Sandgrouse rose from the dusty trails and flew from us with their usual chorus of guttural croaking.

We left the main highway by an extremely dusty cart-track through heavily browsed wild Olive trees to inspect Khabbaki, a brackish, shallow *jheel* of about one square mile, in the Khushab District. This, according to Christopher Savage, is one of the most valuable wetlands areas in West Pakistan and is the favourite wintering place of enormous numbers of wildfowl.

There were indeed nearly 6,000 ducks and grebes on the *jheel* when we arrived. Among them were 250 White-headed Ducks; this was probably the largest number of these extremely rare birds to be found in a single locality anywhere in the world to-day. None of us had seen them in the wild since our expedition twelve years previously to the Coto Doñana, in Southern Spain.[1] Very little is yet known about the behaviour of this amusing little 'stiff-tail' duck and it is exceptionally difficult to raise in captivity. It has a discontinuous distribution in small numbers around the Mediterranean and Black Sea and in south-western Asia. This interrupted pattern suggests that its breeding areas are relics of a once much wider and continuous range. It is a winter migrant to Pakistan, where uncontrolled shooting severely threatens its survival. Those on Khabbaki *jheel* were feeding busily and their snow-white cheeks stood out brilliantly among the thousands of darker-hued ducks with which they were swimming and diving. Examining them with binoculars we could see that they were just beginning to moult, and that the bills of the males were less bright blue than those we had seen in the breeding season in Spain. Christopher Savage had not only discovered that Khabbaki was the chief wintering area of the White-headed Ducks in south-east Asia, but that during their two-month moulting period, when they became

[1] See *Portrait of a Wilderness* by Guy Mountfort. David & Charles, Newton Abbot.

flightless, they were particularly vulnerable. We later recommended that the area should be given strict protection and soon afterwards the Government gazetted it as a wildlife reserve.

The numerically dominant species on the *jheel* were Pochard (2,000) and Coot (3,000), but there were also some Wigeon, Tufted Duck, Teal, Mallard and a few Pintail, some of which were still in breeding plumage. Black-necked Grebe were very numerous, Little Grebe being scattered among them. Five Bar-headed Geese, four Grey Herons, a party of eighteen Flamingoes and innumerable small waders completed the fascinating assembly. It is interesting to note that when later in the day Tom Roberts visited Uchhali *jheel*, which is not very far from Khabbaki, he found another big concentration of ducks, including a few Shelduck and about 1,000 Shoveler, which we had not yet recorded in such numbers. He also found 212 Flamingoes, nearly all of them swimming in deep water. It is a surprise to some people to be told that these long-legged birds swim with ease and grace when occasion demands. When they do so they look not unlike very long-necked swans.

Tom parted from us at Khabbaki to attend to business affairs, while we drove on to Kalakaha, where Peacocks, which were regarded as sacred guardians of the local shrine, were reported to have established themselves in a feral state in the surrounding woods. Three of these beautiful birds were in fact seen in a wood as we approached the town. We were told that there were about 500 within an area of four square miles and that, being unmolested, they were breeding freely. We applauded the community which gave them sanctuary and sped on our way. Truly wild Peafowl can now be found only occasionally in West Pakistan, in the Murree Hills.

Kalakaha was a busy little town and we had the usual contests of will-power in negotiating the dense traffic. It requires an iron stamina to maintain one's right of way when a Pakistani truck driver decides he will make better progress by driving on the wrong side of the road—and at top speed. However, we saw only one head-on collision between two local citizens of evenly matched resolution.

The town council was obviously modern in outlook. One road bridge carried a poster, 'Get your family planned and get prosperous!' More pungently another proclaimed, 'Only a fool shares his house with bugs!' Birth control and public hygiene are taken seriously in Pakistan.

We halted for lunch at a pleasant rest-house on the outskirts of the town. While the cook was catching and preparing some lean chickens for our meal, we watched the usual cloud of Black Kites which feed as confidently as sparrows around towns and villages in Pakistan. Every time fresh scraps were thrown through the open window a dozen birds swooped down in spectacular manner to secure them.

During the afternoon our route took us through a desolate area of barren loess between Chakwal and Rawalpindi. Some of the erosion channels in the parched ground were 100 feet deep, giving the scene the nightmarish quality of a lunar landscape. This was part of the great Potwar Plateau, which had been created during the Pleistocene period. But already on our right the high peaks of Azad Kashmir were beginning to appear above the horizon, snow-capped and rising to more than 20,000

13 *Above* Goshawks are frequently used for falconry in Pakistan, their usual quarry being hares or partridges. *Below* A Pathan falconer with a Goshawk on the estate of the Nawab of Kalabagh.

feet, and as soon as we joined the Grand Trunk Road, which links Rawalpindi with Delhi, we were back in verdant country. Huge Shisham trees lined the route with welcome shade and villages became more frequent.

We reached Rawalpindi by evening and were soon wallowing in the luxury of baths and air-conditioned rooms. After dinner we were visited by the inevitable local merchants laden with carpets, embroidered shawls, precious stones and other attractions of the region. We gravitated to Eric Hosking's room, which quickly took on the appearance of an oriental bazaar, with merchandise heaped all over the floor and bed. The voluble flow of salesmanship, which I remembered so well, was devised to part the tourist from his money as speedily as possible; but to old hands among us who knew the East, time was an essential element in the bargaining process. Again and again the crestfallen merchants were sent packing. The bundles were tied up to the accompaniment of loud protestations that 'the Sahib is a hard man' and five minutes later the merchants were back. If we swore not to tell anyone, they said, or they would be ruined, special concessions might yet be made. And eventually, an hour or so later (who cares when money is involved?) the bargains were struck at about half the prices originally asked and everyone was well pleased. Duncan and I both bought rather fine rugs at less than half the price asked in England— and for the remainder of the expedition frequently wished we had not added their weight to our already heavy baggage.

At breakfast next morning we were all smartly dressed in

14 *Above* The beautifully marked Russell's Viper is one of the many poisonous snakes found in Pakistan. *Below* A four-foot Tricolour Caspian Monitor, one of several species severely exploited by skin traders.

clean lounge suits for the flight to Lahore and Dacca and, apart from our deeply tanned faces, looked, as George Shannon remarked, 'almost civilised, for a change.' Eric grumbled that he had been unable to sleep in such unaccustomed comfort, whereupon Jimmy retorted that 'our leader has so brain-washed us that we now automatically get up and dress at three-thirty am and don't *need* more than four hours' sleep.'

We flew from Rawalpindi an hour later. As the plane soared into the clear sky we had an impressive view of the towering crest of Nanga Parbat, lying to the north among ridge after ridge of snowy lesser peaks. At least thirty-one lives were lost in attempts to climb this great mountain, which finally yielded to the German–Austrian expedition of 1953, when Hermann Buhl made a solo dash to the summit. The second highest mountain in the world, K–2 (also called Mount Godwin Austen), rising to 28,250 feet, lay far to the east in the Karakoram Range beyond our sight; but if my plans matured for visiting the Himalayas on our next expedition I hoped to see both these mountains from the ground. Meanwhile, the present expedition was only half completed. We were now heading south-east across the vivid green patch-work of crops in the wide flood area between the Jhelum and Chenab rivers, which, like the Ravi and Sutlej, merge before flowing into the Indus below Bahawalpur. The interest of East Pakistan was yet to come.

Our connection to Dacca was scheduled to take off only fifteen minutes after we landed at Lahore and there was an unseemly rush to meet Chris, who was waiting for us with the first batch of mail we had yet received from England. Soon everyone was eagerly reading and exchanging domestic news. Fortunately, as it turned out, the public address system then announced that the plane to Dacca would be delayed until four o'clock. This suited us quite well, as it enabled us to see something of Lahore, the capital of West Pakistan.

With Chris as guide in his home town we visited the sixteenth-century Old Fort, the Sikh Temple and the Grand Mosque. Built of glowing red sandstone in 1634 by Aurangzeb, the last of the great Moguls, the lofty Grand Mosque of Badshahi Masjid is one of the most splendid treasures of Pakistan. Apart from being one of the largest mosques in the world, it is notable for its magnificent *kashi*, or encaustic tile work. Its immense enclosed courtyard holds one hundred thousand pilgrims at the time of religious festivals. Although some of the palaces and shrines in Delhi can perhaps boast more ornate interiors, we found the great inlaid marble halls of the mosque with their high arched ceilings extremely impressive. Outside the tall main gateway, fretted and intricately inlaid with marble tracery, the prospect was unfortunately spoilt by a maze of overhead electric cables, which must constantly infuriate thousands of visiting photographers and lovers of places of historical interest.

Our final visit was to the famous *Zamzama*, immortalised by Rudyard Kipling as 'Kim's Gun,' a massive bronze cannon which was cast in Lahore in 1761 and now stands rather forlornly guarding a main thoroughfare opposite the Punjab University, with busy traffic hurtling past it. By now, with the temperature standing close to 90°F, we repaired to a hotel, where a number of prominent people had assembled to give us lunch. Among them was Amir Ahmed Khan, Secretary of Agriculture, a shrewd man with a great sense of humour, who had shown particular interest in our work. Also Syed Babar Ali, a prominent industrialist whose brother was Pakistan's representative at the United Nations; he too was keen to see the introduction of a vigorous new programme of wildlife conservation. We also met a distinguished geologist, Professor Rees-Davies, who had extensive knowledge of the regions in which we had been working. Our discussion at lunch ranged over many aspects of our work and I was greatly encouraged to find how strong was the support expressed for an organised effort to strengthen the preservation of animals and habitats in Pakistan and for the proposals which Duncan and I were tentatively beginning to outline.

Every seat was taken on our plane to Dacca. The majority of the passengers were well-to-do peasants or shopkeepers, many of them with babies in shawls, or small children who shared seats or sat on the floor. Cooking pots, bedding and large bundles filled every available space. Seats had been reserved for us, however, and we were well cared for by the pretty little stewardess in the long emerald-green jacket or *kameez* and white pyjama trousers or *shalwar* of the becoming PIA uniform.

An excellent dinner was served on the plane. Having handed me my tray, the stewardess asked if I would like some 'Polly-fussy.' Perplexed but always willing for a new experience, I said, 'Yes please,' whereupon she poured me a refreshing glass of imported Pouilly-Fuissé.

The flight across India was made at 25,000 feet, so we could not see much of the scenery below us. The journey was enlivened, however, towards sun-down, when all the Muslim men spread their prayer mats in the aisle and quite unselfconsciously turned to face Mecca for the ritual of their customary devotions. We found this a rather impressive interlude and respectfully kept silent.

It was more than twenty years since I had last visited Dacca and the Chittagong Hill Tracts, which in those days had been part of the Indian province of East Bengal. The Burmese campaign was then at its height and I had had little opportunity for sight-seeing. But I could still remember the curious blend of the ancient East and modernity which is so typical of the picturesque city of Dacca, now the capital of East Pakistan. Chittagong had been a vitally important seaport and air base. I had first landed there when an over-laden Dakota in which I was flying had failed to gain sufficient altitude to cross the Arakan Yoma mountains during a blinding monsoon storm. We had circled back over the Bay of Bengal for the approach to Chittagong and had witnessed a terrifying waterspout, which had momentarily linked the boiling sea with the black monsoon clouds. My recollection of Chittagong was of chaotic congestion in the narrow streets and of a desperate shortage of everything which made life bearable in those unpleasant days. The region has always suffered from natural disasters. Shortly before our expedition left England it had been hit by yet another major typhoon, which had wrecked the port and caused heavy loss of life. But inland lay some of the most beautiful primary forest in the world, a jungle stretching all the way to the frontiers of Assam and Burma. I remembered the hill tribes, the delightful Buddhist Chakmas, the Moghs from the Arakan, and the Murangs and the Tripuras. I was impatient to see them again and to know whether the Tigers, Elephants and other large animals which used to inhabit the Chittagong Hill Tracts still survived.

East Pakistan came into being as a homeland for the Muslims from eastern India in 1947. Hindus, however, still represent

20 per cent of its population. Jinnah had presided over the birth of the new State, but few westerners at the time could believe that the two halves of Pakistan, separated by 1,200 miles of generally hostile Indian territory, could become a truly unified Republic, let alone be governed successfully. Yet the twin provinces, each so dissimilar in almost every respect save the dominant Muslim religion, have undeniably linked hands and achieved nation-hood. Their birth pangs were no less severe than India's. Idealism and the shining goal of independence were not enough in themselves, however, to create a new nation. Inflexible determination was needed to forge a new identity and to cast off the suffocating weight of the past. Strong leadership and above all political stability emerged in the person of Ayub Khan and the remarkable twin Republic of Pakistan had stepped firmly forward into the competitive hurly-burly of the mid-twentieth century. Remembering that the President described Pakistan in his autobiography as 'probably the greatest mixture of races found anywhere in the world,' his achievement was certainly great.

The sophisticated British Trident jet aircraft in which we were flying was proof of this. It symbolised Pakistan's deter-mination to link its two territories by the most modern and efficient means. A Government subsidy enables the inhabitants of East and West Pakistan to fly back and forth cheaply. In 1966 PIA carried nearly one million passengers and, with its inter-national connections, showed a healthy profit. Its pilots were typical of the new young technocrats who are emerging from Pakistan's universities and they were set very high standards by their vigorous chief, Air Marshal Mohammed Asghar Khan. At forty-seven he must have been one of the youngest and most athletic international airline Presidents. He was also one of the very few who regularly captained passenger-carrying flights on international routes. A graduate of the Imperial Defence College he, too, served in the Burma campaign, before becoming Commander-in-Chief of Pakistan's air force in 1957.

It was dark by the time we reached our hotel in Dacca. Here the atmosphere had scarcely changed in twenty years. The moment I entered my bedroom, with its wide, creaking fan mounted in the ceiling, I smelt the familiar musty odour of damp mosquito netting. The humidity, like the temperature, stood close to the ninety mark.

We had drinks in the bar with Colonel Angus Hume, a prominent local businessman who was also an extremely well-informed ornithologist. He knew the Chittagong Hill Tracts and the local tribes from long experience and gave us a fascinating account of the changes which had occurred in recent years. From him we heard the first report of the disastrous fate which had overtaken the Karnafuli jungle reserve after the flooding of the Kaptai Dam, which began in 1960. Extensive losses of wildlife had resulted and apparently no precautions had been taken to drive the jungle animals out of the valleys which had been inundated. The headquarters of the reserve, at Pablakhali, was to be our base for the next week.

Our first stop on our flight next morning was at Comilla, where the war-time pierced steel runway was still in use. The countryside here was very different from that of West Pakistan. There was water everywhere and the paddyfields were either shimmering like thousands of panes of glass, or were unbelievably emerald-green with young rice. Between the Meghna and Lakya rivers the land was flooded and hundreds of frail canoes and sampans were plying back and forth. Here and there isolated homesteads built of bamboo and surrounded by palm trees stood disconsolately in the water. For countless generations the riverain people of the delta had been fighting a losing battle with the capricious power of two of the mightiest rivers in the world, the Ganges and the Brahmaputra, which every year flood thousands of square miles of rich land. New islands are formed and new channels cut, decade after decade, and many ancient cities lie buried by these changes. Both these great rivers rise in the Himalayas. Their power can be judged from the fact that the Brahmaputra alone discharges half a million cubic feet of water per second from its mouth. The delta begins 300 miles inland and extends from Calcutta in the west to the estuary of the Meghna nearly 300 miles to the east. Along its southern border, where its multiple channels reach the Bay of Bengal, lie the low tidal swamps of the Sunderbans, one-third in India and two-thirds in Pakistan. The famous Sunderbans, now one of the last refuges of the Bengal Tiger, was to be a primary objective of our second expedition to Pakistan, which will be described later.

When we landed at Chittagong the airport was crowded. The scene was more colourful than at any previous stop. Many of the men wore turbans and all the women *saris* of vivid hues. Here and there matrons from the stricter castes sat like statues, heavily veiled and remote in their narrow world; but the majority of the younger women were unveiled and vivacious. One or two Pakistani businessmen, looking uncomfortably hot in

15 *Above* The design of fishing craft varied from region to region; those at Chit-Morong were particularly picturesque. *Below* A typical banana barge used by the Mogh tribe in the Hill Tracts.

dark lounge suits of western cut, still wore the traditional tinsel garlands with which they had been presented by their local customers or friends.

Outside in the hot glare of the sun we loaded the vehicles which had been sent to meet us and drove slowly to town through the heavy dock traffic. Many buildings had been destroyed during the recent typhoon and the road was still under repair. Long lines of coolies wearing nothing but loincloths were coaling the ships tied along the wharves and, as the coal dumps were all on the landward side of the road, they added greatly to the congestion. Streams of heavy trucks and hundreds of bicycle rickshaws wove in and out, to the accompaniment of shrill vituperations from drivers and passengers alike. There was noise and dust everywhere. In fact, the scene had changed remarkably little since my war-time visit and the seething shanty-town on the outskirts of the city was as dreadful and squalid as ever.

The day being still young, we paid a visit to the Bayazid Bustami shrine, on the farther side of town. Here, in a turbid pool, hundreds of monstrous Sacred Black Mud Turtles were the centre of attraction. We entered the shrine down a narrow alley flanked by open stalls selling a gruesome array of raw offal, from which Black Kites and House Crows were snatching samples whenever the owners' backs were turned. Pilgrims to the shrine, armed with dripping pieces of cow's lung, were squatting at the edge of the pool, feeding the turtles by hand. Some of the fungus-encrusted monsters must have weighed close

16 *Above* The Black-headed Shrike *Lanius schach tricolor* of East Pakistan is a distinctive local race of the Rufous-backed Shrike. *Below* The Common Myna is a close associate of man throughout the subcontinent.

on two hundred pounds and were obviously thriving on the diet. Their species is thought no longer to survive in a wild state.

Karim, who was completely at ease in negotiating the tortuous maze of Chittagong's streets, led us to what at first appeared to be an open-fronted machine shop for lunch. However, on climbing the stairs, we found ourselves in a Chinese restaurant overlooking the busy street. The food was exotic but excellent. A dead Flying Fox hung by its feet from the overhead tramwires which had electrocuted it opposite the window.

Later, when our convoy of vehicles had fought its way out of the dusty turmoil of Chittagong's traffic, we soon entered attractive cultivated country, where everything was green and sweet-smelling. The Black Kites and grey-necked House Crows which are so typical of human habitation disappeared and were replaced by more interesting birds. Snow-white Cattle Egrets and Pond Herons stalked the paddyfields. Drongos, Mynas, Babblers and Bulbuls dotted the telegraph wires. Magpie Robins and Brown Shrikes were numerous and we had our first sight of a beautiful Black-headed Oriole. Flocks of Green Bee-eaters were skimming the irrigation ditches and Spotted Doves were repeatedly flushed from the roadside. These very attractive little doves are all too easily caught and we saw several peasant children carrying them to market in wicker baskets, after having pulled out their flight feathers to prevent their escape.

We reached the Rangamati rest-house well before sunset. It was a picturesque building, more than a hundred years old and once approachable only by elephant transport through the jungle. Originally built on the bank of the Karnafuli River, it now stands on the edge of the flooded area of the Kaptai catchment, an artificial lake of some 456 square miles. A number of skeletons of drowned forest trees still stood forlornly above the level of the water. The house, with its wide veranda, woven split-bamboo walls and roomy lounge chairs, was a welcoming place after our long ride. Having changed into long sleeves and mosquito boots and with long drinks beside us, we sat and watched a magnificent sunset filling the sky with glowing colours. Only Eric was working, pounding away at his typewriter and surrounded by a cloud of moths and mosquitoes attracted by the light. Drums began to throb in a distant village, where fires were twinkling. A big Flying Fox flapped slowly across the water, looking completely bird-like. Geckos scurried noiselessly about the ceiling, enjoying the harvest of moths above the lamp. We were near the edge of the jungle and from now on could no longer use wheeled transport. Travel would be by launch or on foot. I felt excitement mounting for what the next week had in store for us.

Blackbuck

5

The Chittagong Hill Tracts

As the crow flies it is only forty-six miles from Rangamati to Pablakhali. I decided that if we embarked at mid-morning, we would have time for a quick look at the region of the rest-house beforehand. We were out and about at dawn and soon wished we could spend several days in such attractive surroundings. When I stepped out on to the veranda, just as the sun was breaking the skyline, a perky Magpie Robin was singing on the rail, a White-breasted Kingfisher was sitting somnolently on the prow of a moored canoe below and a long line of Pond Herons was passing low over the glassy water. Big fish were rising in every direction and an amazing volume of birdsong was coming from the trees.

Shortly afterwards I heard an excited cry from Eric and found him and George gazing up into an *Artocarpus* tree (a relative of the Breadfruit), which was literally bowed down with roosting Flying Foxes (plate 21a). Their orange bodies were gleaming in the early sunlight and gave the tree the appearance of bearing a heavy crop of large fruit. A quiet chittering and squealing was coming from the roost. The animals were seldom completely still—stretching and folding first one long wing and then another, or searching their fur for parasites, shifting the grip of their hind feet by which they were suspended. At rest, with their beady eyes shut and their wings tightly shrouding them, obscuring the shining fur, they resembled mummies from an Egyptian tomb; but there was something very engaging about them when awake, particularly when they swung, like acrobats on a trapeze, from branch to branch with the aid of the powerful hooks on their thumbs. Later, when the sun had warmed them, they fanned themselves constantly with half-open wings. Flying Foxes live chiefly on fruit and nectar. We saw some of them carrying figs or bananas in their strong jaws. These big bats serve a very useful purpose by fertilising the flowers of certain jungle trees, particularly Mangoes, with the pollen shed on their heads while taking nectar; their habit of carrying away fruit to their communal roosts also makes them useful agents in seed dispersal.

Little is yet known about the lives or social behaviour of bats and almost nothing of their migratory movements. In the Indo–Pakistan subcontinent their species are very numerous, ranging in size from the tiny Pipistrelles to the Flying Foxes, which have a wing-span of four feet. Some species are insectivorous, some carnivorous and some, like the Fruit Bats and Flying Foxes, are frugivorous. Some, such as the Horseshoe Bats, have short, broad wings and fly in a weak, fluttering manner, whereas others, such as the Sheath-tailed Bats, have narrow swallow-like wings enabling them to fly with great speed and grace. The Flying Fox and Fulvous Fruit Bat have relatively small external ears; their lack of the highly developed faculty of sound perception which is found in the smaller species results in a rather blundering navigation; this is why they are so often seen electrocuted on overhead power lines. The False Vampire and Leaf-nosed Bats, on the other hand, have huge up-standing ears and sensitive, hairy facial crests which help them to locate their flying prey in darkness with such uncanny accuracy.

Most bats have sombre colours, as one would expect from their habit of hiding by day in dark caves or hollow trees. The exception is the beautiful Painted Bat, which has been described by the great naturalist S. H. Prater as the most vividly coloured mammal in the world. It has vermilion and black wings and bright orange fur and is extremely conspicuous in the hand. It is nevertheless perfectly camouflaged when in its favourite roost among brightly coloured foliage. The Flying Fox attempts neither cryptic coloration nor concealment, indeed its bright fur, conspicuous roosting behaviour and powerful odour suggest that it fears no enemies. Obviously it could be an easy prey to many predatory animals, yet one never hears of it being attacked, whereas all the other smaller bats are frequently taken by owls, hawks and various tree-climbing carnivores. It is puzzling to know what limits the numbers of these very successful animals.[1]

Sixty million years ago there were bats on earth similar to those seen today; this means that these wonderfully adaptable winged mammals have inhabited our planet thirty times longer than the human race. The Order Chiroptera, to which they belong, consists of nearly 230 species, or rather more than a quarter of the world's present total of mammals. With the exception of the blood-drinking Vampires of Mexico and tropical South America, which being the major vectors of paralytic rabies cause immense losses to cattle farmers, all bats are to a greater

---

[1] For an excellent description of the bats of Pakistan and India, see *The Book of Indian Animals* by S. H. Prater, published by the Bombay Natural History Society.

or lesser degree beneficial to man. Life might be intolerable in the tropics without the presence of the numerous insectivorous species, which consume half their body weight in insects every night.

After breakfast we walked down to the village. The vegetation was lush and colourful. Exquisite butterflies of half a dozen species were feeding on the white, jasmine-like flowers of the *Tabernae montana* bushes and on the hanging trumpets of *Hibiscus schizopetalus* which reminded me of frilly little scarlet ballerinas (plate 7*a*). During our half-mile walk many new species of birds were seen, including Red-whiskered Bulbul, Gold-fronted Chloropsis, Blue Rock Thrush and Yellow-fronted Pied Woodpecker.

The smiling Chakmas in the village gave us cheerful greetings. We inspected their decorative earthenware pots and intricately woven baskets, which were strictly functional and decorated for pleasure rather than for sales promotion. Naked and very sturdy-looking children were playing among the goats and chickens outside the bamboo huts. Most of the men were busy with the banana and wild cotton crops, or were hewing wood, which the women carried away in enormous bundles on their heads. We photographed a shy young couple smoking their pipes; the mixture of locally grown tobacco and what appeared to be dried cow dung produced a dense aromatic smoke which they inhaled deeply and with obvious satisfaction.

At ten-thirty, accompanied by a native cook and half a dozen squawking hens for our later consumption, we boarded our two sleek motor launches. They were powerful American-built craft, capable of considerable speed and, on the dead calm water, steady enough for us to take both still and movie photographs. As soon as we left the shade of the overhanging trees and reached the open water, we realised that we were going to be well roasted by the sun before we reached our destination. However, there was so much of interest to occupy our attention that we were soon enjoying ourselves. We passed a number of dugout canoes and sampans with colourful square-rigged sails, heavily laden with bananas on their way to market (plate 15*b*). Although the considerable wash of our fast craft must have rocked them badly, we were always given enthusiastic greetings.

We also began to pass enormous, slow-moving rafts of bamboos, some a hundred yards long, on which whole families were living in little lean-to shelters made of matting. The head man usually sat at the extreme stern of these picturesque craft, sheltered from the hot sun by an ancient umbrella and smoking his pipe majestically, while the young men plied the paddles. No two craft were ever alike and the photographers found themselves loading film after film into their cameras.

We had lunch while crossing the main part of the lake, which was so large that we could not see the opposite shore for more than an hour. Presently, ahead of us, a vast expanse of huge dead tree skeletons appeared, standing gaunt and white on the horizon, drowned by the flooding (plate 22*b*). It was not until we were among them that we could appreciate their enormous size, and we wondered why such valuable timber had not been extracted before the flooding. We learned later that although most of the timber had been extracted, the ultimate height of

17 *Above* White-backed Vultures provide an efficient *corps sanitaire*, quickly disposing of carcasses of cattle. *Below* House Crows (with grey necks) and Jungle Crows (all black) are also good street cleaners.

the water level had been miscalculated. Here were birds galore, using the naked trees as vantage points for fishing. Kingfishers, ablaze with iridescent colour, were seen every few minutes and we logged no fewer than five different species—the tiny, jewel-like Blue-eared, the Lesser Pied, the Bengal race of the European Kingfisher, the White-breasted, and the big Stork-billed, with its startlingly blue wings and grotesquely large scarlet bill. Flocks of Blue-tailed and Green Bee-eaters and as many as 250 Rose-ringed and Red-breasted Parakeets at a time swept past our launches. There were also many species of herons and birds of prey perched on the trees, and nearer the shore, several Rhesus Macaque Monkeys, which gazed at us with a disingenuous air. Tufts of orchids and the abandoned nests of Weavers hung from many of the tree branches.

The heat of the sun, the steady hum of the motors and the smooth motion of the launches on the still water had a distinctly soporific effect. We lay back almost surfeited by the beauty of the constantly changing panorama which streamed by on either hand. We were now entering a wide channel and the banks were steadily becoming higher. Secondary growth and old abandoned plantations began to give way to forest. Now and then we passed little native settlements, where bamboo huts on stilts clustered at the water's edge and shouting, naked children shrilled greetings. Around these we saw ample evidence of the harm done by shifting cultivation. Patches of forest trees were cut down and burnt and as soon as the bananas, cotton or bamboo which replaced them had ceased to yield, the area

18 Although ungainly and cumbersome on the ground, the White-backed Vulture is a superb master of soaring flight, sailing for hours on end on almost motionless wings, watching for carrion.

was abandoned and the slash-and-burn procedure was repeated elsewhere. Little by little the rich primary forest was disappearing, for mile upon mile along the shores, giving way to useless scrub. This so-called 'swidden' system of agriculture, in which land is cleared, cultivated for a year and then allowed to revert to bush, is a familiar problem to conservationists throughout the tropical regions. The abandoned clearings have the temporary advantage of providing fresh browsing for deer species, but the natural regeneration from adjacent forest trees is inhibited by the inevitably rapid advance of blanketing vines and other undergrowth.

It was not until late in the day that we began to see large tracts of untouched forest, towering to a great height and densely interwoven with impenetrable vines which cascaded in vivid green right down to the water. Here one felt a sensation of isolation and insignificance—a feeling I had not experienced before except in the wide open desert.

In this entirely different scene we were at last in the real jungle. The vegetation was a solid green wall and we had to crane our necks to see any sign of wildlife, most of which was restricted to the highest part of the tree-tops (plate 27a). Occasionally a turtle or a water snake would slither off a root projecting into the water, or a kingfisher would flash past, like a jewelled arrow from a bow; but apart from these there was little movement at eye level. Presently, however, a sudden commotion among the branches revealed a pale golden monkey with a very long tail and limbs, which made a graceful thirty-foot leap across a gap in the foliage. It was our first sight of a young Capped Langur. The adults are grey, and have a distinctive crown or cap of stiff hair. Their range is from the Chittagong region and Assam to upper Burma and five different races have been described. Jerry Wood-Anderson had warned us that there is considerable variation in the colours of immature Capped Langurs and we later saw several which were so like the colour of the Golden Langur (*Presbytis geei*) that we at first believed them to be of this species, which, however, is restricted only to the Sankosh and Manas River region near the Bhutan frontier.

Another interesting primate, the Slow Loris, inhabits the Chittagong Hill Tracts. It is a very self-effacing and strictly nocturnal little animal and therefore seldom seen; but Eric later made a good portrait of one which he found in captivity (plate 53*a*). An ape, the only one inhabiting the Indo–Pakistan subcontinent, also occurs here: the Hoolock, or White-browed Gibbon. We failed to see it, but one morning in the hill forest behind Pablakhali I heard the unmistakable chorus of howling which is so characteristic of these charming black creatures. I had become very familiar with them in northern Assam and Burma during the Second World War.

Later in the afternoon the banks again receded and, after making our way rather uncertainly through a labyrinth of seemingly identical lagoons among the tall dead trees, we caught sight of a wooden bungalow with an invitingly deep veranda, standing on a small promontory in a backwater among low, heavily forested hills. At the small landing stage a notice-board proclaimed it to be the headquarters of the Karnafuli reserve. This was Pablakhali, where we were to stay for several days.

A flight of steps, made by pinning logs in the steep bank, led up to the bungalow. As we toiled up it, carrying our heavy kit, we suddenly realised how much the movement of the launches had tempered the blazing heat of the sun. When we reached the deeply shaded veranda we stripped off our shirts and lay back in the comfortable cane chairs to take stock of our new surroundings. Amid cheers Karim quickly changed into the cool, sarong-like *lunghi* of East Pakistan, of which he is a native.

The view across the water was wild and romantic in the extreme, with occasional canoes gliding smoothly past among the giant trees. To the left a winding track above the reed beds led to the small native village of Pablakhali, which lay hidden among the trees. To the right and behind us were wide, marshy pools, fringed with tall reeds and almost covered by flowering Water Hyacinths. A semi-tame female Sambur, one of the typical deer species of the Chittagong Hill Tracts, was browsing at the edge of the nearest pool (plate 52*b*). And beyond, surrounding us on three sides, was the hilly jungle—immense, mysterious and vividly green—a veritable cornucopia of hidden treasure awaiting us.

As the sun descended, flight after flight of Red-breasted Parakeets and both Red-rumped and Wire-tailed Swallows passed over us, heading for their roosting places. Scores of smaller birds were settling in the vegetation around us and a big Gecko lizard, called Merten's Tokay, began its evening incantation—a quiet chuckling, followed by a loud '*Gec-ko . . . gec-ko . . . gec-ko . . .*' (plate 29*a*). A Fruit Bat flew past and a Barred Owlet called. The sky and the water turned vivid yellow, then pink, then flaming crimson, while the skeleton trees, with their writhing, twigless branches jet-black against the fading light, formed a fantastic pattern in the foreground. The last dugout canoe, pencil-thin and with a single figure wielding a paddle from the stern, crossed the eye of the sun as it dipped behind the far shore. And suddenly, so quickly that it was like magic, it was night.

We dined well that night, our enterprising new cook taking his duties seriously. With some difficulty I then rounded up the team and we went on to the veranda to write the diary. Only two paraffin pressure-lamps were available, one of which was quickly commandeered by Eric for his typing. The rest of us gathered around a table under the other lamp—and were speedily joined by thousands of mosquitoes, moths and beetles, including several huge Rhinoceros Beetles. Leafing through the diary pages now, I see the trace of mosquito corpses on almost every page, for this was to become a nightly purgatory.

The local manager of the reserve joined us as we were finishing the diary and was introduced to us by Siddiqi. He gave us an account of the history and problems of the reserve and of the present status of its larger animals. It was a sad story.

In 1954 the reserve had been planned to embrace 800 square miles around the Kassalog River and Maini headwaters. Work on the Kaptai Dam project began in 1960 and by 1963 the area of the reserve, having a lower priority, had been reduced to 500 square miles under Pakistan's Second Five Year Plan. Later, it was twice further reduced and by the time the flooding of the dam was completed only 172 square miles of the original reserve remained. Most of the best forested valleys were drowned and although the water rose slowly, considerable losses of wildlife occurred. Many Elephants, Tigers and various species of deer which escaped drowning were unable to retreat across the 3,000-foot ridge of the Lushai Hills to the east, and therefore moved either north into Assam, or west across the Kassalog River into Tripura. Some of the best of the remaining land along the

margins of the flooded area was then taken over for tribal cultivation and ten square miles were planted with Government
controlled plantations. Under present plans, an additional thousand acres per annum were to be taken from the reserve for
planting Teak.

A monoculture of Teak, however desirable commercially, is
a death-knell to wildlife conservation. No species of deer or
monkey can find food in such vegetation and they are forced to
abandon the area. In the absence of deer, Tigers and Leopards
turn to preying on cattle and goats around the villages and are
therefore soon shot. Some of the abandoned plots of shifting
cultivation along the water's edge of the Kaptai Dam provided grazing for a while, but not for long. The establishment of
marsh vegetation on the banks was inhibited by the thirty-foot
fluctuation in the water level, and ducks were therefore relatively
uncommon. The extremely rare White-winged Wood Duck,
which used to be found here before the flooding, had now
vanished. A few Gayal (a subspecies of the Gaur, or Indian
Bison) and Chital, or Axis Deer, and Sambur had been successfully introduced and there was a small remnant population
of Barking Deer, or Muntjak. Tigers and wild Indian Elephants
had become rare and the Marsh Crocodiles had all been killed.
The reserve's staff of twenty-five men were chiefly concerned
with controlling poaching, though there was now so little left
to poach apart from Rhesus Monkeys, which were still taken
for medical research, that this was no longer a great problem.
Obviously what had once been planned as a major jungle
reserve had now lost all prospect of fulfilling its proper function.

We were rather depressed by this account. Nevertheless, we
soon learned that the variety of lesser forms of wildlife which

remained was still so great that we had plenty to keep us occupied. Our visitor's parting words to the effect that a Tiger had just killed a Porcupine near the village provided a tantalising stimulus for the following morning.

It was not, however, a Tiger but a Leopard which had made the kill. We distinguished the killer's tracks among the blood-stained quills which we examined at dawn near the village. Unlike the Tiger, which sometimes incautiously attacks Porcupines and is severely maimed or even killed by their needle-sharp quills, the Leopard always goes for the unprotected head and seldom comes off second best. The Crested Indian Porcupine is a powerful and self-reliant animal which, when full grown, can exceed three feet in length (plate 59b). Its method of defence is unique and terrible in its effectiveness. Instead of running away, it suddenly runs backwards at great speed, driving its fully erected quills into the face of its pursuer. Tigers and even Leopards have been found dead with quills deeply embedded in their lungs.

The local villagers were convinced that a Tiger had made the kill and were scared of using the track at night. Several of us walked the track at dawn and dusk during the following week in the hope of seeing the Leopard, but without success.

The beautiful Clouded Leopard still occurs occasionally in the Chittagong Hill Tracts and some cubs had recently been taken not many miles from Pablakhali. The species is essentially arboreal, with short limbs and a very long tail (plate 59a). Although only about half the weight of a full grown Leopard, its powerful build and enormous canine teeth, which are closest among the present cats of the world to those of the long extinct Sabre-toothed Tiger, enable it to kill large deer such as the

Sambur with apparent ease. The Clouded Leopard represents the link between the large cats of the genus *Panthera* and the small cats grouped in the genus *Felis*; its scientific name *Neofelis nebulosa* shows that it has been placed in a separate genus.

We devoted our first day at Pablakhali to exploring the surrounding lake by launch, our two boats working in opposite directions. When we set out at 5.30 a slight mist over the water made the air refreshingly cool, but by noon when we checked the temperature we got a reading of 90°F in the shade and 125°F in the sun. It was difficult to believe that this was winter and that the region had an annual rainfall of 120.4 inches. Photography was made difficult by the brilliant glare reflected by the water; however, birds were so numerous that we took hundreds of pictures. Among many new species seen were Ashy Swallow Shrikes, which are pale-grey birds with a sweet song, long wings, short tails and a very graceful, swallow-like flight. Also seen were Orange-breasted Pigeons, Emerald Doves, Pied Crested Cuckoos and Chestnut Bitterns. It seemed as though the majority of the birds in this wonderful region were either outrageously brightly coloured, such as the various parakeets, bee-eaters, orioles and kingfishers; or had striking head ornaments or tail streamers, such as those worn by the perkily crested Racket-tailed Drongo, which trails two feathered ornaments on the bare shafts of its long, forked tail. When I first saw a Racket-tailed Drongo in flight I thought the two objects fluttering behind it were a couple of the big black Carpenter Bees of the region chasing it. Even the normally austere birds of

19 *Left* The Indian race of the Honey Buzzard *Pernis ptilorhynchus ruficollis*. *Right* A pair of Pallas's Fishing Eagles mating near their eyrie at Haleji Dhand, which they had occupied for seven years.

prey included the boldly coloured Brahminy Kite, resplendent in reddish-chocolate with a white head and breast, and the Crested Hawk Eagle and Crested Serpent Eagle, both with conspicuous, though quite dissimilar, crests.

The following morning Eric, Siddiqi and I made a ten-mile journey on foot into the hills, where it was reported that several Gayal had recently been seen. We took a native guide and two porters to help us. After so much riding in Land-Rovers and motor launches it was good to be exploring as pedestrians again and, of course, much more rewarding in terms of seeing the wildlife of the jungle.

Laden with equipment and to the good-natured jeers of our other colleagues, we set out briskly past the native village and into the Teak plantations. But as soon as the sun rose our pace slackened and we found ourselves stopping more and more frequently in patches of shade. The Teak saplings were only ten feet tall and provided little shelter; there were, however, occasionally large trees beside the track and these proved to be the best places to see birds. Our most notable discovery was a party of delightful little Scarlet Minivets feeding in a vine. The scarlet and black males and grey and yellow females, combined with the mauve flowers and bright green leaves of the vine, made a breath-taking picture. As often happens in the tropics, my attempt to photograph them in colour was unfortunately foiled by the intense brilliance of the light on the dense foliage among which the birds were constantly flitting.

Two other jewel-like small birds were seen later on our

20 Like all the species of cats in Pakistan, the Caracal has now become a rare animal. Its last strongholds are in the Thar Desert and the remoter parts of Baluchistan.

walk—a Purple Sunbird and a Scarlet-backed Flowerpecker. Among the larger birds, a Golden-backed Woodpecker with a crested crimson crown took pride of place.

About mid-morning we reached the area where the Gayal had been reported. Several Mogh tribesmen were waiting for us by the track and they led us into an area of steep little hills, among which wound a sandy trail, with tangled jungle on either side. It did not look like a very good place for observing a shy animal with an uncertain disposition, unless we met it face to face on the narrow trail, which we did not particularly relish. However, we followed our guides closely and silently, hoping we would presently come to more open country. Suddenly, with no warning at all, our guides stood aside, pointing—and then melted into the trees, leaving us face to face at sixty paces with two magnificent Gayal bulls. One was considerably larger than its companion and weighed, I judged, well over 1,000 lb. Their massive bodies, with a high dorsal ridge, were a shining, purplish-black, and their characteristically rather small feet were white, with white 'stockings.' Their horns were short and only slightly curved (unlike those of the Gaur, which are strongly curved). They were grazing quietly and had neither seen nor heard us. Without a word, Eric and I immediately began photographing them.

Knowing that the Gayal is usually regarded as at least a partially domesticated form of the Gaur, which it closely resembles, I was quite unprepared for what happened next. Both bulls evidently caught our scent, or heard our shutters clicking. Throwing up their heads, they snorted and charged straight at us, thundering along the trail like express trains (plate 8b). Encumbered by heavy cameras, we had no chance of out-running them. On our left the overgrown ground fell away too steeply to negotiate. On our right it was also steep and the undergrowth too dense to climb. Simultaneously we came to the same decision and, leaping as high as we could up the bank, cowered behind the nearest tree. In a cloud of dust the Gayal thundered past and disappeared into the jungle. Quaking with fright, I snapped them at twenty feet as they passed and obtained quite a good picture.

Excited shouts came from the undergrowth and our guides emerged, grinning broadly. They had evidently enjoyed the incident highly and chattered among themselves, slapping their thighs with obvious relish. We grinned back at them and made our way up to the main track again. Half-way there, a sudden commotion in the undergrowth showed that the Gayal were still close by. This time we all sprinted up the remaining slope at a very creditable speed and collapsed, laughing, in the shade of a big tree to get our breath back. Eric and I then passed a pleasant half-hour photographing the butterflies which swarmed over a patch of sunlit flowers, before we set out on the home-ward journey.

The following morning George Shannon and Jimmy Hancock, in spite of the probably exaggerated account of our adventure with the Gayal, made the same journey, found the same animals and photographed them at fairly short range without eliciting the least sign of aggression from them. After that George and Jimmy firmly believed we had been pulling their legs, until they saw our pictures of the charging Gayal on our return to England.

There is still some uncertainty about the true relationship of the Gayal *Bos frontalis* and the larger Gaur *Bos gaurus*. Some authorities such as George B. Schaller, whose studies of the Gaur were very extensive, still cautiously refer to the Gayal as 'believed to be a domesticated form' of this species. E. P. Gee, who has studied both the Gaur and the Gayal, also leaves an element of doubt in stating that 'nowadays only the Gaur is regarded as a wild species and the Gayal is thought to be a domestic or domesticated animal ... either the domestic survival of an extinct wild species, or else a cross between the wild Gaur and the domestic cow—a hybrid which breeds true (perhaps in the fourth generation and afterwards).' He then draws attention to the puzzling fact that the Gayal has never been known in central and south India, where the Gaur and local domestic cattle are most numerous: in other words where a cross would be most likely. On the other hand, in areas where Gayal chiefly occur, notably in north-east India and Burma, they often interbreed with domestic cattle. The degree of their domestication is at best very slight, for, as Gee points out, they are never used for ploughing, nor as beasts of burden, nor for milking, though occasionally serving for barter or ceremonial sacrifice. Whether a true species or a subspecies, whether or not originally or occasionally crossed with domestic cattle, the Gayal which charged Eric and me that morning in the Chittagong Hill Tracts seemed splendidly unconcerned about their scientific status.

Returning to the bungalow in the full heat of the midday sun was exhausting. After stripping and pouring several buckets of lukewarm water from the lake over myself, I had lunch and passed the remainder of the afternoon watching the constantly changing scene around the building. In the nearest pool a five-foot Ocellated Water Monitor with a laterally flattened tail was gliding sinuously among the Water Hyacinths. Presently it climbed out on to a floating log and I was able to examine its handsome black body patterned with yellowish spots. Its long, bluish, forked tongue was constantly flickering in and out and it yawned to reveal a cavernous pink mouth. In the flowering tree under which I was sitting, golden-yellow White-eyes and Black-headed Munias were busily feeding, daintily picking insects from the yellow blossoms. A Blue Whistling Thrush and a Malabar Whistling Thrush were singing contrapuntally on either side of the pool and Spotted Doves were crooning a soft accompaniment. Huge black and white butterflies glided everywhere, sometimes alighting in half-dozens to suck the juice of a fallen fruit with their watch-spring-like probosces.

George Shannon, Duncan Poore and Jimmy Hancock returned at dusk after an arduous day exploring a tract of primary forest up-river. Determined to do more than examine it from the comfort of a launch, they had landed and cut their way into the dense vegetation. They had succeeded in obtaining glimpses of Elephants, Capped Langurs and Indian Pied Hornbills and a number of other interesting creatures. But they discovered that their underclothing had been soaked with blood by the leeches which abounded in the jungle and had been exhausted by the physical effort required to penetrate even a short distance from the river bank. The leeches had certainly had a bonanza in finding human blood. In such dense vegetation these largely immobile creatures, which science has shown are capable of living without food for years, normally have to wait for the passing of a Wild Boar, or a Wild Dog, which are the only likely mammals to be found there, before attaching themselves to a victim.

Stimulated by the news that Elephants were still in the region, we planned that the whole party should visit the Rangibara region where George's group had located them. Few wild Elephants now remained in Pakistan. When we discussed this with the manager of the reserve, however, he strongly advised us not to attempt it. There was a rogue male in the neighbourhood which had chased several tribesmen and we would certainly not be able to approach undetected in such difficult jungle. He advised us to wait a day or two until the herd, perhaps by then minus the rogue, moved into easier country. We accepted his advice and settled for a launch trip up the channel of the neighbouring Shishak River.

In some respects the excursion which we made the following day was the most enjoyable of the whole expedition. To begin with, the scenery was constantly beautiful and constantly changing as we followed the winding course of the river through the jungle. At times we passed open backwaters, surrounded by the white, waving plumes of *Saccarum* grasses, where fallen trees sprawled picturesquely and Little Green Herons, Spotbill Ducks, Purple Gallinules and various sandpipers were feeding (plate 54b). But for most of the way the river banks were high and the boundary of the jungle towered for hundreds of feet above us. Here and there the pale trunk of a gigantic Teak, or the heavy foliage of a climbing fig soared above the bright green wall; or a group of shining banana trees, or a clump of feathery fifty-foot bamboos, broke through the enveloping vines which trailed down to the water. Duncan said that the dominant vine, *Michania scandens*, had appeared quite suddenly in 1958 and had spread like a forest fire, smothering the forest verges and river banks from Assam and the Chittagong Hill Tracts to Malaya.

During our expedition the following year we found it had spread to the tea gardens in Sylhet. It inhibits the production of nitrogen in the soil and has become a major problem in the rubber plantations. The many species of jungle figs, on the other hand, some of which began life as epiphytes, are of immense value and their fruit a favourite food of many species of monkeys, fruit bats and birds such as hornbills and pigeons. The fig is therefore an important factor in the food chain of many larger animals which prey on these lesser creatures.

After several hours we reached the reserve watch-house at Gonacheri, a simple bamboo hut on stilts at the mouth of a small tributary. A small group of Mogh tribesmen wearing colourful *lunghis* led us up the steep bank to the hut, where they provided us with fresh lemons, with which we made cool drinks. To our chagrin, they told us that shortly before we arrived a large Python had been seen crossing the river. They had scarcely done so when a boy rushed up the steps gesticulating wildly. The Python had been spotted on the bank of the creek below. We rushed down to the water and I jumped into a dugout canoe with one of the tribesmen, who quickly paddled across to the opposite bank, where three men were peering into the vegetation. With a shout of triumph, one leaned forward and grabbed the snake's tail. The other two soon seized its head and a tug-of-war ensued. The snake was a big and powerful one and had wrapped one coil around a tree; but amid a chorus of shouted instructions it was finally dragged down to the canoe and carried across the water. Dugout canoes are incredibly unstable craft at the best of times and this one was barely twelve inches wide. How we reached shore without capsizing I shall never know, for the Python was thrashing the free parts of its heavy body violently from side to side in the grasp of its triumphant captors. Once on shore, we examined and photographed it with great interest. It measured more than fourteen feet in length and had a massive head with wide jaws (plate 23*a* and *b*). Pythons are now by no means numerous and suffer severely from the demands of the skin traders, who use their beautifully patterned skins for handbags and shoes. We released our captive on the river bank and watched it swim powerfully across the Shishak, none the worse for its adventure.

It was not until we returned to England and sent Jerry Wood-Anderson our photographs that we learned the importance of our discovery. It was not, as we had thought, the familiar Rock Python *Python molurus*, but a Reticulated Python *Python reticulatus* which we had captured. This snake had never previously been recorded nearer to the Chittagong Hill Tracts than southern Burma and Malaya, and we had added a new species to Pakistan's list. Two years later, however, Tom Roberts found this species again in the Ukhia jungle, in the southern Hill Tracts near Cox's Bazaar. In this remarkably richly endowed area he also found a Marbled Cat (which is very rare), some Gaur bison and that curious, donkey-like animal with horns, the Serow, a goat-antelope whose normal range is from Kashmir southward through the Burma hills to southern Malaya and Sumatra, and eastward to China.

We thanked our Mogh friends for their help and hospitality and continued our explorations. An hour later we noticed a commotion in the tree-tops and found a number of Rhesus

21 *Above* We found a large roost of Flying Foxes in the garden of the rest-house at Rangamati. *Below* The Bloodsucker Tree Agama gets its strange name from its reddish throat, not from sucking blood.

Macaque Monkeys and Indian Pied Hornbills feeding on the ripe fruits of a fig. Unfortunately the foliage was too dense to enable us to get good pictures, but Eric managed to catch a Hornbill in flight, which provided us with a reasonably satisfactory record (plate 24a). They were very striking birds, with powerful black and white wings and grotesquely large horny casques above their bills.

While watching the Hornbills we saw a minuscule Streaked Spiderhunter feeding among the flowers of a banana. It was only eight feet from our moored launches and I marvelled at the delicacy with which it picked minute insects from the flowers with its slender, sickle-shaped bill. Its head was white with pollen and it was obviously doing a useful job as a fertilising agent.

That evening the sunset was the most spectacular we had seen on our travels. Minute by minute the flaming colours changed and we watched spellbound until the sun's final quick plunge. Long after we had retired to bed, after an excellent dinner of local fish, chicken, yams, pumpkins and the delicious little thin-skinned bananas of the region, Karim and Siddiqi entertained some of the local wardens to a party. Judging by the noise, which continued far into the night, it was evidently a success.

Just before sunrise next morning, while we were having breakfast, George invented a new beverage. Having put a generous spoonful of Nescafé in his cup, he found we had run out of hot water. Nothing daunted, he seized Eric's pot of strong

22 *Above* A pair of Spotted Owlets at their nest-hole waiting for dusk. *Below* A huge area of primary jungle near Pablakhali was flooded by the Kaptai Dam project, drowning many rare animals.

tea and poured it over the coffee, which he then drank with relish, pronouncing the resultant 'teafee' to be excellent. Most of us often took liberties with our diet during our expeditions, eating all manner of unusual local foods, though maintaining strict discipline in boiling our water. Only Eric, who was staunchly conservative, denied himself the pleasure of experiment. If, as sometimes happened, we paid for our experience with a bout of colic, we fasted, while George, as medical officer, restored us with Kaolin, Sulphathiazole, or Paregoric.

That day we divided into three parties. George, Eric and Karim, having heard that the Elephants had moved to a more accessible locality, went to try their luck at photographing them. Duncan, Jimmy and Siddiqi went to explore the drowned forest region. As I was anxious to study the many puzzling small warblers which inhabited the *Saccarum* and *Arundo* marshes, I decided to concentrate on these. Even after hours of careful observation, however, I was still left with several which I failed to identify, because of the difficulty of holding them in view for more than a few seconds among the tangled grasses in which they skulked. Nevertheless, I was able to compile a fairly respectable list, which included Fantail Warbler, Franklin's Longtail Warbler, Plain Longtail Warbler, Striated Marsh Warbler, Indian Great Reed Warbler, Paddyfield Warbler and the East Pakistan race of the Yellow-bellied Longtail Warbler. The many *Phylloscopus* Leaf Warblers completely defeated me and I doubt that anyone could have named them with certainty without examining them in the hand. I regretted that I had not brought mist-nets with me.

While waiting for the return of my colleagues that evening, I strolled down to the village. In a clearing not far from there I found the red earth had been freshly tunnelled by a large animal. Suspecting the occupant to be a Porcupine, I knelt down and peered into the hole. As I did so I heard the unmistakable rattle of quills and caught a brief glimpse of these powerful armaments disappearing inside. But what immediately struck me was that the animal had an undeniable tail, with a tuft of stiff spines on it. The Indian Porcupine *Hystrix indica* (plate 59*b*) has no tail and although I would have preferred to see the whole beast I felt sure that the occupant of the burrow must therefore be a Brush-tailed Porcupine *Atherurus macrourus*. This species, which is rare and little known, is said to occur in parts of lower Bengal, Assam and southward to Malaya, and undoubtedly should be present in the Chittagong Hill Tracts. However, as my observation was so brief, I felt obliged to put square brackets around the entry in our diary (our formula for an unconfirmed record), though I had very little doubt about it.

The Elephant party was unlucky. The place where the herd had been feeding was located with the aid of local tribesmen and very fresh droppings were found; but the trail led into thick jungle and as there was still uncertainty as to the whereabouts of the rogue male, the attempt had to be abandoned. Had the party arrived half an hour earlier the herd would have been in clear view. Nevertheless, the long journey was not wasted. Eric had photographed a splendid Red Jungle Fowl (plate 53*b*). The first records of a Bronze-winged Jacana, a Grey-headed Fishing Eagle and a Large Green-billed Malkoha were obtained and a number of Capped Langur and Rhesus Monkeys were seen. Duncan's party also added several new species of water birds and raptors to our list, including Pallas's Fishing

Eagle and some high-flying geese which were almost certainly
the rare Forest Bean Goose *Anser fabilis middendorffi*.

There had been some doubt about the bookings for our
return flight from Chittagong to Dacca and Karachi. As no
message had reached us (neither mail nor telephone penetrating to our lonely outpost), Karim tried unsuccessfully to contact
Air Commodore Dass by radio. In the absence of news we
decided that it would be a wise precaution to curtail our stay
at Pablakhali by one day and move back to Rangamati, where
there was a telephone. We hated to leave such wonderful surroundings, but consoled ourselves by organising a farewell party,
sustained by our last bottle of whisky. Our Muslim friends, de-
barred by their religion from sharing the whisky, nevertheless
entered into the spirit of the occasion with their customary enthusiasm. The big Gecko under the roof also excelled himself,
chuckling and calling lustily from his hidden sanctuary among
the rafters, as though enjoying the party.

As a final consolation I decided that we need not move off
at dawn, but could make a final tour of the lagoons before a
ten o'clock rendezvous at the main pool. To save time we
packed the heavy gear before turning in.

For a footnote to our work in this region it is pleasing to be
able to report that, following our recommendations, the Karnafuli Reserve has now been re-shaped and vastly improved. An
additional hundred square miles of untouched primary forest
adjoining the Burmese border have been added and a further
protective buffer zone of similar size established on the vulnerable western side. The planting of Teak has been restricted and
the accommodation at Pablakhali improved.

The journey to Rangamati next day was restful after our

exertions in the jungle. We had been leading a pretty strenuous life for the past three and a half weeks and had seldom had time to relax. It was surprising how quickly we had become accustomed to a working day of eighteen hours, for we were almost invariably up before the sun and seldom able to get to bed before eleven at night by the time the diary was written and the equipment cleaned and overhauled. Breakfast was always a hurried scramble, with cameras being loaded and the day's work being discussed, and I usually began the diary with the dessert at dinner. On the homeward journey, lying back at ease in the comfortable launch, I felt proud of the fact that, in spite of the demands I made on my team, I had not once detected a sign of friction or ill humour.

Birds of prey were numerous on the journey to Rangamati and we stopped to photograph a Lesser Spotted Eagle which obligingly allowed us to circle it while it watched us from a dead tree standing in the lake. We also had a fleeting glimpse of a Lesser Adjutant Stork flying near the shore—the first we had seen. As we drew near our destination we concentrated on trying to photograph kingfishers, but these quick-moving jewels continued to present us with only distant shots and we never succeeded in obtaining good portraits, though George had already filmed the big White-breasted Kingfisher at close quarters.

We lunched at the comfortable Rangamati rest-house, which looked just as welcoming as before. The Flying Foxes were still hanging in their roost, squealing and twittering and scratching themselves contentedly, and perky Indian Redstarts and Pied Mynas were still hopping on the lawn. It was a supremely peaceful place and we were sad to leave it again so soon.

The run to Kaptai did not take long. As we approached the

big dam we were reminded that we were entering a restricted area, where photography was forbidden. Why this should be necessary so many years after the dam had been completed was not clear, but we dutifully put away our cameras.

We were comfortably quartered in the now empty buildings which had originally been erected for the engineers who had built the dam. Beyond a pleasant garden was a large expanse of wasteland above the dam, on which dozens of big American-made bulldozers, road-rollers and other earth-moving equipment stood in lonely disarray. The ever rampant creepers were already climbing over many of them. Swarms of House Swifts and Red-rumped Swallows were feeding above the placid water beyond the dam and over the flowering Flame of the Forest trees beside the buildings. The site, which must once have swarmed with labourers, was now almost deserted. We were told, however, that the Department of Tourism was taking over the buildings and that there were plans for creating a holiday resort by the dam.

After taking a shower and relaxing in the garden we were driven to a pleasant, air-conditioned club-house, where we dined in unfamiliar comfort. As we were not to continue our journey to Chittagong until after lunch next day I announced, amid cheers, that we should celebrate by breakfasting at the luxurious hour of eight. Such was the force of habit, however, that all of us had toured the dam site the following morning long before we assembled at the breakfast table.

We paid an interesting visit that morning to the riverside village of Chit-Morong. The inhabitants were Buddhist Chakmas, who made a modest living by fishing (plate 15*a*). Among the trees in the centre of the village stood a small temple, with the typically decorative curving roof and lattice windows of a Burmese pagoda—in fact only the carved dragon-like *chinthay* guarding the four corners were lacking. An elderly priest with a shaven head and wearing the saffron robe of his office heightened the impression of an authentic Burmese scene. All the boys of the village, on reaching the age of fourteen, entered the monastery for one month's religious tuition. For a couple of rupees one of these shaven-headed young acolytes willingly posed for us on the steps of the temple, despite the disapproving mutterings of the old priest who had retired and was watching him through the lattice window.

The villagers were at first shy and the women quickly scrambled up the ladders into their thatched huts; but when George set up his cine-camera their curiosity overcame their timidity and they gradually emerged again. Soon George was surrounded by smiling children and able to photograph them and their pipe-smoking mothers, some of whom were strikingly beautiful in their brightly coloured *lunghis*. He particularly wanted to film a delightful but shy little boy, aged about three years, whose only adornment was a circlet of small bells around his organs of masculinity. As soon as George's intention was apparent, the child's grandmother, a toothless old witch in a frayed straw hat, dragged the boy forward. The boy burst into howls of anguish and the scene, alas, was spoilt.

That afternoon, when we began our journey back to civilisation, there was a tiresome delay at the police post guarding the exit from the dam site. It required the combined efforts of Siddiqi and Karim to convince the guards that our baggage need not be searched for hidden bombs or contraband. The arguments went on interminably, while a long line of trucks and bullock carts piled up behind us. However, common sense eventually prevailed and we were on our way.

We added only one new species to our lists during the journey to Chittagong—a Small Indian Civet, which had been run down by a passing car. These handsomely spotted, rather cat-like animals are numerous around villages in the farming areas, where they readily develop a fondness for poultry, though normally feeding on small birds, rodents and fruit. The less brightly marked Palm Civet, or Toddy Cat, also occurs in the Hill Tracts.

We flew from Chittagong soon after four o'clock, reaching Dacca two hours later, and Duncan, Jimmy and I took off for Karachi just before midnight. It was a tiring journey and the plane was very crowded, many of the passengers being accompanied by fretful babies with astonishingly well developed vocal capacities. The cabin reeked with the sweet scent of the enormous bunches of bananas and bundles of earthenware pots of spices which a number of passengers nursed in their laps. It was nearly dawn before we finally got to bed. The remainder of our party followed next day, having toured the Dacca region in company with Colonel Angus Hume and obtained some excellent pictures of White-backed Vultures feeding on the carcass of a dead buffalo (plate 17*a*).

I was awakened at eight by a telephone call from Chris Savage, who was flying down from Lahore to meet us that evening. With typical efficiency he had arranged a number of meetings and interviews for us and hoped that Duncan and I

23 *Above* A Reticulated Python was captured on the Shishak River and released after examination; it was the first one ever recorded in East Pakistan. *Below* The massive head of the Reticulated Python.

might be invited to meet President Ayub Khan during the day. This was what I had been hoping for. For the past few days we had been discussing the preliminary recommendations which we wanted to make to the Pakistan Government and I felt that if we could present them to the President personally, as we had done with King Hussein after our Jordan expedition, the prospect of their speedy implementation would be immeasurably increased.

We now had to move quickly. I phoned Duncan who, in spite of having had so little sleep, willingly agreed to prepare a rough draft of our recommendations. As soon as we had put the finishing touches to this he hurried off to find a typist and presently returned with the document neatly typed. It had been quite a *tour de force* on his part and the paper reflected his particular skill in this kind of work. I was thankful that we had reached firm conclusions before returning to Karachi, so that their commitment to paper could be made so speedily.

After fulfilling a number of official appointments, we learned that we were to meet the President the following morning. We therefore had time free until dinner. The ever-willing Department of Tourism quickly produced a couple of vehicles for us and we made a quick dash to the Haleji reservoir, which Chris had recommended as a good centre for water birds.

Haleji Dhand, in the Thatta District, is a large bunded reservoir supplying water to Karachi. A tree-lined dirt road borders it and there are flourishing crops in the extensive seepage areas. The reservoir already enjoys protection under Public

24 *Above* The Indian Pied Hornbill has a remarkable flight silhouette and boldly patterned wings. *Below* Red-wattled Lapwings were seen in most of the paddyfields and marshes of East Pakistan.

Health regulations and we learned that there were plans for developing it as a wildlife sanctuary. The numbers of wildfowl on the water suggested that this could be a valuable project, though we felt that the food resources of the lake might perhaps not be suitable for some species. Apart from several hundred birds of various species, we noted twenty White Pelicans and a flock of thirty Cranes flying overhead. In the flooded margins, Curlews, Bar-tailed Godwits and hosts of small waders were feeding. Perhaps our most unexpected discovery was an immense occupied nest of a Pallas's Fishing Eagle. The nest had been tenanted for the past six years. The female was sitting on eggs and we watched the male in flight, snatching leafy branches from a nearby tree and adding them to the nest, which was already nearly six feet deep.

Well pleased by the outcome of our final ornithological excursion, we drove back at high speed to Karachi, arriving in time to meet Chris and change for dinner, to which we had been invited by Naser-ud-Deen Khan, who was one of our strongest supporters. We dined at the Sind Club, once the haunt of diplomats and senior army officers under the British Raj and still one of the most exclusive clubs in the city. Here we met a number of people interested in our work and were able to give them an account of our travels. We had had a very tiring day; nevertheless at 2.30am Chris and I drove to the airport to meet the plane from Dacca, on which George and Eric were returning.

Our last day in Pakistan was also a full one. Apart from our audience with the President we were to attend an important luncheon given by Air Marshal Asghar Khan, at which a number of Chairmen of Government Commissions, leading industrialists, bankers and High Court judges had been invited to meet us. In the evening we were to be the guests of Mr Masud Mahmood, Director General of the Department of Tourism.

The interview with the President, to which Duncan, Christopher and I had been invited, was extremely encouraging. I was looking forward to meeting the remarkable soldier who had led the Republic so successfully since 1958. I was not disappointed. The man who came from behind the big desk to greet us was instantly impressive. Neither the passage of time nor the burdens of State had detracted from his essentially soldierly appearance. His handshake was powerful and his manner forthright. After exchanging civilities he said he had welcomed the proposal that the World Wildlife Fund should send an exploratory expedition to Pakistan and that he was well aware of the need to improve the conservation of the rapidly disappearing major animals. He had been kept in touch with our progress and would now be interested to hear our recommendations. His slightly disconcerting conciseness reminded me of Field-Marshal Wavell, to whom I had once had to make a verbal report in New Delhi during the last war. Like Lord Wavell, the President had little time for small talk.

Taking my cue from his manner and without preamble, I first expressed our appreciation for the generous help we had received from the various Government Departments concerned with our work. I then quickly outlined our findings, making no attempt to minimise the seriousness of the losses of wildlife and habitats which Pakistan had suffered in the past twenty years, nor the urgent need for action to be taken to preserve what remained. I said that our full report would follow, but that we had drafted certain preliminary recommendations which I would now ask Duncan Poore, as our technical expert, to describe.

Duncan then took him through the substance of our paper, emphasising that in the time at our disposal we had been able to make no more than a first reconnaissance of the very varied wildlife habitats embraced by West and East Pakistan.

Our paper recommended steps which we hoped might be taken by the Central Government, to enable it to come to grips with the problems of conservation within the context of the country's overall plans for land-use. Not least of these was to gain control over the main causes of the losses of wildlife and habitats, which we enumerated. There was at that time no central authority in Pakistan concerned with wildlife. We therefore suggested the formation of a Government Commission, to advise on the legal, administrative and other measures likely to be involved in the changes which we advocated and the creation of national parks and wildlife reserves. Once this was formed, a focal point would be established for the technical and scientific aid which Duncan and I could muster from international sources on its behalf.

A number of other subjects were included in our paper, including proposals for overcoming the difficult problem of the serious shortage of qualified manpower for the management of wildlife and habitats, which, of course, involved technical training. Our final recommendation was that in order to educate the general public and enable it to participate in the national conservation effort, Pakistan should take part in the activities of the World Wildlife Fund, by launching its own

National Appeal. We hoped that, following the examples of other Heads of State, the President himself would agree to act as President or Patron of the Appeal.

Duncan had presented our proposals with his usual quiet sincerity; I had merely elaborated one or two details to give him a break. The President had listened attentively, occasionally nodding his approval or interjecting a brief comment. He now asked several questions concerned with the pressure of shooting on game animals and for a few minutes conversation widened. Then, turning to Air Marshal Asghar Khan who, with Masud Mahmood, was also present, he said briskly, 'Well, there is nothing in this report with which I disagree. We must set about implementing it.' Turning to us, he thanked us and our colleagues for our efforts and said he would look forward to reading our more detailed report. We were delighted by his quick grasp of essentials in our recommendations and by his evident determination to take action without delay. It would have been all too easy for him to have referred the matter to his Ministers for further consideration before reaching a decision, but having weighed the evidence, he had given his verdict without hesitation. He now wished us a safe journey home and we took our leave. The local papers reported our meeting in the evening editions.

The Air Marshal's lunch party, like the interview with the President, provided ample evidence of the interest which our work had created. Assembled around the table were some of the most influential men in Pakistan and their support for our objectives was abundantly apparent. I was able to talk with many of them while we were having drinks beforehand and was greatly encouraged by the promises of support which I received. We all felt that conservation in Pakistan was about to begin a new chapter.

We were looking forward to a gay farewell party with Masud Mahmood, with whom we were to dine. He had put all the resources of the Department of Tourism at our disposal wherever we went. His choice of Karim, an experienced member of his staff, to accompany us could not have been bettered. We were greatly indebted to him and I was glad we should have this opportunity to thank him.

It was therefore more than embarrassing that we were an hour and a quarter late, the car which was to take us to him arriving at our hotel only after a number of frantic telephone calls. I fear we ruined the sumptuous dinner which had been kept waiting so long. Nevertheless our host and hostess gave us a splendid send-off.

Our plane was due to take off for London at midnight, but was delayed for two hours by generator trouble. We then flew as far as Baghdad and turned back because of difficulty in maintaining the correct pressure in the cabin. The remainder of the night was spent uncomfortably at Karachi airport and we eventually transferred to another aircraft, which took off after breakfast. On the journey home we passed through a variety of weather conditions. After the heat of Pakistan we landed at Tehran in bitter cold, surrounded by snow-clad mountains. At Moscow it was snowing and the temperature was at freezing point. At Frankfurt we landed in dense fog and when we finally reached London it was pouring with rain. Our first expedition to Pakistan was over.

6

The Second Expedition

With Duncan Poore's help I completed our detailed reports for
the Pakistan Government by mid-January. In February my
wife and I toured the game reserves in Uganda, Kenya and
Tanzania, where we quickly found ourselves involved in a
number of local conservation problems. I then joined a group
of enthusiasts led by the remarkable businessman turned con-
servationist, Lars-Erik Lindblad, for a visit to the Galapagos
Islands. The World Wildlife Fund is one of the supporters of
the Charles Darwin Foundation, which, 600 miles from civilisation, is doing such valuable biological research on the unique
animals of the islands. On my way home I stopped off in Peru
for a few days' bird watching in the Andes and realised a lifetime's ambition by seeing no fewer than six of the rare Andean
Condors soaring over the snowy peaks. Even in South America
conservation had begun to function.

During these travels I had time to reflect on our work in
Pakistan. I was increasingly dissatisfied by our failure to obtain
a sufficiently broad appreciation of the very varied habitats to
be found in the two Provinces. We had seen nothing of the
western Himalayas, nor of the high-altitude animals which
inhabit them. Neither had we visited the tidal jungle of the
Sunderbans, or the great mangrove swamps of the Indus

Delta, each of which embraced a unique community of vegetation and animal life. If we were to help Pakistan to introduce a comprehensive programme of conservation and to create reserves in the most threatened areas, these gaps in our knowledge would need to be filled. My half-formed plans for a second expedition gradually took shape.

I consulted my colleagues and found them instantly enthusiastic. By correspondence with Christopher Savage and Tom Roberts a proposal was soon submitted to the Pakistan authorities, who said they would welcome a continuation of our studies.

This time I was determined not to repeat the breakneck pace of the first expedition, which had imposed a strain on everyone and had frustrated much of our field work. I therefore doubled the length of time in the field and reduced the number of regions to be studied. The main centres would be the Gilgit Agency in the western Himalayas, the Indus Delta and, in East Pakistan, the Sunderbans. Two subsidiary objectives were the Kirthar Range, between Sind and Baluchistan, and the forested area of Sylhet Division, near the frontier with Assam. As planning progressed we found that by dividing forces for the Gilgit and Kirthar sectors and doing them simultaneously, we could probably manage all five regions in about eight weeks.

Timing for the start of the expedition was decided by balancing two factors: the need to avoid the monsoon period and choosing the most likely date when access to Gilgit would be possible by air. The tiny air-strip, which is 4,755 feet above

25 *Above* The White-collared Kingfisher is one of the most colourful of the twelve species occurring in Pakistan. *Below* The big Brown-winged Kingfisher has an immense scarlet bill.

sea level, is hazardous at the best of times and often inaccessible for weeks on end because of violent storms. However, it was reported to be reasonably safe to approach over the 20,000-foot peaks which hem it in, during the first week of November. We ruled out going by road when we heard that the Babusar Pass, which winds through the mountains at 13,500 feet, had been open for only thirty-six days during the previous year. I decided on 30 October as the date for reaching Karachi and that if weather reports were favourable the advance party would proceed immediately to Gilgit.

Logistics this time would require very careful planning. As the study areas were widely spread and we wanted to reduce time lost in travelling between them, maximum use would have to be made of flying. This involved eleven different flights, with varying numbers of people and varying weights of baggage (at maximum numbers we carried nearly 500 lb of equipment, to say nothing of food and bedding). At each stop we needed road transport. Short wheel-base Jeeps were the only vehicles which could negotiate the narrow Gilgit mountain trails. For the Kirthar sector, where there were no rest-houses, we needed camp equipment. For the Indus Delta a steamer with a shallow draft would be required to negotiate the shifting sand-bars in the mangrove swamps, while the labyrinth of narrow creeks in the Sunderbans called for motor launches working from a headquarters ship on which to sleep. Finally, for Sylhet, we needed not only Jeeps but elephants for exploring the great marshes. This was a pretty tall order, yet we were to learn that the

26 *Above* At Naltar an attempt was being made to breed the increasingly rare Monal Pheasant in captivity. *Below* Wall Creepers were common at Gilgit and one was caught in the rest-house.

Pakistan Government was not only willing to supply all these things, but that when we later asked for a helicopter this, too, was miraculously forthcoming. This was the ninth expedition I had organised to various countries and never were we to be better equipped.

Since our return from Pakistan Jimmy Hancock had assumed important new business responsibilities which made it impossible for him to take part in our new explorations. In his place I was fortunate to be able to recruit John Buxton, a well-known naturalist whose estate in Norfolk is among the best of the bird sanctuaries in England. His particular value to the expedition lay in the fact that he was a top-ranking wildlife cinematographer. He would therefore be able to take some of the load which George Shannon had previously carried single-handed.

By lengthening the duration of the expedition, however, I ran into difficulties. Neither Eric Hosking nor George Shannon could spare more than five weeks away from their professional responsibilities, while Duncan Poore was so heavily involved with work at the Nature Conservancy that he could take part for only an even shorter period. I therefore recruited Lord Fermoy, a remarkable young Irish Peer who had resigned a commission in the Blues (Royal Horse Guards) in order to devote himself to farming and the conservation of wild-life. I liked his infectious enthusiasm and, although I knew little of his capabilities at that time, I felt he would fit in well with the team. I asked him to take on sound recording, the lack of which we had felt keenly on the previous expedition. His later performance in this role was to astonish us and he also gave me invaluable help in the administration of the expedition.

On 30 October Edmund Fermoy, Duncan Poore and I took off as the advance party for the Gilgit explorations. John Buxton, Eric Hosking and George Shannon left a week later for the Kirthar Range. We planned to join forces at Karachi on 14 November before setting out for the Indus Delta.

We left England on a clear, crisp morning, with the trees in the full splendour of their autumn colours. Our route was by way of the Austrian Alps, Bulgaria and Turkey to Beirut and Karachi. It was dark before we passed Dhahran, where hundreds of gas flares from the rich oil deposits of Saudi Arabia were illuminating the empty desert.

Karim and his assistant Hemayut-ud-Din Khan met us at Karachi airport. During the previous two weeks Karim had made a pilot run round the entire route of the expedition, to make sure all arrangements for our accommodation and travel were in order. Now, exhausted but triumphant, he was eager to take the field with us and we were more than happy to be having his company again.

The following day was devoted to official meetings and we dined that night with our old friends Air Commodore Dass, Naser-ud-Deen Khan, Pir Mahfooz and Sifatullah Siddiqi, who brought us up to date with events. The most important news was that three of our previous recommendations had already been implemented. The largely ineffectual Game Department had been closed down and the responsibility for wildlife management taken over by the highly efficient Department of Forests. The formation of the Wildlife Enquiry Committee (in effect the Government Commission which we had advocated) was about to be announced. Perhaps most important of all, the prohibition of the export of skins of all wild animals had become law.

This was a tremendous achievement by the Central Government and one which would be applauded all over the world as an example to other nations. Finally a move was afoot to form a wildlife society. I had already had discussions about this with the energetic Dr Quraishy, Curator of the Karachi Zoo, who was the prime mover. It all sounded most encouraging.

We flew early next morning to Rawalpindi, where we were joined by Tom Roberts and Brigadier Aslam Khan, a distinguished soldier who knew every inch of the Gilgit region and was keenly interested in the conservation of the animals inhabiting it. Tom had, of course, already explored these remote mountains before and the detailed planning for this sector had been largely in his hands. We were also joined here by Dr Rahman Beg of the Institute of Forests at Peshawar, who was to be attached to the expedition for the time we were in the Gilgit Agency.

The approach by air to Gilgit is always spectacular. From Rawalpindi we flew up the Kaghan Valley and over the Babusar Pass. The Brigadier invited me to take photographs of Nanga Parbat from the cockpit of the plane as we drew near and we were fortunate enough to pass its 26,660-foot crest in brilliant sunshine (plate 30a). It used to be called Diamin, the Fairy Peak. Down one side flows one of the greatest glaciers in the world. Beyond it lay the Karakoram Range and the great peak of Rakaposhi, or Dumani, the Mother of Clouds. As we crossed the Indus, which here is a mere stream, we could see on our left the frowning mass of the Hindu Kush, the point where three nations meet—Pakistan, China and the USSR.

As we dropped sharply down into the narrow trench of the Gilgit valley, the air-strip looked remarkably short. I was not surprised to feel the brakes being applied hard as we came to a halt, with the view ahead completely obscured by a massive mountain.

It was bitterly cold when we stepped out of the plane. The valley was, however, bathed in sunlight and the Walnuts, Oriental Planes and Black Poplars were gay with orange and yellow foliage. The rest-house where we were to stay overlooked the Gilgit River not far from where it swung left towards the opening of the Hunza Valley. Our little garden was gay with late Zinnias and Marigolds and the lawn was still green. Blue Whistling Thrushes and Streaked Laughing Thrushes were calling in the trees and a flock of Pale Crag Martins was wheeling overhead. The surrounding mountain spurs, of a mere 15,000 feet, were not yet snow-capped; but in a gap among towering cumulus thunderheads we could see the shining crown of Bilchar Dobani rising to 20,126 feet against the blue sky. We could scarcely have had a more magnificent setting for the opening stages of the expedition.

The Gilgit Agency has had a long and turbulent history. Ptolemy was apparently the first to describe the warlike Dards, as its inhabitants used to be called. The Chinese pilgrim Hsuan Tsang, describing the scenery after ascending the region from Swat in AD 631, wrote: 'Perilous were the roads and dark the gorges ... here were ledges hanging in mid-air; there flying bridges across abysses; elsewhere paths cut with the chisel, or footings to climb by.' More than thirteen hundred years later our first journey from Gilgit to Naltar over the 'ledges hanging in mid-air' convinced us that this description was still no exaggeration.

According to tradition Gilgit was originally ruled by the

Rajas of Trakane. When these died out, a long succession of foreign invasions followed. There were at least five different dynasties between 1810 and 1842. In 1846 the whole of Kashmir and Gilgit were placed by Lord Hardinge under the control of the Maharaja Gulab Singh of Jammu, ruler of the Dogras. The fierce Dards of Gilgit staged an uprising in 1852 and slaughtered the army of occupation to the last man. They managed to hold the territory until 1889 when the British, to forestall an advance by the Russians, established the Gilgit Agency under a resident British Political Agent. But when in 1947 the British withdrew from the subcontinent and the long *pax Britannica* came to an end, a Kashmiri governor was unwisely appointed. The famous Gilgit Scouts, originally raised as the Hunza Levies by General Sir George Cockerill and regarded as a *corps d'élite*, instantly revolted and proclaimed Gilgit's accession to the new nation of Pakistan. Although India then bombed Gilgit, rather ineffectually, the transition to Pakistan was accomplished with none of the terrible bloodshed and suffering which Partition brought to other parts of the subcontinent.

One of the best written and most interesting accounts of life in Gilgit in the early years of the present century is Tom Longstaff's *This My Journey*. As a subaltern Longstaff, whose whole life was devoted to mountaineering, was appointed as Assistant Commandant of the Gilgit Scouts in 1916. He made his entry on mule-back after a journey of three arduous weeks crossing the mountain ranges which we had taken less than an hour to cross by aeroplane.

The Agency embraces a number of small principalities between the borders of Chitral, Afghanistan, the USSR and the Chinese province of Sinkiang. Many races and languages occur there, though the Shins are the dominant race and theirs is the language most widely spoken. The winter costume of the typical Gilgiti is a long felt coat called a *chogha*, with sleeves which reach below the knees and can be used in cold weather as a scarf. Baggy pyjama trousers are tucked into puttees. A distinctive, close-fitting cap called a *khoi* is worn, with the brim rolled into a kind of sausage around the head. The women, who in this essentially man's world live lives of unremitting toil, are distinguished by brimless pillbox hats. Life is far from easy in Gilgit, which is an isolated community, often cut off from the outside world for weeks on end. When the roads are closed, supplies have to be flown in and this results in very high prices. Salt, for example, costs eight times more than it does in Rawalpindi. Money, however, is less used than barter between the producers of foodstuffs and livestock.

Having unloaded our baggage at the rest-house, we were taken by Brigadier Aslam Khan to meet the Political Resident, who had reserved seats for us at the finals of the local polo tournament. We were ushered into the crowded stand to find the two teams lined up and waiting for our arrival. The Resident handed me the ball and invited me to throw it between the forward lines to start the game.

Polo, as played at Gilgit, is a spectacle which has to be seen to be believed. It is wildly exciting and the horsemanship is superb, with more than a touch of wild-west rodeo about it. There is only one rule: the game must be played for one hour nonstop, or until one side has scored nine goals. There is no nonsense about changing ponies between chukkas, nor any rules to protect riders or their mounts from injury. Because of the scarcity of flat ground in the valleys, the stony polo fields are long and narrow and are enclosed by stone walls, into which players think nothing of driving their opponents. A player may catch the ball in mid-air and ride with it into goal, but at the risk of having his hand smashed by a polo stick, or of being dragged bodily from the saddle and dropped among the flying hooves. The game is, in fact, a free-for-all equestrian punch-up, with no holds barred. Tom Longstaff, whose career at Gilgit was terminated by a blow on the temple while playing this game, called it 'a kind of rugby football on horseback.' In his day play did not begin until a popinjay, a gourd filled with flour, had been shot down from the top of a flag-staff by a rider firing at full gallop.

Sticks were often knocked out of players' hands. When I asked why wrist loops were not worn, I was told that this was to prevent wrists from being broken, or shoulders dislocated. The Gilgit stick differs from ours in having a much smaller, curved head mounted obliquely, instead of at right angles to the shaft.

Polo is a passion with Gilgitis and every valley has its team. Even bare-footed boys play a pedestrian version, using a stone instead of a ball. At the match we were watching, several thousand tribesmen, who crowded every inch of the mountain slope, kept up a continuous roar of encouragement (plate 30). The applause was deafening each time a goal was scored, and we were exhausted with excitement by the time the match ended. I was then invited to present the massive Ayub Khan challenge cup, but feeling this might be breaking with tradition, I declined.

27 *Above* The jungle at Pablakhali rose like an impenetrable wall along the banks of the river. *Below* We explored the shallow creeks and backwaters of the Shishak River by dug-out canoe.

It was dark when we returned to the rest-house and extremely cold. A landslide had deprived Gilgit of its electricity and we dined by candlelight. Our sitting-room had a large fire-place, but we were informed that the chimney had been blocked up in order to keep out the cold. This curious excuse was apparently true, so we huddled around the table in our outdoor jackets, planning our work for the following day.

We were presently joined by Wing-Commander Shah Khan, the Commandant of the local Air Force Ski School. Like the Brigadier, he had expert knowledge of Gilgit and its wildlife. He had created his own reserve at the head of the Naltar Valley, where he was breeding Ibex, Shapu and Markhor, in addition to Monal Pheasants. We gladly accepted his invitation to make our first excursion to his reserve next day. We then had a long discussion with him and the Brigadier about the status of the major animals of the region.

In the opinion of our two friends all the animals of Gilgit had suffered severe losses in recent years. The reasons, which we later confirmed from our own observations, were a compound of several factors. Obviously the increasing pressure of hunting was one of these, though as hunting under licence was reasonably well regulated and sportsmen normally sought only mature males, this was not a controlling factor. Shooting by local landowners, officials and officers of the armed services who often did not bother about licences was more difficult to evaluate, but it was undoubtedly much too heavy. We had heard, for example, that a local officer had shot no fewer than

28 *Above* The Gilgit Valley was bathed in sunshine which heightened the brilliance of the autumn colours. *Below* Graceful Nipa Palms fringed the margins of the mangrove jungle in the Sunderbans.

eighteen Ibex in a single excursion and every house we visited had its collection of trophies (plate 33). However, uncontrolled shooting, trapping and poisoning by local villagers was probably the most important factor. It had proved to be almost impossible to control the possession of firearms in the hundreds of little communities scattered throughout the remote valleys. A gun is easily concealed and there was little doubt that the majority of the hill tribesmen had one hidden away somewhere. It was also easy to obtain weapons from the industrious backstreet gun-smiths of Kohat or Peshawar, who still do a roaring trade copying anything from a 12-bore Purdy to a submachine-gun.

Unlike the licence-paying sportsmen, the hill tribesmen kill animals for food, for the protection of crops or cattle, or for the sale of skins or heads. If they need meat, they shoot males, females or young of the Markhor, Shapu or Ibex indiscrimi-nately, in or out of season. If a Snow Leopard is near a tribes-man's goats, he does not hesitate to set a trap for it, knowing that the skin will fetch a high price in the local market.

The prices offered by skin traders are another big factor and certainly the main cause of the frightful losses suffered in recent years by the numerous species of cats inhabiting Pakistan. In Gilgit the chief victim has been the Snow Leopard, probably the most beautiful of all the cats, with its soft, greyish-white fur and very long tail. Just how serious this persecution has become can be judged from the fact that during a visit to Peshawar I learned of a skin trader who was offering for sale the skins of 60 Snow Leopards, 30 Lynxes, 1,500 Leopard Cats and 1,000 Stone Martens. There are many such traders in both West and East Pakistan.

The demand for skins is, of course, predominantly from

western countries and notably the United States, where those of the cat family are promoted as 'fun furs.' Big money is involved in a trade no less barbarous than the trade in 'aigrettes,' which came within an ace of exterminating the egrets of the world before public opinion revolted against the senseless slaughter. American importers were in 1967 selling dressed skins of Snow Leopards at the equivalent of £100. One can scarcely blame the needy hill tribesmen of Gilgit for taking advantage of the demand. Fortunately, however, the United States Government has recently introduced legislation to curb the importation of skins of endangered animal species. The prohibition of imports is the best answer to this horrid problem and it is a matter of grave concern that the United Kingdom and other European countries have not yet followed the lead given by Pakistan and America.

Another factor, which affects the mountain goats and sheep, is the competition of domestic goats for their limited grazing. We later saw domestic flocks at above the 14,000-foot level; in other words well above the lower levels at which Markhor and Shapu sought food at that time of year. The rare Marco Polo's Sheep, which keeps to the highest grazing, is the only species which escapes this competition. Further and more serious harm has recently arisen from domestic goats introducing an outbreak of anthrax into the wild flocks.

We got out our maps and Brigadier Aslam Khan indicated where we were most likely to find the high-altitude animals. His estimate of numbers, which was supported by the Wing-Commander, was that the Markhor had declined to not more than 1,000; the Ibex population was about 3,000; but the more easily shot Shapu had suffered badly and he doubted that more than 500 remained in the Agency (plate 32*b*). A few of the severely exploited little Musk Deer still frequented the high forests. The Snow Leopard, Leopard Cat and Lynx were present in small numbers. Brown Bears were disappearing, though a few occurred above the tree line, and Himalayan Black Bears could be found in the high forests around Chilas and Astor. Wolves were numerous. Hill Foxes occupied the northern valleys and Desert Foxes the southern parts. There were Otters in most of the rivers and Stone Martens were still fairly common in spite of being constantly trapped by villagers using fruit as a bait.

The Brigadier cherished the idea that a protected reserve might one day be created to save the wildlife of the Gilgit Agency. As we listened to him we became increasingly determined to bring this about if it were humanly possible. We pored over the maps and between us drew boundaries around an area in the Deosai Range, which appeared to offer the maximum advantages in terms of the existing animal populations it enclosed and in terms of seclusion and natural boundaries, such as rivers. This was the genesis of our subsequent plan for the Gilgit National Park, which I shall describe later. Chief credit for the idea must be given to the imaginative Brigadier Aslam Khan.

7

Wildlife of the Himalayas

Before the sunlight had dipped into our valley next morning we had explored our immediate surroundings. The little town of Gilgit, which has a single tree-lined main street of open-fronted shops, is picturesque and animated. On the outskirts are a number of modern houses where the officials live. There is the headquarters of the Gilgit Scouts, very trim and well kept as befits its tradition, and near it a substantial prison. A long line of prisoners in clanking leg-shackles and accompanied by armed guards passed us on the way to work. They looked relaxed and cheerful and greeted us unselfconsciously. 'All murderers' we were informed casually and somehow in this strange, romantic valley, where blood feud killings were a matter of honour, the information did not shock us.

After saying good-bye to the Brigadier, who unfortunately had to return to Rawalpindi, we set off in three Jeeps for Naltar. As an introduction to travel in the Himalayas the journey could not have been better chosen, nor more hair-raising. The first part was deceptively easy going, though the road was rough. After crossing a long, narrow bridge over the Gilgit River we began to climb an awe-inspiring gorge leading into the heart of the mountains. The road rose, at first gently and then at an alarming angle as we crawled round shoulder after shoulder of the soaring peaks, twisting and turning constantly. Now and then we plunged back down to river level again, only to face a zig-zag climb up the next spur. Then we came to the first of a succession of fragile suspension bridges back and forth across the gorge. These were so narrow that extreme caution was needed in turning the Jeeps on to them without demolishing the hand-rails. As our vehicles began to clatter slowly across the wooden floor of the first bridge, the suspension wires creaked and groaned and the whole thing swayed alarmingly. One bridge had collapsed and we had to pick our way down a one-in-three gradient to the river, which we crossed with water up to the floor boards. The climb up the boulders of the opposite bank was even steeper. Almost every time we crossed a river in these parts we caught sight of immense trout in the pools and wished our relent-less programme permitted us to spare an hour for fly-fishing.

The mountain tracks were masterpieces of local engineering, though obviously designed for horses rather than vehicles. None was more than a few inches wider than a Jeep. Around the outer curves of the mountain spurs they had been cut bodily out of the almost vertical rocks, leaving barely a three-inch clearance above the roof of a Jeep. The crumbling outer edge of the track hung at times over a sheer drop of 1,500 feet to the river. Often sections of the outer edge had collapsed and had been rebuilt with piled up and uncemented rocks, revetted casually here and there with crooked Juniper branches. Why they did not immediately collapse again the moment we passed over them we could not imagine. Fortunately, during the whole period of our explorations we only twice met other Jeeps nose to nose in the mountains and on both occasions had to back only a few hundred yards to enable them to squeeze past.

Our drivers were experienced in these hazards and usually drove with considerable skill. Their chief failing was an inclination to delay engaging four-wheel drive until the last possible moment when ascending steep gradients. This almost invariably resulted in the Jeeps running backwards on hairpin bends. They were also inclined to rush at full throttle up particularly bad slopes, regardless of the fact that these usually ended with a blind corner. On one such occasion when I was sitting next to the driver, the gradient was one-in-one; as the bonnet of the Jeep reared up, it completely obscured the driver's vision and had I not shouted to him to swing hard left we would have dived off the track into space. He grinned, rocking his head from side to side to show his embarrassment and said, 'Bad accident!'

As we climbed towards Naltar the Artemisia steppe on the mountain slopes was replaced by a magnificent Spruce forest. Here we took a side track leading across a bridge to the Wing-Commander's reserve. Signposts announced that all hunting was prohibited. We came to a halt among picturesque wooden buildings scattered around a plateau on the forest edge. Examining the map I noted that the reserve was 9,800 feet above sea level and that we had averaged less than seven miles an hour for the last two hours.

The Wing-Commander led us first to a paddock containing several immature Shapu and Ibex and a splendid specimen of a four-year-old Markhor (plate 32a). This was of the local race, the Astor Markhor *Capra falconeri falconeri* and quite distinct from the other two races which occur elsewhere in Pakistan. Its spiral horns were already massive in growth and it had a handsomely tufted beard. With small yellow eyes it watched us cautiously and when we entered the paddock it lowered its head and drove us out. All the animals were in fine condition.

We then went to another enclosure to inspect the Monal, or Impeyan, Pheasants which the Wing-Commander was hoping would breed, so that he could re-populate the reserve with these really spectacular birds. They are indigenous in the Gilgit Agency, though now scarce and found chiefly in the Bunji region. The pheasants were very shy. The cock, resplendent in shining purple and orange, was too wary to be approached in the paddock; when it scuttled back into its enclosed sleeping-quarters I took its picture nevertheless (plate 26a). It is unfortunate that the Gilgit Scouts wear a tuft of the shining purple crest feathers of this bird, surmounted by the white feathers of the Snow Cock, behind their cap badges. The decorative effect is striking, but the species is now much too rare to serve this purpose. The Royal Bodyguard of the Ruler of Swat also wear the Monal's crest in their caps and represent a further threat to its survival.

We congratulated our host on his reserve, which was the only one in the Agency. He was obviously skilled in the management of animals and we encouraged him to try his hand at breeding Horned Tragopan Pheasants if he had any opportunity. These very beautiful birds are now nearing extinction. They are, however, native to the Hazara district and two were shot in the Khagan Valley near Balakot recently, which suggested that a few might still survive. Their best chance of escaping extermination probably lies in being bred in captivity.

29 *Above* A large gecko called Merton's Tokay serenaded us every evening from the rafters of the rest-house at Pablakhali. *Below* Rock Pythons are disappearing under the demand for python-skin handbags.

Peter Scott first demonstrated the efficacy of this technique with the Ne-Ne Goose of Hawaii, which by careful breeding in captivity was increased from a world population of fewer than 50 to more than 500, the birds being successfully returned to a protected reserve on the Island of Maui. Philip Wayre is now repeating this success with the equally rare Swinhoe's Pheasant, some of which he has already restored to Taiwan (Formosa). Pakistan's disappearing pheasants could be saved by the same techniques.

Very little is known about the Horned Tragopan, which many authorities have regarded as an extinct species. News travels fast, however, and reports that it still occurred in Gilgit attracted the attention of an American collector, who arrived armed with printed handbills offering one hundred dollars to anyone who could procure a specimen. Such a vast reward in a poor community could have resulted in every hill tribesman in the entire region catching or shooting every bird even remotely resembling a pheasant. Fortunately the authorities intervened to prevent a major tragedy.

We then drove on up the valley, until the trail vanished among the great Spruces. The scene here was very beautiful and we stopped for a while to watch birds. During our journey we had seen many interesting species, such as Wall Creepers, Rufous-breasted Accentors and both Pine and Rock Buntings. Yellow-billed and Red-billed Choughs had been numerous, their flocks often mixed and we had watched them hungrily feeding on the orange berries of the Sea Buckthorns along the

30 *Above* Flying to Gilgit we passed the 26,660 foot peak of Nanga Parbat. *Below* Polo as played at Gilgit is very spectacular and resembles a kind of ferocious equestrian rugby football.

river edges. In Europe we tend to regard these two species as having quite distinct ecological niches, divided by differences in altitude, the Yellow-billed being a bird of the high mountains and the Red-billed preferring sea cliffs and hills. In Gilgit there was no such distinction and they were foraging side by side, though doubtless breeding apart.

In a tall Blue Pine we found our first Nutcracker, swinging from the tip of a branch to open the hanging cones and scattering the husks in showers below. It differed greatly from its European counterpart, its dark back being so closely speckled with white as to give a pale grey impression. Tom identified it as the Himalayan race, which scientists have blessed with the tongue-twisting name *Nucifraga caryocatactes multipunctata*.

Beneath a Spruce we noticed many fallen cones which had obviously been gnawed by an animal. This, said Tom, was characteristic evidence of the presence of Flying Squirrels, which he knew inhabited the region at this altitude (we were now at 11,000 feet). Unfortunately, as Flying Squirrels are nocturnal, we did not see any. However, when I was later watching some Black Crested Tits, I disturbed a small animal with a dark face which I saw only momentarily as it ducked back into a hollow tree; it had the loose-skinned look though not the colour of the Smaller Kashmir Flying Squirrel. Although I could not be certain, it was probably one of the Woolly Flying Squirrels, which also occur in the Gilgit and Chitral regions.

We were now at the snow line. When we resumed our journey, picking our way as best we could among the trees, we soon found ourselves having to jump out and push the Jeeps up steep inclines deep in snow. The ground was very undulating and before long we could progress only by strewing the ground with branches. Often the Jeeps would slide back again, bringing the branches with them (plate 31*a*). At one point my vehicle slewed sideways, leaving one wheel suspended in mid-air; we had to lift it bodily back on to the track. We were all feeling tired by the time we reached our destination, a beautiful little frozen lake called Koti. It was surrounded by ancient Birches with frosted leaves. Here we lit a camp fire and had lunch.

Afterwards we went exploring. Duncan and Rahman Beg were in their element, deep in discussions about ecozones and microclimates as they tramped off in the snow. Tom and Edmund headed straight up the mountainside into the sparse Juniper scrub. There they were soon rewarded by finding fresh tracks of Snow Leopard, Ibex and Wolf. Snow Leopards often hunt by daylight, but one would be very fortunate to catch sight of such a constantly hunted animal.

I took the opposite direction and also soon found numerous Wolf tracks weaving among the trees. These animals were obviously thriving in the Agency and we were told that they often attacked goat-herds if they had a chance. A flock of Black-throated Thrushes came whistling through the trees and settled on a pink-barked Rowan tree to feed on its berries. High over the peaks a number of Himalayan Griffon Vultures were soaring on straight wings; when I raised my binoculars to them I saw several more far above them, so high that they were quite invisible to the naked eye. I calculated that they must be flying at 20,000 feet. During the Everest expeditions vultures were noted at even greater altitudes and I remembered that Sir John Hunt had seen Choughs at 26,000 feet. How do birds survive the lack of oxygen at such heights when they expend so much energy in flying?

Our return to Gilgit was delayed by the time we had to spend man-handling the Jeeps during the difficult descent from Koti. It was dark before we reached the rest-house. The journey nevertheless produced some more new bird species. The first of these, seen at a torrent near Naltar, was a Little Forktail, a charming and very active little black and white bird. We found several others later, all in river beds, for they are essentially aquatic in habitat, behaving like the many Brown Dippers which we saw perched on rocks in midstream. Another new bird was a White-capped Redstart, very attractive in Burgundy red and with a shining white crown. These were, however, quite overshadowed by some even more magnificent birds called Güldenstädt's Redstart. I came across the first of these in a Tamarisk swamp. Superficially resembling the White-capped though with a more extensive white crown, they are distinguished by the lack of a terminal band on their flaming red tails and by large white panels on their wings, which are well displayed during their characteristic sallies into the air when singing. During our stay in Gilgit we also saw Blue-headed and Plumbeous Redstarts.

As we approached the Gilgit Valley the sun was setting, gilding the Walnuts and Poplars with an extraordinary brilliance of colour (plate 28). The river was steely blue and the distant peaks glowing with pink radiance. Hot curried goat was awaiting us at the rest-house. Although we did not know it, this was to be our invariable mainstay for the next seven days.

We decided to spend the following night at Gupis. This involved a journey of sixty-five miles through the mountains and it took nearly ten hours of hard driving. The road was every bit as difficult and dangerous as the road to Naltar and we thought we did pretty well to average nearly seven miles an hour. We took with us a remarkable old *shikari* who was a great favourite with our drivers. He was reported to be ninety years old, but was as tough and agile as the Ibexes and Markhor which he had stalked all his life. We were to appreciate his skill later when we went after Markhor ourselves.

On the way to Gupis we stopped for lunch at a delightful little rest-house at Singel and while we rested a Walnut tree showered us gently with crisp golden leaves, like a priest sprinkling holy water. Grey Tits and Himalayan Tree Creepers kept us company, while Jungle Crows watched for scraps, calling 'owk-owk-owk' at intervals. Tom's interest in entomology was aroused by the many butterflies flitting around the garden at such an altitude and so late in the year. He was excited by the discovery of all three races of the Clouded Yellow. I was equally surprised to see a number of green dragonflies, some of them *in coitu*, and I wondered how they could breed when most of the ponds were already freezing over.

Resuming our journey, we presently came upon a herd of hardy little cows being driven down to the valley. We were in a section where it would have been suicidal to attempt to back, as there was barely a hand's breadth between us and a deep precipice. After a shouted consultation with the herdsman we gathered that the road behind him was just as bad. To our admiration, however, he backed his herd to an extremely steep gully, down which a small waterfall cascaded to the road. He then drove the cows up it, until they stood shoulder to shoulder. We edged past, with the tail of the lowest animal brushing our windscreens. At any moment we expected a cascade of cows on the roof. No self-respecting European cow would have scrambled

up such a steep waterfall, but the Gilgit animals were moun-
taineers. They lived hard and could find little grazing in an
area overrun with ravenous goats. Such little fodder as the
homesteaders could provide for them had to be stored in strange-
looking haystacks in trees above a barrier of thorns, to keep it
out of reach of the goats. We even saw men laboriously knocking
the big leaves off Oriental Planes with long poles in order to
collect them as winter feed for cattle.

The Jeep carrying our food and bedding then broke down
with a burnt-out bearing in the dynamo. The drivers removed
the dynamo and fitted a new bearing made from a piece of
metal cut from a tobacco tin. As this was too short to go round
the shaft, a small nail was hammered in to close the gap. The
up-ended dynamo meanwhile was supported on its carbon
brushes, one of which broke under the hammer blows. The
bearing was then found to be too tight, so oil was poured in,
thus quickly penetrating the electrical connections and render-
ing the whole thing unserviceable. Nevertheless, the dynamo
was replaced with the aid of a large rock, which was hammered
between it and the crankcase in order to tighten the belt. Two
holding-down bolts were left over after this operation was completed and the driver, unable to find where they came from,
shrugged his shoulders and tossed them into his tool-box.
Needless to say, the engine would not start.

But Edmund turned out to have done a course of vehicle
maintenance with armoured scout cars when he was in the
Blues. Almost in hysterics watching the efforts of our drivers,
he finally could bear it no longer and took command. Under his
expert hands the dynamo was cleaned and refitted and miraculously made to work again.

Gupis is barely thirty miles from the Chinese border. Up to the time of the First World War it was the northernmost outpost of the British Army in India and in those days its little mud fort used to be defended by two muzzle-loading screwguns. The locality has only three inches of rainfall a year. The air in the valley was noticeably dry when we arrived, and our lips were chapped by the wind. However the small rest-house, screened by tall yellow Poplars, was snug and warm. Our rooms were simply furnished, with string *charpoys* and rush chairs. The kindly Raja of Gupis had sent tea and cakes for us, which were more than welcome after our long ride. We then wrote the diary by candlelight, everyone crowding into my small room to enjoy the warmth from an aromatic fire of Juniper logs which I lit in the grate.

We were invited that evening to dine with the local doctor. His little house, sturdily built to withstand the Himalayan winter, reminded me of a Russian *dacha*; in the centre of the living-room was a pot-bellied iron stove with a samovar bubbling contentedly on top. After an excellent dinner we sat drinking sweet green tea and listening to his account of the life of a doctor among the primitive mountain villagers. Although there was a hospital at Gilgit, the roads were closed for much of the winter and he had to deal with every type of emergency singlehanded. He was unable to treat any women patients, who were forbidden to expose their bodies to a stranger. Childbirth requiring Cæsarean operation therefore invariably led to an agonising death and epidemics were almost uncontrollable. Although the mountain folk were so hardy, illness arising from dietary deficiency was frequent, as well as tuberculosis, jaundice and eye complaints such as cataract and trachoma.

The following morning Tom, Duncan, Rahman Beg and Siddiqi left at seven to explore the surroundings of Phandar Lake which was situated at 10,500 feet, half a day's journey from Gupis. To reach it they had to wade an icy river. The effort was made worthwhile by the discovery of some domesticated Yaks at a remote farmstead and by the sight of Tufted Ducks and Teal on the lake. Tom also obtained reliable evidence of the presence of a Turkestan Eagle Owl, by finding an unmistakable feather of this magnificent bird.

Edmund and I explored the Gupis area. There were many Chukor Partridges scampering among the jumbled rocks and Wrens kept popping out of crevices as we passed. Flocks of Choughs, Goldfinches and Rock Buntings were frequent. Along the banks of the Gupis River we found Magpies, Blue Whistling Thrushes and Brown Dippers, and occasional Grey Wagtails. Streaked Laughing Thrushes (which are not related to the European thrush family but rather to the Asiatic babblers) were often found creeping in a rodent-like manner in and out of the dry-stone walling along the roadside. Our most interesting birds were a very striking black and white wheatear called Hume's Chat and a tiny wren-like creature with a long, cocked tail; on closer examination it revealed astonishing colours. Its crown was reddish, its throat lilac, its breast shot with purple and its tail with blue. This exquisite little bird was Stoliczka's Tit Warbler and it certainly deserved a more attractive name. How I dislike the striving after immortality practised by our earlier naturalists, who attached their often unpronounceable

31 *Above* In the snow at 11,200 feet, near Naltar, it was difficult to keep our Jeeps moving. *Below* Our ninety-year-old *shikari* (*right*) spotted some Markhor descending the opposite side of the gorge.

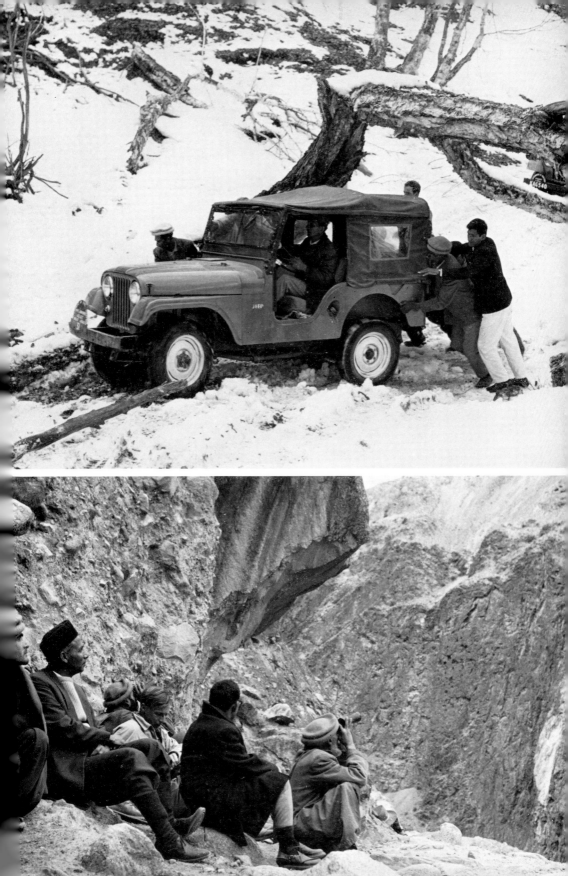

names to species of the animal kingdom. Stoliczka's Tit Warbler and Güldenstädt's Redstart are bad enough: but it is horrible to contemplate that the famous wild horse of Mongolia must in perpetuity be called Przewalski's Horse—assuming that future generations can get their tongues around it.

Down in the wide flood track of the river we came across two huge boulders liberally covered with fascinating chiselled designs of men shooting Ibex and Markhor with bows and arrows. Judging by the weathering of the stone they were of immense age and we thought them either Neolithic or Palaeolithic (plate 35a and b). On the journey to Phandar, Duncan also found rock engravings of a similar nature, though some of these depicted men on horseback shooting backwards with crossbows, in the manner ascribed to the Phœnicians. We longed to be able to date these discoveries accurately.

Driving round a hairpin bend near the rock engravings we disturbed a Bearded Vulture, or Lammergeier, at the roadside. Of all the vultures this is the most magnificent. Indeed, in many ways it is more like a long-winged eagle of great size, for it lacks the hideous naked skin and other noisome head ornaments of most vultures. Instead, it has a forward-jutting black moustache, which contrasts splendidly with the orange feathers of its face and neck. It rose effortlessly and circled back to inspect us before sailing majestically on motionless wings for a thousand feet up the side of the mountain and into the blue sky (plate 37a).

We breakfasted next morning with the Raja of Gupis, an

32 *Above* A Markhor of the distinctive Astor race, aged about four years. *Below* Excessive hunting has reduced the population of the Shapu mountain sheep in the Gilgit Agency to about 500.

elderly man of great charm, wearing the traditional long, embroidered *chogha* with sleeves almost reaching the ground. Like
all the men of Gupis, he had a noble, hawk-nosed face and
great natural dignity. After answering his questions about our
work we sought his views concerning the animals of the region.
The Shapu, he said, had now disappeared from Gupis. Ibex,
yes, and there were still a few Lynx in the mountains, but not
many. Snow Leopards were a nuisance raiding the goat flocks
and he paid a bounty in grain for every one shot or trapped, as
he did for Wolves.

I was interested in the barter system practised at Gupis and
asked how it worked. This was quite a simple matter, he said.
He fixed the rate of exchange with the village elders according
to the current availability of the commodity concerned. For
example, at the present time one goat was worth 28 lb of grain.
Twenty pounds of grain could be exchanged for $2\frac{1}{2}$ lb of butter.
Two female goats were worth one male and six goats one cow.
Two cows would buy one ploughing bullock and three bullocks
one polo pony. It sounded a very practical arrangement in a
region where money had little significance.

Gupis was a poor community and, because the laws of
inheritance were based not on primogeniture but on an equal
division between all the sons, land was constantly being divided
into smaller and smaller parcels, so that few could now make a
profitable living. When I asked why the laws of inheritance were
not changed, he smiled gently and said. 'Traditions are very
strong here.' Thinking of the tradition which condemned women
to die in agony rather than be seen by a male doctor, I felt sad
for the proud people of the Gupis mountains.

When we took our leave, the Raja made a touching little

speech of farewell and picked each of us a red carnation from his garden as he walked to the gate with us.

Our next appointment was with the Raja of Punial, one of the hereditary princes of the Gilgit Agency, the others being the Mir of Hunza and the Mir of Nagar. The northern boundary of the principality lies at the junction of the Ishkoman Valley and the high peaks of Hunza and extends southwards across the Gilgit River.

On the way to Punial I idly began counting the number of hairpin bends as we climbed the shoulder of a mountain which jutted out over the river. There were seventeen in quick succession going up and twenty-one going down the other side. It was interesting to think that although these roads were of ancient origin, it was scarcely twenty years since the first four-wheeled vehicle had penetrated the Gilgit Valley. Even to-day nothing larger than a Jeep could negotiate most of the roads and, as our drivers enjoyed reminding us, many of these had fatal accidents.

The approach to the Raja's house was dramatic. Having plunged down to the river, we crossed a little bridge over a torrent and found ourselves in a courtyard flanked by a small medieval fort, beside which was a more modern house. I recalled that in Tom Longstaff's book about Gilgit the bridge had been described as a frail spider's web of only three strands, one for the feet and two for the hands, woven of birch twigs. The Raja of those days was a great practical joker and his favourite trick was to wait until his guests were half-way over the bridge and then cut the main support, dropping them into the river. Wild and romantic scenery surrounded us and with the music of the waterfall in our ears we half expected to come face to face with Kubla Khan himself. The valley of Punial is known as 'the place where heaven and earth meet' and it fully justified the description. The local people are tall, fair-skinned and hawk-nosed Shins.

The Raja, with a beaming smile, came down the steps to meet us. A man with twinkling eyes, a large grey moustache and captivating good humour, he nevertheless had the lean physique of his people. I could imagine him scaling high mountains with the best of them. In this I was not far wrong, for I was told later that he had been a great *shikari*, though he now preferred to watch animals rather than shoot them.

We were given an excellent lunch of curried chicken and lamb with red persimmons, followed by enormous locally grown apples and sweet yellow grapes. I was again struck by the modesty of the standards of living of the notabilities of Gilgit. The Raja's house lacked all trace of the regal splendour which one normally associates with the hereditary princes of the sub-continent. It was comfortable and full of character, but, like its owner, completely unostentatious. Over the mantelpiece were photographs of the Raja's father and grandfather. The latter, who must have been photographed at the turn of the century, was an extremely impressive figure, with a fierce black beard and a curved sabre, wearing traditional costume and cross-over puttees.

After lunch we inspected the garden, where white geese and domestic poultry scratched contentedly among the flower beds. The Raja then produced a ring which he had removed from the

33 Pictures from the game book of the Gilgit Scouts, showing (*above*) fine heads of Ibex, Shapu and Marco Polo's Sheep and (*below*) Markhor, as well as skins of Snow Leopard, Wolf and both Brown and Black Bears.

leg of a Bar-headed Goose shot in the region of Sher Qilah in April 1966. It bore a Russian inscription and was therefore of particular interest to us as a recovery. Christopher Savage later reported it to the Russian ornithological authorities and learned that the bird had been ringed as a juvenile at Chatyr Kul Lake, in Kirgiz SSR, in July 1959.

Punial was certainly one of the most interesting places we had visited and we wished we could have stayed to explore it more thoroughly. The sun had set long before we reached Gilgit. Our return journey was enlivened when we switched on our head-lights and found that our driver, succumbing to the Pakistani's love of decoration, had rigged up a chain of Christmas tree lights over the windscreen. The effect was very gay, but when presently one of the lamps shorted and set fire to the cable, we decided that he was no better an electrician than he was a mechanic.

Kargah Nullah was our objective the following day. Our old *shikari* said it was the best place for seeing Markhor and that we should approach it in late afternoon, when they came down to drink from the river. Accordingly we reached the yawning gorge at about three o'clock, leaving time for climbing to good vantage points. Where to stop was decided for us when we came to a point where the entire road had been carried away by a huge landslide. After surveying the scene with expert eye, our *shikari* pointed to a projecting spur about 1,500 feet above us and indicated that this would be an admirable spot from which to watch for Markhor. Craning my neck I wondered

34 Where to halt at Kargarh Nullah was decided for us by a landslide which had carried away the road. By climbing the mountain on the left we ob-tained our first sight of the Markhor wild goats.

T.V.J.   L how we should reach it, but our guide seemed in no doubt about this and set off at a fast pace across the fallen rocks and straight up the mountain (plate 34). He looked very old and frail and his feet were clad only in tattered sandals, but he moved like a young man.

It was by no means a difficult climb, though very steep. I kept up reasonably well for the first half and then found myself lagging behind. Tom, Edmund and Duncan were well up in front and Siddiqi, who was not as young as they were, was also going well. After ascending a thousand feet or so I was puffing like a grampus and I reached our destination exhausted. I have always loved mountains, but climbing at the 10,000-foot level imposes a certain strain even on the young. Nevertheless I felt a sudden overpowering sense of frustration that just because I was on the eve of my sixty-second birthday I no longer climbed with the easy gusto of my youth. I sat disconsolately on a boulder to regain my breath and looked down into the distant gorge, where the Jeeps looked like miniature toys beside the narrow ribbon of the river. My companions, perhaps sensing my feelings, did not comment on my late arrival and the mood soon passed.

We divided into two groups. Tom took half our number round the soaring needle of rock on our left and over the next ridge, while the old *shikari* and I, with Siddiqi and a couple of Gilgit Scouts who had somehow attached themselves to our party, climbed to a vantage point and settled down to watch the opposite side of the gorge (plate 31*b*). The vast cliff rising to twin peaks was honeycombed with hundreds of caves, in which the Markhor often sheltered during snowstorms. The sun was now well down in heavy clouds and the light was failing. It was bitterly cold and a strong wind was blowing, whistling fiercely around the promontory. Presently squalls of sleet began to cut into our faces, forcing us back into the protection of the rocks. The *shikari*, however, still lay full length on the edge of the precipice, his eyes glued to the binoculars I had lent him, apparently impervious to the cold.

Half an hour later the *shikari* gave an exclamation of triumph. The sleet had now stopped and far above on the mountain behind us he had spotted a group of five Markhor coming almost vertically down a fissure in the rocks. They were a long way from us, but I could make out a young male and four females. Soon afterwards another large, bearded male followed by four females came cautiously over the skyline to our left. These were much nearer and I was able to see that the male had great corkscrew horns of well over forty inches and a fine coat of long grey hair almost to his knees.

The other party was also able to see a distant group of Markhor and we returned that night to Gilgit delighted with our excursion, though several of us had caught severe colds from exposure after getting over-heated during the climb.

Fresh snow fell on the mountains around Gilgit that night and we decided to pay another visit to Naltar while the roads were still open. We were lucky, for when we reached the Spruce forest the snow lay heavy on the road and the big trees were transformed into towering spires of new beauty under their white mantle. When we trudged knee-deep in the soft snow along the edge of the forest, a whole new population of birds greeted us. Thousands upon thousands of twittering Hodgson's Mountain Finches were sheltering among the trees, looking very like the Snow Buntings which congregate along the British coasts in winter. There were also many Rufous-bellied Crested Tits and

White-cheeked Nuthatches, as well as flocks of Black-throated Thrushes, driven down by the snow. On our journey we had already seen another rare new species when we came across a party of Mongolian Trumpeter Bullfinches, birds which have a curious bleating call.

With the coming of the first winter snow the Gujars, a hardy nomadic tribe who spend the summer in the Himalayas and Kashmir, had begun descending from their mountain settlements to seek shelter in the valleys. We met several large parties of them, driving their flocks down the winding mountain trails. All the oxen and horses carried enormous loads of household chattels and the children were walking barefoot in the snow. Each time we met such a cavalcade, the cattle and children were driven up the rocks to make way for us and I hated to see the additional hardship we caused them.

After a strenuous week of almost continual travel I thought it time to give the team a rest. We therefore spent the next day on foot around Gilgit. Edmund took the opportunity to make some admirable recordings of the Blue Whistling Thrushes which were still singing in the trees around the rest-house. Tom and I walked the banks of the Gilgit River and the surrounding fields.

While examining a mixed flock of buntings feeding in the stubble, we made a startling discovery. Among them was a female Chaffinch, a bird so far from its normal range that at first we could hardly believe our eyes. We examined it closely and when we consulted our text-books found that the only

35 *Above* Lammergeiers, the most splendid of the vultures, were seen at Gilgit and the Kirthar Range. *Below* The Persian Wild Goats (locally called Sind Ibex) proved to be extremely difficult to photograph.

previous record for Pakistan was of a vagrant Chaffinch shot at Kohat by Whitehead in 1906. Out of all the 423 species of birds which we saw during our two expeditions to Pakistan this, the most numerous bird of the British Isles, was certainly the most rare.

The next three days were rather frustrating. We were booked to fly back to Rawalpindi and then to Peshawar, where Duncan and I were to have important meetings with forestry officials. The weather, however, grew steadily worse and flying impossible among the obscured peaks. Again and again we heard that an aircraft was coming in and rushed down to the airfield with our baggage, only to be told it was a false alarm. We dared not go far from the rest-house and had to content ourselves with local observations.

During this time we were not idle, however. Edmund seized the opportunity to have a ride on one of the Gilgit polo ponies. He said its mouth was like iron. A very accomplished steeplechaser, he had played polo with the Duke of Edinburgh at Windsor and would obviously have given a great deal for a chance to try his hand at the extraordinary local game. We also had time to photograph a young Himalayan Black Bear which we had found chained in a back yard, moaning quietly to itself. The Pakistan zoos were glutted with bears which hunters sent them after shooting the parents. Another useful find was a beautiful Wall Creeper, which obligingly allowed itself to be caught in one of our bedrooms (plate 26). It was the first time I had had an opportunity to examine one of these superb

36 *Above* Exploring the Indus Delta. From left to right, Lord Fermoy, John Buxton, George Shannon. *Below* A Sindi chieftain came aboard to present me with two kids as the traditional gift of welcome.

little crimson, grey and black birds in the hand. I was surprised to notice that its black legs were so long and delicate. One would expect a bird which spends its life creeping up vertical rock faces to have short, sturdy legs like a Nuthatch's. Perhaps its rock-climbing was after all a relatively recent evolutionary development. I was not surprised to learn from Tom that these delicate little birds did not stay through the long, hard Gilgit winter, but descended to the milder slopes of the Salt Range and the hills around Lahore.

On the third day and already two days behind our planned schedule, a powerful military troop carrier succeeded in landing. We rushed to the air-strip in the hope of hitching a ride. We were already too late for our appointments in Peshawar, but an audience with President Ayub Khan had now been arranged and I was determined not to miss it.

Alas for our hopes. Arriving at the air-strip we found about a hundred Gilgit Scouts lined up waiting to board the plane. Karim, whose responsibilities in looking after our needs had prevented him from joining most of our excursions, now showed his persuasive powers to the full. Seizing the advantage of our appointment with the President, he succeeded in obtaining two places for Duncan and me and assurance that the remainder of our party would be lifted later in the day. I thanked the Colonel commanding the unit and within a few minutes we found ourselves squeezed into the already overcrowded plane. The interior had been gutted and most of the troops sat on the bare floor. We sat in relative comfort among the kit-bags.

We had previously watched the perilous process of taking off from Gilgit. Planes were pulled back to the very edge of the tarmac and full throttle was applied before releasing the brakes.

As they raced down the runway it was impossible not to think that they would fly straight into the mountain at the far end. At the last possible moment the pilot would bank the aircraft right over and climb obliquely up the face of the rocks, finally scraping through a gap on the crest with a very few feet to spare. Our troop carrier followed the same procedure and as we breasted the gap I could see the very texture of the snow below us. In this exhilarating manner we concluded the Gilgit sector of the expedition.

Soon after returning to England after the expedition we learned that our new friends the Political Resident and the Commandant of the Gilgit Scouts, with twenty-three others flying in an aircraft similar to ours, had been caught in one of the violent storms for which Gilgit is notorious and had crashed into a hidden peak. There were no survivors.

Cholistan dancing camel

8

The Swamps of the Indus Delta

The hot sunshine of Rawalpindi was more than welcome and it was strange to see people in shirtsleeves less than an hour's flying time from the snow and icy winds of Gilgit.

Several changes were now made in our group. Dr Beg unfortunately had to leave us and return to Peshawar. When we reached Lahore, however, he was to be replaced by Mr Z. B. Mirza, Curator of the Natural History Museum, who would accompany us on the Indus Delta explorations. Duncan Poore was to fly back to England after our meeting with the President. The second echelon of the expedition was by now completing its work in the Kirthar Range and I was looking forward to our joining forces in Karachi.

As no official meetings had been arranged for that afternoon, Duncan and I headed for the beautiful Murree Hills, the famous resort of the wealthy of Rawalpindi and Lahore during the heat of summer. Tom, who knew the area well, had told us where to find the best localities for wildlife and we found them without difficulty. The best of these, Chikka Gali, was a delightful spot at an elevation of 6,000 feet among tall pines. It produced for us one of the most spectacular birds of Pakistan—the

Yellow-billed Blue Magpie, which has sky-blue and white plumage and an astonishingly long tail, which often seemed to get in its way. While we were watching it feeding on the ground, we also saw three different species of woodpeckers, the Himalayan Pied, the Fulvous-breasted Pied and the Scaly-bellied Green, all from the same spot.

Most of the Murree Hills area is now a well managed forest reserve. Where goats had been excluded there was good natural regeneration and plenty of undergrowth, with superb Gentians starring the roadside. However, on the other side of the valley through which the main road climbs, the hills had been stripped as bare as the proverbial billiard table. It was a dramatic object lesson in conservation. We wished our friends in Gilgit could see it, because most of the forests there were deprived of any chance of regeneration by constant over-grazing by goats.

Our meeting next morning with the President, at which Air Marshal Asghar Khan was also present, was this time completely informal once the television cameras had withdrawn. We had been warned not to exceed fifteen minutes, but the President showed such interest in our work that it was fully forty-five minutes before we took our leave. His comments were constructive and very helpful, particularly when we came to the subject of National Parks, which involved questions of local economics and land-use. His reaction to our proposal to create a major National Park at Gilgit was immediately favourable. He questioned us closely about the potentiality for attracting tourist revenue and the restrictions which would be necessary in the area reserved for the protection of wildlife. There was no doubt in our minds that the National Park could be one of the most spectacular in the world and that the opportunities for tourists to enjoy skiing, climbing, photography and trout fishing in such amazing scenery would bring them from the far corners of the earth. The notion that we would provide increased employment for the local population in road making, building and servicing the park obviously appealed to the President. As to the question of the wildlife reserve which we wanted for the centre of the park, we pointed out that there would be plenty of room for this in the 800 square miles which we recommended as the extent of the plan. We agreed to make detailed recommendations, based on the natural boundaries provided by the Indus and Gilgit Rivers, with the southern boundary formed by a line between Astor and Skardu.

The President then told us what steps had been taken to improve conservation since our last visit. We were astonished that with so many affairs of State to consider he had all the details at his fingertips and that he had no notes in front of him. He said he had arranged a special meeting of State Governors in three days' time, at which the formation of the promised Wildlife Committee would be announced. We had always regarded this as the keystone to the new conservation programme. It was momentous news.

The President was in excellent spirits and made several asides in the course of our discussion which revealed a strong sense of humour. It was, however, apparent that he was determined once he had given a decision to brook no undue delay in its execution. When speaking of the Wildlife Committee he expressed impatience that it had taken so long to bring it into being. For our part, we assured him that in England the progress of Government Commissions was usually measured in years rather than months.

As we rose to go I presented him with the gold head of the Arabian Oryx, the emblem of the Fauna Preservation Society, on behalf of the Marquess of Willingdon who is its President. They were old friends and the gesture obviously pleased him. Saving the Arabian Oryx from threatened extinction had been one of the most successful joint ventures of the Fauna Preservation Society and the World Wildlife Fund and the President said he looked forward to reading the account of this in the Society's magazine which I gave him. In parting, he asked me to convey his thanks to Their Royal Highnesses the Duke of Edinburgh and the Prince of the Netherlands for their interest in the conservation of wildlife in Pakistan and the work of the World Wildlife Fund expedition, about which they had both been in touch with him.

Duncan and I felt the meeting had been not only enjoyable but a great success so far as our work was concerned. The prospect of creating a protected reserve for the magnificent animals and vegetation of the western Himalayas sounded almost too good to be true; but we had little doubt that the President intended our proposal to be followed through.

We lunched with the Air Marshal and his brother Brigadier Aslam Khan, and a number of interesting people they had invited to meet us. Among them were the Minister of Defence, Vice-Admiral A. R. Khan and Mr H. A. Twist, representing the British High Commissioner, Sir Cyril Pickard, who was away at the time. Mr Twist kindly arranged to circulate the Pakistan Press with copies of the speech I was giving later at the University of the Punjab.

We had time that afternoon to make a quick visit to the new reservoir known as Rawal Lake, near Islamabad, the new

Government centre. The lake, of about 1,700 acres, provides an attractive recreational area for the people of the new town and we hoped that part of it might be set aside as a wildlife reserve. Already it had attracted a large number of birds, including the first Great Crested Grebes we had seen. A new Natural History Museum was to be built at Islamabad, where Siddiqi would make his headquarters. The lack of a representative collection of skins was a severe handicap to scientific work in Pakistan and the new museum and library were greatly needed. Siddiqi said that there were plans for a similar centre at Dacca, to serve East Pakistan.

Duncan then left for London. I said good-bye to him with great regret. The loss of our vegetation ecologist for the remainder of the expedition was a considerable matter and I was also going to miss his cheerful companionship; but I knew I could count on his expert help with drafting our reports when we returned.

Next morning all the papers carried illustrated reports of our meeting with the President. From now on there were frequent references to our work in the Press and I had to give interviews, broadcasts and Press conferences at all the major cities through which we passed. These often tiresome activities undoubtedly played an important part in rousing public opinion to the need for conservation and I did not begrudge the extra effort they involved.

Christopher Savage had now joined us and we flew to Lahore soon after breakfast. The high peaks of Azad Kashmir

37 *Above* Curlews were seen in thousands in the Indus Delta and many other species of waders streamed past our boat. *Below* A Dunlin and a Terek Sandpiper rose to inspect us.

were gleaming with fresh snow on our left beyond the flood-waters of the new Mangla Dam, which the President was to open the following week. As we approached Lahore a dozen Egyptian and White-backed Vultures were soaring over the airfield. Vultures have a great liking for airfields because the hot tarmac provides excellent thermals on which to soar. This results in many collisions with aircraft and has become a major problem throughout the world.

Our new member, Mr Z. B. Mirza, met us at the airport and we drove to Faletti's Hotel, where arrangements had been made for us to do some sight-seeing. This included Lahore Fort, which is so vast an edifice that a week would be required to do it justice. Begun in 1556 in the reign of Akbar, it was enlarged and embellished for more than a hundred years, each succeeding Emperor vying to outdo his predecessor in magnificence. Like good tourists we duly admired the ornate little balcony with its notice-board reading 'Here stood the Eunuchs.' We also visited Jahangir's Tomb, one of the most beautiful of the royal mausoleums in Pakistan, with a profusion of intricately inlaid marble. Hundreds of Rose-ringed Parakeets were flying around the gardens surrounding the tomb and Edmund took the opportunity to make recordings of their shrill voices.

Masud Mahmood honoured us with a dinner party that night at the International Hotel, where the atmosphere and food are authentically Pakistani. A number of our friends were there, including Justice Feroze Nana, Sayed Babar Ali and Naser-ud-Deen Khan.

38 *Above* Reef Herons were seen chiefly in the typical dark blue-grey plumage, but also in pale grey and pure white. *Below* The acrobatic Mud Skippers were a source of constant interest.

We sat talking for more than an hour after dinner and I was able to learn from Justice Nana some of the interesting customs of the mountain people of Pakistan. As a Circuit Judge he had frequently to try men accused of murder, a crime which he said was almost invariably connected with disputes over land, water or women. The tribal laws of the Pathans permitted them to kill their wives if taken in adultery. In some regions it was regarded as obligatory also to kill the lover, providing this was done within the 'law of seven paces.' This meant that if the wronged husband caught the guilty pair within seven paces of each other he could kill them both without any questions being asked. If the lover succeeded in escaping, the husband was in duty bound to pursue him; but outside the seven paces rule he was liable to conviction for murder if the police heard about the killing and could apprehend him. Sometimes the guilty pair both escaped, thus triggering off a savage vendetta which in the old days often led to a tribal war. Justice Nana knew of an instance in which the lover had been forced to flee to a mountain top, where the wife built a pillbox of rocks around him, leaving only slits through which he could fire at his inevitable pursuers. At the risk of her life she kept him supplied with food through the gun-slits, until the husband tracked them down and killed them.

Justice Nana was a kindly man and told these stories with compassion rather than condemnation. The hill tribes were basically fine people, he said, and he was always saddened when he had to pass sentence on them as convicted murderers. He always made a point of talking to them after the trial and asking if they wished to see their relatives before being taken away. Frequently the condemned man would take the opportunity to harangue his relatives and instruct them how to continue the vendetta against the family of his unfaithful wife, or her lover. Few of them thought much of losing their lives and took the sentence stoically. One of them, when asked if he would care to see his relatives, shrugged and said, 'No—they live a long way away. But I really must insist that I get my shoes back. The police took them from me and they were a very nice pair. If you could get them back for me I should be most obliged.' The kindly Judge sent a policeman fourteen miles to the gaol to fetch them and the condemned man then went quite cheerfully to his death.

We had a number of important engagements next day. The first of these was with the Secretary of Agriculture, Amir Ahmed Khan, who had been very helpful to us during our previous expedition. He had summoned a number of his senior officials to the meeting, which he described as a working session. After the Press photographers had withdrawn, we enjoyed talking to a man who so obviously understood the technicalities of conservation.

'Tell me how we can help and I will see that it is done,' he said. 'And let's see if we can't cut some of the red tape!'

Between this meeting and our appointment at the Punjab University we dashed off to see what birds we could find in the surroundings of Lahore. We were accompanied by John Tyack, a young British ornithologist who had been working in Pakistan for several years. He took us to a derelict brick-works on the edge of cultivated fields, where we quickly ran up a very respectable list. Very hot and dusty, we then drove to the University, where I gave my lecture and showed the film of our first expedition. The film was only roughly edited and I was not very proud of it, but it was well received. I was very flattered to see the Secretary of Agriculture in the audience and even more so when he told me he wanted to publish my speech in the forestry journals.

The subject I had chosen was the value of the wildlife of Pakistan to the nation. I gave evidence of the serious losses which had occurred among the major animals and their habitats during the past twenty years and analysed the causes in relation to the expansion of human activities. Afterwards I sensed an undercurrent of obvious anxiety and even protest in the questions which were asked by the students. They were intelligent questions which showed that there was a genuine interest in knowing what was being done to curb the thoughtless exploitation of the natural heritage of the nation. I was encouraged by this, because the students represented the new generation which would be the custodians of what little my generation leaves of the wildlife of the world.

Tea was served under the trees on the campus, where I talked to the students. Unfortunately we had to hurry to catch our plane and having left at the last minute had a hectic ride to the airport. I was feeling rather exhausted after the quick succession of meetings, at which I was always having to lead the discussion, and was thankful for the brief respite of the flight.

Eric Hosking, George Shannon and John Buxton met us at the Hotel Intercontinental in Karachi and we had an animated reunion, each eager to hear the other's adventures.

The Kirthar Range party had been dogged by difficulties and frustrations. The experienced *shikari* who was to have

39 Near Gupis were primitive rock engravings of men hunting Ibex, Markhor (*left*), Lynx (*right*) and Snow Leopard (*bottom centre*). Near Phandar Lake were engravings of equestrian hunters.

accompanied them had been replaced by a man who did not really know how to locate the Persian Wild Goats (also called Sind Ibex) which were the chief animals to be studied. One of the vehicles had failed to turn up, so that the remaining Jeeps had been uncomfortably overcrowded. Two precious days were lost trying to overcome these difficulties. Although they had not been caused by any fault in the planning by our hosts, there was no doubt that the absence of Karim, who had been with the Gilgit party, was keenly felt. Nevertheless the agile Wild Goats were eventually located and some excellent film sequences obtained of them (plate 37), running with amazing ease up and down apparently vertical cliffs. These animals, whose scientific name is *Capra hircus blythi*, bear a close resemblance to the Himalayan Ibex *Capra ibex sibirica*, though their colour differs and their long, arched horns do not reach the spectacular fifty inches which have been recorded at Gilgit.

A number of valuable observations had been made in the Kirthar, particularly of the many eagles, sandgrouse and chats which inhabit the mountain slopes and the adjoining desert where the party camped. Eric obtained some excellent pictures of them and found time also to photograph one of the interesting Bloodsucker Tree Agamids which are common in the region (plate 21). Their rather sinister name has nothing to do with sucking blood, but is derived from their reddish throats, which do rather suggest that this is their habit. The males change colour from grey to red during combat with their rivals. There was no time to do any work on other animals, though

40 While some of us were in Gilgit, others explored the rugged mountains of the Kirthar Range, where chief interest lay in studying the Persian Wild Goats which inhabit the peaks.
    T.V.J.   M

Leopards, Wolves, Jackals, Porcupines and Ratels (Honey Badgers) are all fairly numerous in the Kirthar Range. The two lost days unfortunately robbed the party of any chance of seeing the Baluchistan race of the Urial Mountain Sheep, which were only a few miles farther along the range.

We found the Hotel Intercontinental full to bursting with a large party of sheiks from Abu Dhabi, each of whom had brought with him a Saker Falcon, or a Shahin, or a Peregrine. Stately figures in flowing white robes stalked the corridors, carrying their falcons on their wrists, causing no little distraction to the hotel staff who followed them round anxiously with mops and pails. We heard that at least sixty falcons were to be flown after Houbara Bustards in Cholistan and were horrified that this additional persecution was to be imposed on these rare birds. Later, however, we learned that the falcons had in many instances 'hacked back to the wild' as the British falconers would say and that few Houbaras had been taken. We were delighted to hear it. Having exterminated all the game in their own country, the sheiks should not be permitted to hunt in other lands.

The following year, however, two more parties of sheiks with falcons killed between them 600 Houbaras, which that winter had arrived in unusually large flocks. This slaughter caused such a commotion among the growing number of officials who were interested in conservation that representations were made to prevent the sheiks from receiving any further invitations to practise their sport at the expense of Pakistan's wildlife. German falconers had also been busy that year, trapping Sakers on migration through West Pakistan. Several foreign diplomats had also shot some particularly endangered animals. No opportunity was now lost in bringing these abuses to the attention of the authorities. This at least showed that progress was being made in the general attitude towards wildlife.

After lunch next day we drove to Korangi Creek, to board our ship for the Indus Delta explorations. It took two hours to ferry our baggage and stores out to the *Sima*, a rather dilapidated looking vessel lent to us by the Department of Forests, which, however, proved quite adequate to our needs. The little ferry-boat was barely eight feet long and when loaded had a freeboard of only one inch; but the last load, a basket of squawking chickens, was eventually hauled on board and we headed out into the shallow creek. It was a relief to smell fresh air again after the appalling stench of effluent on shore.

We now encountered a quite new spectrum of bird life, among which gulls, waders and terns predominated. Even as we began to move, a large flock of White Pelicans was seen and as soon as we entered the mangrove swamps new species came thick and fast.

Our plan was to sail the whole length of the huge swamps, which extended for some hundred miles or so from Karachi to the open sea. We were then to turn back up the main channel of the Indus to the region of Keti Bundar and Shahbundar, where big colonies of the various species of storks, herons, ibises and egrets were reported to nest. All these birds had suffered severe losses and we were anxious to create a reserve for them. Very few storks, cranes or ibises are seen in Pakistan to-day, though they were plentiful only twenty years ago. Most of their breeding places have been destroyed and birds of passage are constantly harried by hunters or trappers. But for this persecution, Pakistan could still boast a larger diversity of species than almost any other country. Eight storks (Painted, Openbill, White, Black, White-necked, Black-necked, Adjutant and Lesser Adjutant); four cranes (Common, Sarus, Siberian and Demoiselle); and three ibises (White, Black and Glossy) used to be either residents or winter visitors. In all our travels in West and East Pakistan we ultimately found only six out of the original total of fifteen species in these three groups. All are more or less dependent on mangrove swamps for their food and shelter.

I should perhaps explain at this juncture what is meant by the term mangrove. It is a type of forest found in the tidal estuaries, salt marshes and muddy coasts of many tropical countries. Its chief characteristics are the production of adventitious roots arching out from the main stem and radicles growing down to the mud from the ripening fruits, thus constantly spreading the growth over an ever widening area. Erect, spike-like 'breathing roots,' or pneumatophores, are produced by the genus *Sonneratia*; these emerge in thousands above the surface of the mud and carry oxygen to the true roots below and also expel carbon monoxide. The spider's web of roots around the trees gradually trap flotsam and silt from the water at each high tide, eventually building fertile soil. As the soil increases and the mangroves advance into the water, other species of trees less tolerant of salinity are able to establish themselves on the drying land behind. The species of trees which have the characteristics of mangroves number about thirty in the Oriental region and all are evergreen. The majority belong to the salt-tolerant genus

41 *Above* Lesser and Greater Sand Plovers had never before been photographed side by side. *Below* A host of different birds of prey was attracted by the colonies of Little Sand Jirds.

Rhizophora. The graceful Nipa Palm, which we were to see in the Sunderbans later, is also a typical species of the mangrove jungles of south-east Asia (plate 28).

A few miles out from Korangi we passed the little fishing village of Rerhi, where, standing forlornly on the roof-tops were half a dozen young Painted Storks. These had undoubtedly been taken as nestlings from the breeding colony at Keti Bundar. This at least was evidence that some of these increasingly rare birds had bred there during the previous year (plate 44).

At sundown we anchored for the night and a huge full moon rose to bathe the misty marshes in brilliant light. I was thankful to be back in the wilds again and away from meetings, speeches, flashbulbs and formalities. My team was now complete except for Duncan and Christopher Savage; the latter would be joining us for the last stage of the expedition in Sylhet.

At dawn, just as we were about to hoist in the anchor, a canoe put out from the shore and a very imposing figure came on board. Tall, hawk-nosed and black-bearded, he looked like a Biblical character or a Barbary pirate. He was, in fact, the head man of the local Sindi tribe, a riverain people of mixed Arab and Pakistani blood, whose territory we were entering. He carried under each arm a silky-skinned little goat with a snub nose and long white ears. These he formally presented to me as the traditional offering of goodwill to distinguished visitors to his domain (plate 38). With Karim as translator we exchanged speeches of greeting and he then paddled majestically back to the shore. The kids were an instant success with us all. Their

42 *Above* A Darter, or Snake Bird, showing the characteristic kinked neck in flight. *Centre* A thousand Cormorants waiting expectantly for fish to be landed. *Below* A Cormorant in flight.

appetites were catholic and it was not long before one of George's shirts, a tablecloth and the upholstery of one of our chairs had been nibbled and the cable release of John's camera well chewed. They wandered around the ship at will. At night they were inclined to put their heads down the companion-way and bleat loudly just as we were dropping to sleep, but we forgave them because their little black baby faces were so adorable and their long ears so silky.

The ship's crew watched the kids with a quite different interest. Next morning we could find only one of them and when curried goat was served for lunch we knew why. None of us would eat it and we raised such a rumpus that the lonely survivor succeeded in staying alive for the remainder of the voyage, though I have no doubt it went straight into the pot the moment our backs were turned.

On the second day out I had a nasty accident when descending the vertical iron ladder from the top deck to the main deck. The ladder had a handrail which ended seven feet from the bottom and when I found myself grasping thin air I fell backwards heavily on to the square-edged iron rail around the deck below. For a moment I thought I had broken my back, though in fact I was only badly bruised and had lost six inches of skin off my spine, which under George's skilful ministrations soon healed.

We were working our way steadily southwards through a maze of mangrove islands. The shifting mudbanks made navigation slow and uncertain and we had to drop anchor every evening. There was never a moment when we could not see large numbers of marsh birds. There were many sightings of the Plumbeous Dolphin and later, when we came in sight of the open sea, of Porpoises too, though we could not be certain of their species.

The most numerous waders were Whimbrels and Curlews which were seen in thousands (plate 39). All the heron species were there, attracted by the immense wealth of food along the margins of the creeks. Reef Herons were the most numerous species of this group and appeared in every morph or variation of their often confusing plumage (plate 40). The majority had the typical blue-grey colour, though others varied from dark slate-grey to pale dove-grey or pure white. In the white morph the Reef Heron is quite difficult to distinguish from the Little Egret except by the shape and colour of its bill and legs. We noticed that many of the birds in the blue-grey morph had an interesting white spot on the fore-wing and that the spots were frequently asymmetrical.

Caspian, Lesser Crested and Gull-billed Terns and Brown-headed Gulls followed the ship constantly, as often did Brahminy Kites (plate 5). Flocks of Lesser Sand Plovers and Redshanks fed busily on the muddy shores and Terek Sandpipers and Little Stints flew in hundreds ahead of us. From time to time a Darter, or Snake Bird, raised its serpentine head above the surface of the water to examine us before continuing its relentless pursuit of fish, which, unlike most birds, it spears with its dagger bill instead of seizing them. Occasionally an unusual new species was added to our list, as for example when we saw in quick succession a Slender-billed Gull, a Great Black-headed Gull and a flock of Crab Plovers. The last mentioned species is a great rarity in Pakistan and we were lucky enough to see another flock later. They are curious birds, with disproportionately large heads and heavy, black, angular bills and pale blue legs.

Another interesting bird seen several times in this region was the Black-eared Kite *Milvus migrans lineatus*. It is a distinctive mountain race of the familiar Black Kite and normally inhabits Ladakh, northern Kashmir, Tibet and the higher ranges of Assam. According to Tom Roberts, who knows it well, it often winters as far south as the Indus Delta.

Near the mouth of the Indus, where the water was more saline, fishing boats became numerous. All of them differed in detail, though the tall, triangular sail and sloping mast were constant. Out on the distant sea a line of much larger deep-water fishing craft was suspended in space by an intervening mirage; their square, lantern sails were gaily patched in many colours. Near the shore was silhouetted a long black frieze of fishermen dragging a net across the shallow bay. A thousand Cormorants waited expectantly in heraldic attitudes on an adjacent sandbank (plate 42).

We took a long time trying to cross the bay, moving first one way and then another to avoid the shoals. Dolphins gambolled around us, heaving their sleek grey bodies out of the water as they surfaced to inspect us. We were now well behind schedule from repeated delays and the captain finally decided to turn back. It was most frustrating to be so close to our objective at Keti Bundar without setting eyes on the nesting colonies of the storks and ibises; but there was nothing we could do to overcome the captain's reluctance to hazard his ship. As a consolation we landed for a brief exploration of the shore before beginning the journey back to Karachi.

We chose an area where the usually swampy ground looked firm enough to permit a landing and drove the bows of the ship into the bank. We then jumped the eight feet or so down to the mud. A few yards from the water the ground was dry and we walked inland into the Tamarisk scrub. A dozen domesticated buffaloes were wandering on the sandy trails.

In every open space there were hundreds of tunnels made by Jirds, which we frequently saw popping back into their holes (plate 41). All around us we heard their alarm signals, made by pattering their hind legs rapidly on the ground. These little rodents had attracted a large number of raptorial birds. White-eyed Buzzards, Long-legged Buzzards, Montagu's Harriers and Tawny Eagles were preying on them and also a fine Black-shouldered Kite, which was hovering like a Kestrel and diving down to strike the Jirds. Later it boldly attacked one of the Tawny Eagles and drove it away—a bird three times its size.

Here and there were patches of Sodom Apple *Calotropis procera*, a shrub with which we had become very familiar during our work in Jordan. White-cheeked Bulbuls, Drongos and tiny, jewel-like Purple Sunbirds were attracted by the insects in the pale mauve blossoms. A Black Partridge, a bird often found in Tamarisk scrub, called cheerfully from a bush-top. It was the only one we saw in Pakistan, though the species was once common in both Provinces.

Mirza said that the Tamarisk area was well known for its Rock Pythons and was also greatly favoured by the now very rare Fishing Cat. Although we failed to see either of these, Tom quickly found fresh tracks of Hog Deer, Wild Boar and Jackal. Jerry Wood-Anderson, who had been with us on the first expedition, had told me an amusing story about a Jackal which had been seen by him in this locality. He found the Jackal apparently trapped on a mud-bank and when he landed to release it, had found its tail in the jaws of a large Moray Eel, lying well hidden in its hole. Jackals are crafty hunters and very fond of crabs and fish. Jerry thought this one had been dangling its tail in the eel's hole as a bait. A more likely explanation, perhaps, was that the Moray Eel, which is a very powerful creature, had caught the Jackal while it was squatting by the hole to defecate.

Eric stayed on board while we were exploring the area. When we returned we found he had seized a unique opportunity to photograph Greater and Lesser Sand Plovers side by side on the shore. Though quite different in size, these two species are very difficult to determine in the field and we had had a lot of trouble with them in Jordan, where we had finally established a new breeding record for the Lesser. Size is always difficult to judge through binoculars and the two species had certainly never been photographed before, so Eric's picture has a particular value to ornithologists (plate 41).

John Buxton meanwhile had been busy filming Mud Skippers and Signalling Crabs. We never ceased to be fascinated by these interesting little creatures. The Mud Skipper *Periophthalmus* is without doubt a figure of fun. It occurs in untold millions throughout the muddy waters of tropical Asia and it was impossible to find a mud-bank in the Indus Delta, or later in the Sunderbans, which was not swarming with them. About five inches long and prettily speckled with pale blue or orange, it has a big head and grotesque up-standing bulbous eyes (plate 38b). Its pectoral fins, which normal fish employ as stabilisers in the water, have been modified to turn downwards on thick, fleshy bases forming sturdy little 'legs,' with which it climbs up the arching 'knees' of the mangroves to feed on insects. This

climbing process is aided by its ventral fin, which supports its
slippery body against the stem to which it clings. Instead of having its air bladder modified to enable it to breathe air like the
Lung Fishes, it inflates its enlarged gill chambers with a mixture
of air and water when about to go on land. In an emergency, the
air is expelled with an audible belch, which we found intensely
amusing. There is of course considerable survival value in being
able to feed on land as well as in the water and the specialised
ability to hold both air and water in the gills improves the Mud
Skipper's ability to survive in the densely muddy, saline water
of the mangrove swamps, which are anathema to most freshwater fishes.

Mud Skippers are extremely agile and we found them impossible to catch, as they jumped this way and that by arching
their bodies so quickly that the eye could scarcely follow them.
Normally, however, they 'rowed' themselves forward across the
soft mud on their leg-like fins, leaving distinctive herring-bone
trails behind them. In water, they often swam with their up-
standing eyes just above the surface and, if pursued, took to the
air like Flying Fish in a series of wild leaps.

The courtship of the Mud Skipper is a delight to watch.
Females are enticed by a series of intricate manœuvres to enter
a hole in the mud made by the male. The male rises on his fins,
blows out his gills until his already large head looks twice its
size, and erects and closes his fan-shaped dorsal fin rapidly.
Sometimes, if the coy female hesitates on the brink of the hole,
the male dashes at her in the hope of driving her in, but she
usually leaps a couple of feet away and the long wooing then
has to be repeated. Mud Skippers are extremely pugnacious,
males threatening each other, nose to nose, with bulging eyes

and raised dorsal fins, often leaping repeatedly at or over each other like fighting cocks.

The Signalling Crabs were almost equally amusing. The male has a single big red claw, which it waves in a beckoning manner above its head, as a warning to other males and as an attraction to females. It builds little mud caves, roofing them over like beehives with skilfully placed pellets. After every tide these homesteads are washed away and have to be painstakingly rebuilt. The females have only tiny anterior claws, with which they feed themselves daintily and with great urgency, while keeping watch on their wooers with eyes mounted on long stalks, like twin periscopes. All the 4,400 species of crabs in the world are interesting and some, such as the scarlet and blue Rock Crab *Grapsus grapsus* of the Galapagos Islands, are extremely colourful; but the modestly coloured Signalling Crab is certainly one of my favourites.

We had by now seen, in the first two and a half weeks of the expedition, as many bird species as we had found during the whole of some of our expeditions to other countries. Working with telephoto lenses from the top deck, our photographers were kept very busy on our homeward journey. In the little used waterways through which we passed birds were unusually tame and often did not bother to rise as we approached. The Great White Egrets were irresistible subjects, standing in always graceful attitudes, with kinked necks poised for the lightning thrust at unsuspecting frogs or Mud Skippers. Strange, unidentified creatures were often glimpsed in the turbid waters, perhaps

43 *Above* A Brown-headed Gull in winter plumage. This species breeds on the lakes of central Asia, wintering along the coasts of Pakistan and India. *Below* A Lesser Crested Tern about to dive.

reptiles, perhaps fishes, or maybe diving birds, tantalising us as we strained our eyes to make them out. One, however, we both saw clearly and photographed—a five-foot snake, banded in yellow and black and with a laterally flattened tail. This was a Banded Sea Snake *Hydrophis mammalaris*, which, like all the Sea Snakes, is very poisonous.

Although we had failed to reach our planned destination, it was obvious that the Indus Delta had considerable potentiality as a wildlife reserve. The degree of human disturbance was relatively small and the villages were limited to only half a dozen small fishing communities. Contractors working under Department of Forests licence were seen only rarely, cutting firewood along the edges of the creeks. The chief threat to wildlife was from hunters in speed-boats, who could make the journey from Karachi much more rapidly than we had done, and from villagers who robbed the heronries at Keti Bundar. Further studies were needed, however, before we could make detailed recommendations and we later asked Christopher and Tom to conduct them for us.

We reached Korangi Creek during the afternoon of the fifth day and spent the evening at the hotel overhauling our equipment. At this juncture Tom had to return to his business affairs and unfortunately was unable to continue with us into East Pakistan. He knew more about the wildlife of the country than any of us and was going to be badly missed. We were also sorry to lose Mirza, who had made a very useful contribution to our work in the Indus Delta.

44 Like all the storks, cranes and ibises, the brightly coloured Painted Stork is now rare in Pakistan. A breeding reserve is being planned for it at the mouth of the Indus.

We had time the following day to re-visit Haleji Dhand, which had tantalised us by its wealth of interest during the previous expedition. We hoped this time to catch sight of the monster Marsh Crocodiles which lived there (plate 49), but were again unlucky. One of them, measuring sixteen feet in length, was shot soon after we left Pakistan and Jerry Wood-Anderson wrote an impassioned letter of protest to the Karachi papers about the stupidity of killing a last survivor of these rare animals in an area which was supposed to be protected. The commercial exploitation of the Crocodile and the Gharial in Pakistan, like that of the Alligator in South America, is chiefly in response to the Western demand for skins. Even in Britain women are still willing to pay highly for the possession of handbags made from them; a leading store in London recently boasted of selling three or four a day, with gold clasps, at £335 each. Such prices are sufficient to guarantee the extermination of any animal, though the proud owners of the handbags would probably be horrified to realise that they had contributed to the loss.

The Pallas's Fishing Eagles were still at the lake and again were nesting. Eric and George quickly decided that they represented the most important subjects for photography. The eagles behaved admirably, bringing a Jacana to an adjoining tree and plucking it in full view of the cameras. This was the seventh successive year that the huge eyrie had been occupied and we were relieved to find that it had not been disturbed.

Edmund obtained a very good tape of the voices of the eagles. Most birds of this family are rather monosyllabic and difficult to record; but the Pallas's Fishing Eagles were obligingly very vocal, particularly during a brief period preceding copulation (plate 19). Their cries had a singularly gull-like, squealing quality.

John Buxton and I went to work on the bund surrounding the reservoir. This year great changes had been caused to the vegetation by recent heavy rain and flooding. Both the *Phragmites* reed-beds and the Water Hyacinths had made vast extensions into the lake and all the vegetation in the surrounding plain was now high and dense. Very few of the thousands of waders which we had seen in 1966 were now visible and ducks and grebes were relatively scarce. The only species which had increased were the Purple Gallinules, Pied Kingfishers and Black-headed Buntings. The last mentioned birds are often a serious agricultural pest in Pakistan, descending in tens of thousands on the millet fields.

We had planned to fly to Dacca next morning, but I was asked to remain behind to meet Air Marshal Asghar Khan and Air Commodore Dass. While the others went ahead I therefore found myself with twenty-four hours to spare. Fortunately Jerry Wood-Anderson happened to drop in at my hotel and I was glad to accept his invitation to visit the farm belonging to his business partner, Mr Robertson, not very far from Haleji Dhand. We had a very pleasant time inspecting the thriving crops and talking about the wildlife of Sind.

The meeting next morning was well worth waiting for. The formation of the Wildlife Committee had just been announced, as the President had promised, and I was given a confidential report on what had taken place. The Air Marshal was good enough to ask my advice on a number of matters concerned with the forthcoming work of the committee, which was to have such an important part to play in the future of Pakistan's wildlife and vegetation. It was to be placed under the distinguished chair-manship of Mr M. M. Ahmad, a politically powerful figure whose reputation as Deputy Chairman of the Planning Commission of the Central Government was greatly admired. I took the opportunity also to talk about the plans which we were already drafting for new reserves and was given valuable suggestions as to the best means of presenting them. I felt elated that the Wildlife Committee was now actually in being. Few, if any, countries in Asia had created a body of such authority to deal with their wildlife problems and in none was the Head of State himself so determined to achieve results. The driving force behind the long negotiations which had led to the formation of the committee had without doubt been the Air Marshal and I congratulated him warmly on his success. I was then driven to the airport by Air Commodore Dass who, with his usual kindness, insisted on seeing me on to my plane.

Grey Mongoose

9

Wildlife of the Sunderbans

My flight across India was uneventful, but as soon as we turned eastwards near the Ganges across the northern reaches of the huge delta area, I saw an immediate change in the scenery below. Between the network of waterways the earth became steadily more rufous and the vegetation a more vivid green.

Karim met me at Dacca airport and handed me copies of the local papers, which carried a report and pictures of a meeting held the previous evening in honour of the World Wildlife Fund team. George Shannon had deputised for me and had obviously handled the meeting well. There had also been a television interview with the team. I had hoped to catch up with my companions at Dacca, but they had taken off ten minutes before my arrival, on their way to Jessore.

I flew on to Jessore soon after five and landed half an hour later in darkness. I was the only westerner on the plane and while I waited for my baggage I felt glad to be back among the gaily clad people of East Pakistan. The hotter the climate, the brighter the colours, I reflected. The temperature and the humidity were both very high in the little waiting-room, which was roofed only with split-cane matting.

My two hour ride by Jeep to Khulna was enlivened by the temperament of my driver, who seemed to take a fiendish delight in risking our lives. The road was narrow and twisting and it carried a considerable volume of traffic. To dip one's head-lights is regarded as effeminate in Pakistan and most native drivers are at pains to elevate their lights so that they play straight into the eyes of oncoming drivers. The road immediately in front of one's vehicle thus remains in total darkness. Again and again my driver, who had a fixed, demoniacal grin, charged oncoming traffic eyeball to eyeball, as it were, swerving with screaming tyres at the last possible moment to avoid collision. Being a fatalist in such matters, I refrained from remonstrating, though I had little doubt that he enjoyed trying to scare a foreigner.

We eventually pulled up with a flourish at the dockside, where I handed him the customary *baksheesh*. His fine white teeth gleamed in the darkness in a broad grin of pleasure which, however, vanished when I said that although I hoped he would have a long and happy life I had serious doubts that he would survive the year as a driver. I was probably wrong, as most Pakistani drivers lead charmed lives.

Eric met me at the gangway to our ship with the news that a large Press conference was waiting for me on board. I was hot and tired after travelling all day and was looking forward to a cool drink and putting my feet up. However, Press support for our work was important, so I dropped my bags on the deck and went straight in. The conference lasted for more than half an hour and some of the questions were less easy to handle than on previous occasions. The local Press representatives were evi-dently keenly interested, but they wanted assurances that East Pakistan would receive the same treatment as West Pakistan. By this they meant Government treatment, in terms of setting up new reserves and introducing wildlife management training schemes. News of the Gilgit National Park had already appeared in the National Press and they felt that East Pakistan also should have a new National Park for its wildlife. When I said that we hoped our forthcoming studies in the Sunderbans might lead to something of this kind they were delighted. The Press of every country likes nothing better than beating the gun, so next morning's papers carried banner headlines proclaiming 'A New National Park for the Sunderbans!' An extraordinary interest had been aroused by our visit and the conference was given extensive coverage.

We had a gay reunion dinner after the Press had left and I then inspected our strange craft. We had, in fact, not one ship but a small armada. In the centre was a large, square-ended houseboat, with a comfortable shaded deck in the bows and plenty of room on top for the photographers. On either side was a powerful diesel-engined tug, tied to us fore and aft. In the wake of the houseboat were tethered a cabin cruiser and two motor launches for exploring the narrow creeks in the Sunderbans. The houseboat was to be the mother ship, in which to sleep and have our meals. It all seemed quite admirably suited to our needs and very comfortable. The combined crews of the various vessels must have numbered more than twenty.

Just before midnight, amid much shouting and billows of smoke from the tugs, we edged our way through the crowded shipping in the harbour and began our voyage down through the heart of the Sunderbans.

The scene which greeted us next morning had a strange beauty quite unlike anything we had seen before in a land where almost every scene was beautiful. On either hand was mangrove

jungle, but mangrove which differed from that which we had
seen in the Indus Delta. It was greener, taller and more dense
and the vegetation far more varied, with stretches of graceful
Nipa Palm arching over the water at intervals. The sky was of an
intense brilliance above long whisps of opalescent mist rising
from the pale green water, which sparkled in the early sunlight.

The immense tidal jungle of the Sunderbans is a mosaic of
islands of varying size among a confusing labyrinth of twisting
creeks and rivers. Towards the close of the last century it was
realised that the extensive felling of trees, which had already
reduced the Sunderbans forests by nearly half, was increasing
the inland devastation caused by typhoons and the tidal bore
from the Bay of Bengal. The forests were then put under proper
management. To-day there are no permanent human habitations
in the whole of the 2,338 square miles of Pakistan's share of the
Sunderbans, though the Indian part has been allowed to
deteriorate badly and has lost most of its original tree cover
under the advance of the human population.

Forestry is the main activity and in Pakistan this is managed
on a rotational cropping basis, followed by rapid natural regeneration. The dominant species is the white-stemmed Sundri
Heritiera minor, which accounts for 77 per cent of the extracted
timber. The most valuable species, however, is the Passur
Carapa moluccensis, which produces excellent wood for panelling
and cabinet making. The Gewa *Exocaria agallocha* and Goran
Ceriops candolleana grow as an under-story to the larger trees and
provide pulp for newsprint and tannin for fishing nets. The

45 *Above* The arched roots of the mangroves trap silt from the river and
gradually build islands. *Below* Air roots, or pneumatophores, expel carbon
dioxide and take in oxygen for the mangrove trees.

fronds of the Nipa Palm *Nipa fruticans*, locally called Golpatta, are extensively used for thatching. Because of the high salinity of the water, many of the tree species have twisted and stunted growth and are of inferior quality; but the energetic Department of Forests is taking advantage of modern techniques of preservation under pressure and for the exploitation of by-products.

Honey collecting from wild bees is another source of revenue in the Sunderbans, though at present the methods used are scarcely scientific. Hives are collected and squeezed to extract the honey and wax, which inevitably are mixed with the juices of the larvæ, thus contaminating the honey and killing the next generation of bees. Other revenue is obtained by the collection of mollusc shells for the production of lime and also from the sale of orchids, which are abundant and very beautiful in the Sunderbans.

Fishing is an important industry in the area and is controlled by the Department of Forests. The boats of some 5,000 fishermen congregate from November to April in the region of Dubla Island, to harvest the fish and crustaceans feeding on the wealth of marine organisms along the shores of the Bay of Bengal. Jew Fish, Lakua, Shark and Ray provide the main tonnage. In the inland creeks and rivers the fishing continues throughout the year. Fishing is, however, largely uncontrolled and yields are steadily declining. By modern standards the methods employed are primitive and inefficient. None of the boats have engines and by the time the catches have made the

46 *Above* On Mandarbaria Island we found our first Tiger pug-marks. *Below* Many of the Sunderbans Tigers are now man-eaters and too cunning to be photographed. This picture of a male and cub was taken in India.

long journey to Khulna they often putrify and have to be thrown overboard. Most of the illiterate fishermen are in debt all their lives to the *Mahajans* or moneylenders who finance them and make them work at prices far below market value. Neither, in the remote wastes of the Sunderbans, are there any facilities for the fishermen to obtain help in case of illness, accident or piracy, though there are now plans to provide them.

In the afternoon we passed Putney Island, near the south-westerly corner of the delta. It was a long, low strip of mangrove, perhaps three miles in extent, and separated from the nearest land by a similar distance. Nevertheless, Tigers inhabited it, being quite capable of swimming there and back. Our objective was Mandarbaria Island, close by, and when we reached it Karim told us he had made arrangements for a *machan*, or tree hide, to be built in the hope that we might be able to photograph a Tiger.

The launches were released from their moorings and we made for a small sandy beach, where we landed. I had not gone ten yards before I saw, with a tremendous thrill, the unmistak-able pug-marks of an adult Tiger clearly imprinted in the sand (plate 46a). Close by were the tracks of a fairly large cub. I shouted to the others, who gathered round to photograph this exciting discovery. We noticed the difference in the size of the great fore-foot of the Tiger, which is where the power lies for pulling down its prey.

Karim, who before he became interested in the conservation of wildlife had shot five Tigers, was elated that his forecast of the presence of this animal on Mandarbaria Island had been so speedily proved correct. He now gave us careful instructions. Most of the Tigers of the Sunderbans were man-eaters, he said.

Therefore nobody, in any circumstance, was to land anywhere unless accompanied by an armed *shikari*, or carrying a gun himself. If we walked in a group, the man in front and the man at the rear must both be armed, because Tigers often attacked from the rear.

We were then introduced to two local *shikaris* who were to look after us. They were small, wiry men wearing the green shorts and shirt of the Department of Forests. They were brothers. The older of the two had an impassive face, large, owl-like eyes and a deceptively gentle manner which belied his reputation. Their grandfather had been a noted hunter of Tigers until killed by one. Their father had likewise been a professional *shikari* with fifty-five Tigers to his credit before falling victim to a *Bagh*, as the Tiger is called in Bengali. The older brother, having now brought his score to fifty, was determined to avenge his father's death by killing at least sixty Tigers. He was armed with a 1908 large-bore shotgun almost as tall as himself and I marvelled that he could handle it with any accuracy. However, I heard afterwards that half the Tigers he claimed to have shot were not killed face to face, but by gun-traps set in their hunting trails. This method is, of course, completely unselective and just as liable to kill a deer or a passing woodsman.

One of the best known Tiger hunters of East Pakistan is Tahawar Ali Khan, who had kindly provided each of us with an autographed copy of his remarkable book *The Maneaters of the Sunderbans*. For sheer excitement it compares well with the writings of the redoubtable Jim Corbett of Indian fame. Some of the illustrations, though sadly spoilt by bad reproduction, are blood-curdling portrayals of what Tigers can do to their human victims.

From long discussions with *shikaris* and forest officers during our stay in the Sunderbans, I was able to piece together an appreciation of the factors surrounding the survival of the Tiger in that area. About forty years ago it was estimated that there were at least 40,000 Tigers in the Indo–Pakistan subcontinent. By 1966, according to the eminent Indian zoologist B. Seshadri, not more than 2,800[1] remained, the majority of which were in the Indian reserves such as the Kanha and Corbett National Parks. In West Pakistan the last Tiger was shot in the Indus Valley in 1886. In East Pakistan we had already ascertained on our first expedition that very few were left in the Chittagong Hill Tracts. A few still occurred in the border region of Sylhet as vagrants from Assam or Tripura, though it was doubtful that any survived as residents. The Sunderbans were, in fact, the Tiger's last stronghold in Pakistan.

The causes of the extremely rapid decline in the population of an animal which had almost no natural enemies capable of affecting its numbers, are clearly attributable to man. The Tiger's habitat varies from the watery wilderness of the Sunderbans swamps, where it is largely aquatic in behaviour, to the high grass thickets of China and the Cedar forests and rocky ravines of Manchuria and the dense jungles of Indonesia. Its tracks have even been found in a 13,000 foot pass in the Himalayas. Yet throughout all these regions man is steadily but surely encroaching on its habitat. Sometimes, as in India and Pakistan, he has already destroyed the greater part of the Tiger's living-space by the wholesale felling of forests and the reclamation of swamps and jungles for agricultural and other needs. Nothing can stop this squeeze continuing. Unfortunately, in spite of its

[1] By 1969 this figure had declined to 1,900.

apparently wide range of habitats, the Tiger is a species which does not readily accept any modification to its ecosystem; in other words it is dependent on the totality of the interactions of the various organisms within its chosen environment.

Probably no other animal has been more highly prized as a sporting trophy. The shooting of Tigers for the protection of human life or livestock has been insignificant beside the enormous numbers killed for sport. The killing was originally chiefly by the Indian princes and the British, but more recently by hunters of every nation, who have regarded the killing of a Tiger as the crowning glory of a hunting career. Some have regarded numbers as even more important than record dimensions. There are reliable statistics to show that two of India's Maharajas each killed well over one thousand Tigers. Even to-day, when it is quite obvious that the survival of the species in the subcontinent is increasingly doubtful, the killing for sport goes on. Most of the shooting is now done not by stalking but at night from the comfort of automobiles or motor launches equipped with searchlights. Poaching in the reserves has been stimulated by high prices obtainable for mounted heads and skins. Last year, apart from Tiger-skin rugs, at least one Tiger-skin coat was sold in New York for two thousand dollars.

The Department of Forests in East Pakistan told us that they estimated the number of Tigers at 300. On the completion of our studies there, based on local information and the number of fresh tracks seen, we reluctantly concluded that this figure was far too optimistic. In our opinion the maximum number was about one hundred, and the total could be as low as fifty.

In the old days there is little doubt that the 'Royal Bengal Tiger' as it was called, so dominated the Sunderbans that humans could enter the jungle only at their peril. Even to-day, though its numbers are now so small, it is still greatly feared and its whole population is widely believed to be man-eating. It is true that many humans are killed and eaten, though the number of victims is too small to suggest that all the Tigers are man-eaters. Tigers rarely take to killing men unless they are either too incapacitated by wounds or old age to hunt their normal prey, or are desperately hungry. If many of those in the Sunderbans have acquired this habit, which is soon taught to their young, it is possible that shortage of preferred prey was a contributory factor. All the Gaur (jungle bison) and the big Barasingha Deer, which used to provide their chief food, have long since been wiped out by hunters. The remaining Chital (Axis Deer) and the Wild Boar are probably insufficient substitutes for an animal which, killing every two to four days, needs an average of 15 lb of meat a day.[1]

The predation of Tigers on humans in the Sunderbans is concerned with wood-cutters, honey-collectors and occasionally fishermen. Armed guards usually accompany parties of men working under Forestry Department contracts; but in the dense jungle it is a simple matter for a Tiger to stalk them, waiting until one of them steps aside to relieve himself and carrying him off before a shot can be fired. The killing of humans is efficient and speedy, the victim being crushed to the ground by the huge fore-paws on his shoulders and having his neck broken by a single bite. The body is then carried away to a safe place, where the buttocks and thighs are eaten first. When such tragedies occur, the Department of Forests immediately organises a hunt for the killer and *shikaris* are sent to track it down. Not

[1] See *The Deer and the Tiger* by George B. Schaller. University of Chicago Press, 1967.

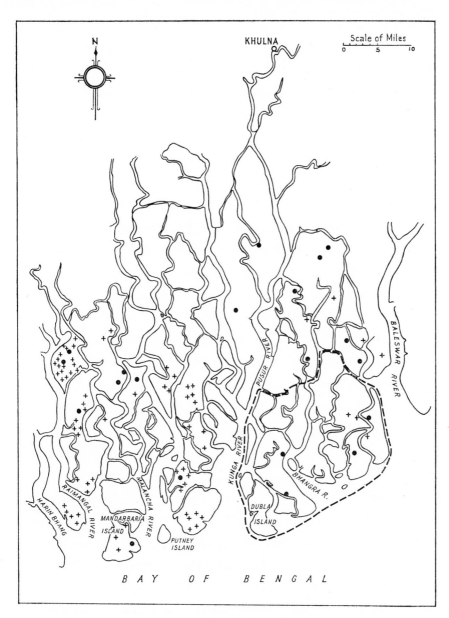

SUNDERBANS FOREST DIVISION Showing localities where, from 1963 to 1967, men are known to have been killed by Tigers (+) and Tigers killed by men (●). Boundaries of the new Sunderbans Wildlife Reserve are shown by dotted line.

Map by courtesy of the Chief Conservator of Forests, Govt. of East Pakistan.

only is no licence required to kill a Tiger, but a standard bounty of 100 rupees (about £8) is paid for every one shot. This is a large sum by local standards and is another not inconsiderable factor in the rapid decline of the species. As much as Rs. 800 has been paid for killing a particularly notorious man-killer which was reported to have killed twenty-one people. The family of a man killed by a Tiger, on the other hand, receives only fifty rupees from the Government by way of compensation.

Careful records are kept by the Department of Forests of all human victims and of the Tigers shot in the Sunderbans. Because of the bounty system, the number of Tigers destroyed can be regarded as accurate; but the figures for humans killed are thought to be much lower than the real totals. Men landing alone in the jungle can disappear without trace except for an empty canoe; such losses are often not reported and some of the men are undoubtedly taken by Tigers. The official records list eighty-two known killings of humans during the last five years in the Pakistan Sunderbans (*map page* 203). The real total probably exceeded one hundred. In the much smaller but populated area of the Indian Sunderbans, losses are much greater, thirty-nine people having been killed by Tigers in 1966 alone. The number of Tigers shot in the Pakistan Sunderbans was forty-eight, plus an undetermined number shot illicitly by soldiers guarding the frontier with India; they were probably not all man-eaters or the human losses would have been much greater.

At this point it is perhaps worth emphasising that the fate of the Tiger in the Indo-Pakistan subcontinent is also threatening

47 There were many White-bellied Sea Eagles in the Sunderbans. Several were seen carrying snakes or fish caught in the river and all the nests we found were overhanging the water.

all the other species of cats, large and small. Even the Leopard, which has a much wider tolerance in its acceptance of habitats than most other species in this family, has suffered a very dramatic decline. Statistics are not available for Pakistan, but in India, according to the expert E. P. Gee, its population has fallen in the last fifty years from 60,000 to only 6,000 (plate 51).

On board the houseboat that night we talked for hours about Tigers. Karim regaled us with hair-raising stories of his experiences with them. We were also able to question the older *shikari*, who had come aboard this time more comfortably dressed in an orange and grey *lunghi*. He afterwards entertained us by his imitations of the characteristic moaning and growling of a Tiger, the high, whistling bark of a Chital and the chattering of Assamese Macaque Monkeys, which were numerous in the jungle. I think he enjoyed the performance as much as we did.

The *shikari* told us he had been baiting the clearings on Mandarbaria Island for several days and that two goats had been taken by a Tiger. He had constructed two *machan* hides, each with a good field of view. As there were fresh tracks at both of them, he suggested we should try our luck the following evening. Eric had brought his electronic flash equipment for night photography, but if we were to obtain any cinema film of a Tiger we would have to try at dawn or dusk, using ultra high-speed film. Trying to photograph such a notoriously wary animal at short notice was unlikely to succeed, but we were determined to try. I asked Eric to share one hide with me, while

48 *Above* The Crested Serpent Eagle was easily identified by its boldly patterned wings and speckled body. *Below* My birthday present from our cook was a paper bag containing a live Jungle Nightjar.

George and John occupied the other. We arranged to enter the hides two hours before sunset and for armed relief parties to release us just before dark. The return journey might be dangerous if a Tiger happened to be in the neighbourhood.

Turning in that night I found Eric already in his bunk, reading *The Maneaters of the Sunderbans*. Holding up a particularly gruesome illustration of the remains of a Tiger's victim, he said, 'I think we must be raving mad!' I was inclined to agree with him, but slept soundly none the less.

Dawn next morning was again an exquisite experience. The rising sun was sending sparkling shafts of light through the Sundri trees, to gild our little armada anchored on the still water. Several Chital were quietly grazing under the trees and a group of Assamese Macaques was busily searching the shore for crabs. One of the monkeys jumped nimbly on to the haunches of a Chital doe, which merely jumped and then went on feeding. These two species had an obvious commensal relationship and we often saw them together, each warning the other of impending danger. I noticed that the Chital stags were all in velvet. We saw very few full-grown antlers, which suggested that the old ones had been dropped during the late summer months (plate 52). The rutting season is very variable with this species and some authorities believe it continues throughout most of the year. There were several Wild Boar in sight of the ship also, powerful beasts with heavy white tusks. When, however, a member of our noisy crew shouted, all the animals faded instantly into the jungle.

I found Edmund leaning over the rail. He had been up most of the night with his recording gear and I was fascinated when he played back some of his recordings for me. His directional microphone mounted in a big parabolic reflector had captured the shrill barking alarm of a Chital perfectly and also the mellow voice of an unidentified owl.

We took the three launches out after breakfast, each group heading in a different direction and made arrangements for calling up to report progress over our walkie-talkie sets at fixed times. We were using these admirable devices for the first time and were also using pocket tape recorders for recording our observations in the field. They proved so invaluable that I wondered how we had managed without them on previous expeditions. It is all too easy for boats or vehicles to get lost in the wilds, or to drop out with mechanical failures, as we had learned to our cost in Jordan; but with walkie-talkies contact was easily maintained.

Eric and I concentrated that morning on the numerous kingfishers, which were to be seen in every creek we entered. Never in my wanderings around the world had I seen so many different species in one locality. There were in fact nine species in the Sunderbans and we could usually be sure of seeing at least five of these in an hour's journey. The two largest were the Stork-billed (plate 54) and the Brown-winged (plate 25); both as large as a pigeon, with vivid orange breasts and immense scarlet bills which looked heavy enough to over-balance them. The blue-winged Stork-billed, which had been the dominant species in the Chittagong Hill Tracts, was here quite scarce. Next in size came the White-collared and the White-breasted, the former dressed in pale greenish-blue and white, with a black crown (plate 25). Then came the most beautiful of them all, the Black-capped, with an almost unbelievably glittering violet and white body, a black cap and bright orange beneath its wings (plate 54). About the same size is the neatly piebald Lesser Pied, which has a shaggy little crest. The smallest was the local race of the Common Kingfisher, which was particularly numerous in the narrower creeks. Finally the Ruddy, a fairly large bird of a uniform bright chestnut colour with a white rump; this was in striking contrast to the kaleidoscopic range of colours and patterns shown by the other species. The only other kingfishers occurring in Pakistan which were lacking were the Greater Pied, the Blyth's, the tiny Three-toed and the jewel-like Blue-eared, which we had seen in the Chittagong Hill Tracts. The larger species were very vocal, the Brown-winged having a very loud cackling cry, not unlike the yaffle of a Green Woodpecker, and the Black-capped a harsh 'chick-chick' alarm recalling the Pied Woodpecker. We obtained pictures of the Brown-winged quite easily, as it usually chose sunlit stumps as its look-out posts. The Black-capped, however, tantalised us by invariably alighting in deep shadow. Although we repeatedly tried, by switching off the motor and drifting up to it, we were never able to get a good photograph except in flight.

In the Sunderbans we had ample opportunity to study that 'difficult' bird the Intermediate, or Smaller, Egret *Egretta intermedia*. This species has given ornithologists considerable trouble in defining its status and distribution, because of the close similarity of its appearance to that of the Great White Egret *Egretta alba*. In winter the two are virtually identical in form and coloration. Both have snow-white plumage, yellow bills and black legs and feet. Their ranges overlap in Pakistan,

49 *Above* The Mugger, or Marsh Crocodile, once a familiar sight in every river, has almost disappeared. *Below* The Gharial, a fish-eating crocodilian, has also been nearly exterminated by the skin traders.

India and Burma and they not only winter in similar localities but breed side by side in mixed colonies, with Ibises, Darters, Cormorants and other water birds. Although their feeding behaviour appears to be identical, they probably catch different prey.

Because of these well-known difficulties, it may be worth recording how we separated the two birds. At first we shared in the general confusion. Then we had an opportunity to examine the species side by side on a mud-bank and the distinction was at once clear. The Great White Egret was very nearly as large as a Grey Heron, whereas the Intermediate was scarcely larger than a Little Egret. The bill and legs of the Great White Egret were proportionately longer and the feet larger than those of the Intermediate and therefore protruded in flight farther beyond the tail. We were seldom in doubt after this fortunate comparison, though isolated birds still required closer examination.

There is little difficulty in separating the two species in the breeding season. While both have blackish bills at that time and highly developed scapular 'cloaks' of long white plumes, the Intermediate has long display plumes also on the breast. The Great White Egret, which we had studied at breeding colonies in Hungary, has orange-pink on the upper parts of its legs when nesting, whereas those of the Intermediate remain black.

During the morning we photographed two very striking eagles, both of which were plentiful in the Sunderbans, feeding chiefly on snakes. The first of these was the White-bellied Sea

50 *Above* The Adjutant Stork eats offal, snakes, rodents, small birds, fish, and almost anything else within reach of its huge bill. *Below* We found Little Green Herons in the backwaters of the Chittagong Hill Tracts.

Eagle, an extremely handsome creature with a snow-white head and under-parts (plate 47). The other was the Crested Serpent Eagle, which has dark, vinous-brown plumage finely speckled with white dots; its wings are very beautifully patterned below (plate 48).

Towards evening we assembled on the shore of Mandarbaria Island for our first attempt to photograph a Tiger. With armed *shikaris* at the front and rear, we set off through the high grass and undergrowth towards the first *machan*, which commanded an excellent view of a grassy clearing. On the branches of the hide-tree hung many empty, gourd-shaped nests of Baya Weavers, compact little globes with the texture of loofah sponges and with long, funnel entrances below. John and George swarmed up the tree and were soon safely established on the well-hidden platform, with their cameras mounted on tripods. From there they had a clear view of the goat which had been tethered as a bait in the clearing. We left one *shikari* with them, wished them luck and proceeded in single file towards the second *machan*.

I must confess that as we made our way through the shoulder-high grass, keeping well clear of the patches of undergrowth which might harbour a hidden Tiger, I felt a thrill of excitement. This was the first time I had been on foot in an area occupied by a man-eater and I hoped I was not unwisely hazarding the lives of my comrades. However, the vegetation soon gave way to more open meadow and we reached our destination without incident.

Our *machan* was in a rather small tree close to the beach on the opposite side of the island and commanding a good view of a lagoon where many waders were feeding. The hide was barely twelve feet from the ground, a height which any determined

Tiger could reach without difficulty if it chose. The branches were not very well clothed with leaves and I felt we would be much too visible not to be spotted from a distance. Nevertheless, we scrambled up with our *shikari* and settled in silence for a long wait. Karim thought it would be safe for us to walk back along the beach afterwards, but warned us not to attempt to return through the high grass.

As the sun set, the first Chital could be seen picking their way cautiously from the jungle to the open meadow behind us (plate 52). Jungle Fowl began to crow, a very authentic 'cock-a-doodle' which emphasised their relationship as the progenitors of the barnyard chicken, and the first Nightjars began their clockwork vespers. Out on the shore Curlews and Whimbrels called their sad, liquid notes. Our sheep, which had been steadily cropping the bush to which it was tethered, scraped a comfortable hollow in the sandy ground and lay down to sleep. Our *shikari*, hunched against the branches with his gun across his knees, was soon also fast asleep. As the colour faded from the sky a great stillness descended on the scene. In the diminishing light we kept scanning the edge of the jungle for the sight of our quarry, but it was quite evident from the tranquil manner in which the Chital were feeding that no predator was in the neighbourhood. Our light-meters had long since registered zero and I whispered to Eric that we might as well call it a day. He nodded and began dismantling his cameras. With relish I lit my pipe and followed suit. Our *shikari* had begun to snore and I wakened him by calling up Edmund on my walkie-talkie.

It was completely dark by the time we had descended from the tree. We made our way to the beach, leading the little sheep, which seemed very disinclined to leave its snug hollow in the sand. With our kit on our backs, we picked a route through the slippery mud pools along the beach, keeping as far as possible from the overhanging mangroves which loomed up black and threatening on our left. The *shikari*, playing a powerful torch on the weirdly distorted shapes of the trees with one hand and carrying his cocked gun in the other, brought up the rear. We had a rather eerie half-hour's walk in total darkness to where the launch awaited us. During the journey the sheep, which had remained completely silent hitherto, suddenly let out a deep, resounding bleat, causing Eric and me to whirl round in instant alarm that a Tiger was at our heels.

John and George had been similarly unsuccessful, though they had exposed some film on the Chital, which had come almost under their tree before the light failed.

Back on board the houseboat we exchanged notes over drinks before doing the diary. I decided that we had taken un-justifiable risks and that if any more night journeys were in-volved it would be foolhardy not to have two guns with each party.

We saw our first crocodile next morning. This was not, as we expected, a Marsh Crocodile, for the water was too saline, but the big, sea-going Estuarine Crocodile, which thrives in salt water. The Marsh Crocodile, or Mugger, used to occupy the inland creeks and rivers of the Sunderbans by the thousand. As elsewhere in Pakistan it had now been virtually exterminated by the skin traders. Even the sea-going species which lives along the estuaries in the Bay of Bengal has become rare and we saw

51 *Above* An adult Tigress. The number of Tigers in the subcontinent has declined in forty years from 40,000 to 2,800. *Below* Leopards have also suffered a 90 per cent decline in fifty years.

only three of them during our stay. The long-nosed, fish-eating Gharial (plate 49) has shared the same fate and can now be found in very few localities.

That evening we put Eric and Edmund into the best *machan* for an all-night session. This time Eric brought his electronic flashlamps, which were carefully rigged to illuminate the un-complaining sheep when the camera was fired. Again the little sheep settled down unconcernedly to await its fate and the occupants of the hide did likewise. Back on board the houseboat we gave them a call on the walkie-talkie and assured ourselves that all was well before leaving them to a twelve-hour vigil. I found it difficult to sleep that night, thinking of them crouching in the darkness, straining their ears and eyes for a sign of the Tiger and I hoped they would be rewarded by a spectacular success.

Alas, when we called them up just before sunrise, Eric's cheerful voice announced that the night had passed with nothing worthwhile to report. It had been bitterly cold in the small hours and a heavy dew had condensed on the lenses and flash equipment. He and Edmund were now ravenously hungry for breakfast and would we please send a launch to fetch them? John set off immediately and within half an hour we were all eating eggs and bacon together.

Nothing would convince either Eric or Edmund that they should turn in for some sleep and we were out in the launches again by eight-thirty. During the afternoon, however, I was glad to see them both on their bunks for a while.

52 *Above* The largest remaining population of the Chital, or Axis Deer, is in the Sunderbans, where it is the chief prey of the Tiger. *Below* A female Sambur at Pablakhali.

In the course of that morning we located an Adjutant Stork, a large, ungainly bird with a balding head and wispy, ginger 'hair,' which made it look remarkably like one of the well-known British Cabinet Ministers. Like the Marabou Stork of Africa the Adjutant is a confirmed necrophile, an unlovely and unlovable creature which spends much of its time standing about with its head sunk between its shoulders in apparently abject misery. Once in movement, however, it becomes a highly efficient scavenger. Nothing comes amiss to its cavernous bill, as it stalks ponderously along, scanning the ground with rheumy, baleful eyes. Snakes, birds, small mammals, frogs, fish or offal are all equally welcome. It was a new species for us, however, so we were pleased to see it (plate 50).

We were now to cross the full width of the Sunderbans, east-wards to the Kotka Reserve. While waiting to weigh anchor we sat on the little fore-deck. The last of the launches was just approaching. It contained the local forestry officer and I noticed that he was carrying a shotgun. One of the crew had a live but wounded Whimbrel by the legs and in the bottom of the boat lay the carcass of the Adjutant Stork.

When the forestry officer came on board there was a pretty lively exchange, in which Karim, as the senior official in our party, took the leading part. He was white with rage that any-one accompanying our expedition, which had come to Pakistan to protect wildlife, should be guilty of the very thing we were trying to prevent—the wanton killing of harmless creatures. The forestry officer was crestfallen but perplexed. If one was carrying a gun and a couple of birds came within range, it seemed to him quite natural that they should be knocked down.

This was harmless enough, surely? 'No!' shouted Karim. 'It was a piece of criminal stupidity!'

Unfortunately young Klaus Roetz, a cinematographer from the Asian Television Service, who had been attached to us while we were working in the Sunderbans, had also been with the luckless forestry officer and had filmed the shooting. This caused another noisy altercation and Karim, well within his rights, insisted that the film should be destroyed lest it brought discredit to us. Klaus objected that he had a right to photograph whatever he chose, whereupon Karim confiscated the film. It required all my diplomacy to cool off this three-sided row; but I eventually made everyone shake hands and peace was restored.

When the shouting died down, I told the forestry officer to have the wounded Whimbrel put out of its misery, which was promptly done by cutting its throat in the Muslim manner so that it could be bled before being eaten. The wretched Adjutant meanwhile was already being dismembered on the after deck and the two birds went into the crew's stew-pot for lunch. Meat was meat, but I shuddered to think what flavour the offal-eating Adjutant added to the stew.

We sailed all afternoon through endless winding channels fringed with luxurious vegetation. On the iron top deck the sun beat down mercilessly and we roasted ourselves as we sat watching the ever-changing scene.

During the afternoon the sky was suddenly full of migrating Swallows. For an hour they streamed overhead, travelling southeastward towards the Burmese coast. It was impossible to calculate numbers accurately as the birds were in very open formation, feeding as they flew, but we reckoned that at least

four or five thousand passed. The date was 24 November and
we remembered that in the second week of November 1966
similarly large numbers had been seen flying south over the
Chittagong Hill Tracts.

The jungle was fascinating to watch, too, for although the
dominant mangrove tree species tended to grow in homogeneous
blocks on each island, there was infinite variety in the undergrowth and climbing creepers. The trees here grew quickly and
were short-lived, dying in about forty years and then usually
being replaced by a different species, so that island blocks were
constantly changing. Strangling plants of many kinds swarmed
over the trees, sometimes completely submerging and killing
them under the weight of their foliage. The impression of
competition for light and space was inescapable—everywhere
green arms were reaching upwards and outwards in a desperate
struggle for survival. There was a kind of urgency in the way the
arching roots of the mangroves stretched out hungrily into the
water, like a million flying buttresses. Urgency, too, in the
tightly wrapped vines, which shot up to the topmost twigs and
raised longing tendrils into the life-giving air. Here, in the tree-
tops, lived the violet Sunbirds, the blue Verditer Flycatchers
and the long-winged butterflies of the jungle, dancing and
flitting from one patch of trumpet flowers to another. Beneath
the leaf canopy, clusters of epiphytes, the famous orchids of the
Sunderbans, clung to the branches, and colonies of white
crustaceans hung like cancerous growths from the pendent
mangrove roots.

Even where the mangroves had succeeded in building soil
from the accumulation of silt and debris trapped by their roots,
there was no unimpeded open ground, for here the spiked

pneumatophores rose like regiments of bayonets, eager for the oxygen which the knee-roots were unable to extract from the muddy water (plate 45). In the cavernous twilight beneath the roots along the water's edge was a little secret world of animal life. Here on the wet mud lived the Otters, the Mud Skippers and a host of snakes, turtles, toads and little scarlet crabs, each preying ruthlessly on its neighbour.

We anchored at sundown in a placid backwater and watched the sunset while we drank our *chota pegs*. On the top deck of the tug alongside, the Muslim crew spread their prayer mats for their evening devotions, facing the dying sun. The Chital and Wild Boar began to wander out from the trees a hundred yards from where we were moored. Above the throb of our lighting dynamo the quavering notes of the first owls were heard. A wonderful sense of peace and stillness enveloped us. When night fell, the sky was filled with brilliant stars, faithfully mirrored in the glassy water. Among them a gleaming satellite moved steadily on its lonely journey through space. Edmund, his glass in his hand, was fast asleep. He fell asleep again during dinner and I packed him off to bed, excusing him from the nightly ritual of the diary.

We were on deck again at five-thirty next morning, muffled in sweaters against the pre-sunrise cold, and by six we had resumed our journey. We were now nearing the junction with the wide Pusur River and as soon as we reached it we began to see fishing boats heading for the open sea. Each day during our stay in the Sunderbans we stopped one of these picturesque craft, which are called *jela maukas* in Bengali, to buy fresh fish. We enjoyed poring over the wonderful variety of strange species they produced for us from the wicker baskets which they towed behind them. The fish, and particularly the big white prawns, were invariably delicious.

Presently we sighted the rest-house of the Kotka Reserve, raised on stilts and pleasantly situated on a sandy shore backed by Keora trees. Because of the lower salinity of the water in the eastern Sunderbans, the vegetation was taller and more lush than it had been at Mandarbaria Island. Some of the islands rose six feet above water level, though of course still subject to tidal flooding; these had grassy clearings which were much favoured by herds of Chital. The reserve, of 46 square miles, was unfortunately located in an area where disturbance from river craft was greater than anywhere else in the Sunderbans. Except for the monsoon period, fishing boats and barges moved in a steady stream through the main channels bordering the reserve. Nevertheless, the concentration of wildlife attracted by the rich vegetation and availability of fresh water was impressive and certainly higher than in the western areas. There were even a few Barking Deer farther inland to the north-east of the reserve—a clear indication of more normal conditions.

Tigers were reported to be plentiful in the region of the reserve and we later found numerous tracks where they had swum creeks and climbed out over the soft mud. Our first task, therefore, was to select the best site for a *machan* hide, for we were still determined to do our utmost to obtain a picture of one. We also put John Buxton ashore with the local forestry officer to find a tree commanding a suitable glade for photographing grazing Chital. Landing was always a difficult problem and we enjoyed watching them wallowing knee-deep in the glutinous mud, surrounded by leaping Mud Skippers.

On our way back to the mother ship, Eric and I noticed a

white, globular object floating in one of the creeks. Stopping
our launch, we found this to be a six-foot Beaked Deep Sea
Snake which had swallowed a Globe Fish (plate 55). The fish,
after being seized, had inflated itself to the size of a small football
and its sharp spines had evidently penetrated the flesh of its
attacker, preventing it from completing its meal. The huge
bulge had already been nibbled by other fish and the snake was
dying. Doubtless it would soon be picked up by one of the
numerous Crested Serpent Eagles in the region and we wondered
if the poisonous Globe Fish might then claim a second victim.

George Shannon and I had a restful afternoon exploring an
attractive lagoon where we had noticed large numbers of
herons and other birds. This proved to have been a very good
choice. On a single fallen tree we found, perched in attitudes of
somnolent repose, a Whimbrel, a Pond Heron, two Little
Egrets, eight Terek Sandpipers and a Chestnut Bittern. Such
was the fantastic wealth of bird life in the Sunderbans. Having
filmed this group, we drifted up and down the edges of the
lagoon trying to film kingfishers. I frankly did not mind very
much whether we succeeded or not, because every minute was
so full of beauty. I have seldom seen a more entrancing sight
than a Brown-winged Kingfisher perched in full sunlight, with
its glowing orange head and breast and great scarlet bill contrasting with the rich evergreen foliage of the mangroves. Every
time one took off in flight, I marvelled anew at the sudden
brilliant flash of iridescent blue on its rump.

Next day I paid a visit to Tiger Point, a lonely outpost on
the shore of the Bay of Bengal, from which a resident warden
controlled poaching in the reserve. I found plenty to occupy me
on the way. My best find was a very striking Green-billed

Malkoha, a large, long-tailed bird with grey plumage and a vivid patch of scarlet around its eyes. It was feeding on berries in a dense vine, but I managed to obtain quite a good picture of it (plate 55). I failed, however, in an attempt to photograph a seven-foot Monocled Cobra, which glided off a mud-bank as we approached. John and Edmund had already had an adventure with an even larger cobra which they had met face to face in the jungle, one day when they had landed on the edge of a creek. The snake had been coiled around a tree at eye level. The *shikari* had been terrified, but John stood his ground and filmed it as it slid away.

We reached Tiger Point by way of the Sapote River. Here we found the guard hut. Like all the buildings in the area it was built on high stilts to escape the monsoon floods and I had to climb a long, rickety ladder up to the bamboo walk to the hut. The warden, a quiet young man who lived a life of considerable hardship, greeted me shyly. The hut was furnished with the barest necessities—a string *charpoy*, a table and a couple of wooden chairs. The unglazed window was heavily barred, a not unwise precaution as a Tiger had been seen prowling beneath the cat-walk only recently. The warden worked for ten months without leave and had neither books nor radio to relieve the tedium. Although he had a canoe and several native boatmen to help him, he had little chance of controlling poaching over so large an area. If he or one of his men fell ill or had an accident, he had no means of summoning help except by sending a canoe to the Kotka headquarters. As for the animals of the

53 *Above* An interesting little nocturnal primate, the Slow Loris, still survives in the Chittagong Hill Tracts. *Below* Red Jungle Fowl, from which domestic poultry are descended, inhabit forests in East Pakistan.

region, he told me frankly that he had had no training and knew little about them, though he was very willing to be taught.

I thought about the reserve on my way back to Kotka. It was obviously a reserve in name only. Not one of the wardens or forestry officers had been trained in wildlife management. All of them, however, were most interested in knowing that their Department had assumed responsibility for wildlife and saw this as opening up possibilities for improving their status and the interest of their work. Proper training facilities were badly needed. At present there was not even a simple text-book available about the animals of Pakistan, let alone instructors in animal and vegetation ecology as an inseparable entity. Nevertheless, since our first expedition several forestry graduates had been sent to the United States on wildlife conservation courses and Edmund had met them there. He reported them to be keen and enthusiastic. Our recommendation that a training syllabus should be introduced as part of the Forestry degree a some of the universities in Pakistan had been well received and this was encouraging. I determined to do everything in my power to speed up the process. If the remaining wildlife and wilderness areas of Pakistan were to be saved, it was essential not only to create adequate reserves, but to staff them with trained men who could work under scientific management plans. This called for proper equipment, as well as proper training. Wardening the Sunderbans obviously required motor launches and two-way radio if commercially sponsored poaching was to be kept in check.

54 *Above* The Black-capped Kingfisher has iridescent violet, black, white and rufous plumage. *Below* The Stork-billed Kingfisher is the largest of all the colourful species in this numerous family.

That evening, in consultation with the very knowledgeable District Forest Officer, we drafted plans for a new Sunderbans reserve. The eastern area had certain physical advantages over the western and these outweighed the disadvantage of the higher incidence of river traffic; this could be fairly easily controlled or even eliminated, as all fishing and wood-cutting was subject to annual licence. The present small reserve was in itself suitable as a nucleus and by extending its boundaries westward to the Pusur River we could include a highly desirable wildlife habitat, amounting in all to some 300 square miles. An area of this size was necessary for animals such as the Tiger, which needed extensive hunting grounds. Although the Tiger is a strong swimmer, both the Pusur and the Baleswar rivers were wide enough to serve as fairly effective natural boundaries. The sea coast would be the southern boundary. The landward northern side, protected only by narrow creeks, would remain accessible for the natural flow of animals into the reserve. Experience in other countries had shown that animals soon learn where safety lies and that if properly managed they remain in the protected areas so long as food is adequate and the pressure of hunting outside the reserve continues as an invisible barrier.

If a suitably large reserve could be created and properly guarded, it would be possible not only to re-introduce the Gaur and Barasingha to provide more adequate food for the Tigers, but also to restore the Indian Rhinoceros, which had once been a typical occupant of the Sunderbans. There was now a surplus of rhinos in the well managed Kasiranga Reserve in Assam and it would not be difficult to transport some of them by boat down the Brahmaputra.

This, in essence, was the plan which I later submitted to Mr Nooruddin Ahmad, Chief Conservator of Forests for East Pakistan, who greatly encouraged me by his constructive interest. With his blessing and with certain modifications which he suggested, we included this as a firm proposal in our subsequent report to the Central Government (see map, page 203).

Edmund and I tried the Tiger *machan* the following night. It was in a particularly beautiful setting, a gnarled old Sundri tree of unusually large size, one of several standing in the centre of a long tract of tawny meadow, which had evidently once been part of the forest which had been clear-felled. Around the edges was dense jungle, through which we had had to pick our way slowly among the rank undergrowth and projecting pneumatophores. A well-worn path led past the tree to a distant water-hole, where tracks of Chital, Wild Boar and Tiger were numerous.

We were settled and ready by four o'clock and the light was still brilliant. A wait of thirteen hours or more lay ahead of us; but this time we were well prepared and had comfortable seats. Our *shikari* sat slightly below us on a branch, with his back to the main stem. There was barely room for us on the platform and we had to take care not to move our seats even half an inch, or the legs would slip between the four boards which supported us. Edmund's tripod and parabolic reflector occupied the space behind us and our rucksacks, Thermos flasks and the tape recorder filled every inch of the remaining space. Karim had insisted on my taking his heavy .375 Magnum, a rifle powerful enough to fell an Elephant, let alone a Tiger. I hung this on a branch within reach, though nothing but dire necessity would have induced me to use it. We had in fact equipped ourselves with every comfort, except, alas, that I could not smoke my pipe without instantly advertising our presence. Our faithful little sheep, who had made the journey with us from Mandarbaria Island, was contentedly cropping the grass. All we lacked was a Tiger. I got out my notebook and began cataloguing the bird calls in the nearby jungle, while Edmund swung his reflector round and recorded them for me.

Soon after five o'clock the Chital began entering the meadow, their beautifully spotted coats shining sleekly in the evening light. A young buck, with its three-tined antlers in velvet wandered close to our tree and was just coming within range of my camera when it caught sight of the sheep. Its head shot up and with a single spring-heeled bound it jumped twenty feet sideways and raced for cover. With the flash of its white tail, every Chital in sight also instinctively ran a few paces. For ten minutes they stood alertly, scenting the air and peering this way and that, stamping nervously; but finding no danger, they resumed feeding. We later saw the same instantaneous herd-reaction to danger when a Chital barked an alarm in the jungle. Every head flashed up as though jerked by a single string and every animal bounded a few steps before stopping.

At five-thirty a band of Assamese Macaques passed noisily along the edge of the jungle, crashing about in the branches as though enjoying the commotion. Soon afterwards the first Red Jungle Fowl 'wound up' with a series of clucking notes and let fly with a strident crowing. Another and another answered and for a while we could hear them from every direction. Then, as

55 *Above* The Large Green-billed Malkoha has a patch of vivid red skin around its eyes. *Below* A Beaked Deep Sea Snake dying from the poisonous spines of a Globe Fish which it was unable to swallow.

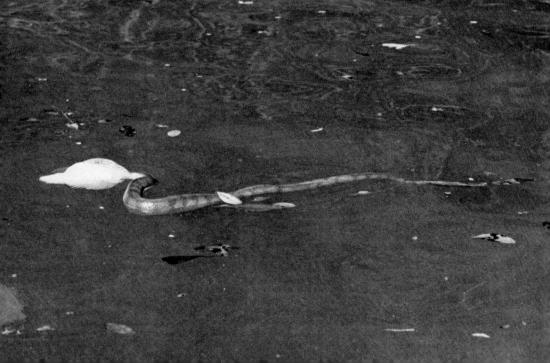

the light faded, a big Gecko lizard began calling a resonant '*gec-ko, gec-ko*' from the trees behind us. Cicadas began strumming all over the meadow, sawing away with the notched ribs beneath their wing-cases to produce an astonishing volume of sound. Finally the Jungle Nightjars struck up their hollow, interminable knocking, like the sound of beating an empty wooden box with a stick (plate 48).

I placed my heavy camera between my feet, tucked up my collar against the cold night air and concentrated my attention on the just discernible blob in the grass which marked the sleeping form of the sheep. There was barely sufficient light from the brilliant stars to enable me to pick it out at a distance of fifty feet. I wished it would bleat to announce its presence, but it remained staunchly silent.

Two hours after sunset the Nightjars and Cicadas ceased singing and there were long periods of utter silence, broken only occasionally by the nervous bark or stamp of a Chital, or by a mysterious cry or disturbance in the distant jungle. I could imagine the thousand pitiless dramas which were nightly enacted in the darkness of its tangled depths, the hunter and the hunted twisting and turning among the clutching roots and vines, the hot blood spilling on the fetid mud. In the sunny light of day the face of the jungle wore an expression of guileless enchantment, where colourful butterflies, shining sunbirds, exquisite orchids and flowering vines masked the dark tragedies of the night.

I shook my head. This was just romantic anthropomorphism

56 Fishermen at Chandpai were using Otters to drive fish into their nets. The Otters appeared to enjoy their work and afterwards groomed each other thoroughly in the bows of the canoe.

and I knew it. The orchids were mere parasites and the scarlet trumpets of the vines could not hide the fact that the plants were vicious stranglers, which killed their hosts as surely, if more slowly, as the Tiger killed the defenceless Chital, or the Shikra hawk struck down the Emerald Dove. It was all part of the natural process of competition for survival.

Soon after midnight the dew began to fall and fat drops of water dripped noiselessly from the waxy leaves around us, saturating our shoulders. It was now intensely cold and I whispered to Edmund that a cup of hot coffee would be a good idea. Very carefully, not to rustle the paper, we unwrapped our sandwiches and enjoyed our refreshments.

The long night dragged on uneventfully and we grew steadily damper and colder. I was too busy with my thoughts to feel sleepy and rather enjoyed the opportunity for reflection after the weeks of intensive work, which usually left me so tired that I slept the moment my head touched a pillow.

Around four-thirty the sky began to pale in the east and a few minutes later the first Black-headed Orioles began to call their liquid notes in the jungle. Within fifteen minutes the whole area was filled with sound and the scene changed from grey and black to gold and green. The Ashy Drongos which had roosted in our tree shook the dew from their feathers and flew off towards the river. Parakeets wheeled overhead, screeching noisily, followed by Green Bee-eaters. Bulbuls, Laughing Thrushes, Jungle Babblers and Racket-tailed Drongos added their voices to the chorus welcoming the dawn and the strident cackling of Brown-winged Kingfishers rang out along the hidden creeks. The tethered sheep rose stiffly and shook its dew-soaked coat, sending a parabola of spray flying. I was glad it had not been sacrificed, though sad that we had had neither sight nor sound of a Tiger to reward our vigil.[1] As the first rays of the sun broke the horizon, the Chital vanished and a new day had begun.

'Well,' said Edmund, 'that was an interesting experience.' The *shikari* grinned sympathetically at us and wrung out the sodden shawl which he had draped over his shoulders during the night. He dropped down from the tree and Edmund began passing down our equipment while I called up Eric on the walkie-talkie and asked him to send a launch to pick us up.

This was to be our last day in the Sunderbans. A radio message had been received, saying that Air Commodore Dass had succeeded in finding us a helicopter, which I particularly wanted, in order that we could film the Sunderbans from the air. It was impossible to portray the vast network of creeks and islands from ground level. The helicopter was available for only a couple of hours and we were asked to return to Khulna a day early in order to use it. We therefore set sail immediately after breakfast.

The return journey was enlivened by sighting a Rock Python and a 15 ft. Marsh Crocodile (plate 49). Near the fishing village of Chandpai we also found Smooth Otters being used to drive fish into nets. They were harnessed by ropes and performed admirably for our photographers. A large square net on two poles was lowered into the water from a fishing boat and the otters jumped in, driving the fish before them into the net. This was then raised and a shower of small fish emptied into the boat. The Otters appeared to enjoy themselves, chirruping

[1] Having failed to photograph a Tiger ourselves, I obtained permission from Peter Jackson and George B. Schaller to include their excellent pictures in this book (plates 46 and 51).

happily in a high falsetto and gambolling in the water. Each of them was rewarded with a fish, which was eaten daintily, clutched as one would hold a banana and being munched from the head downwards. Afterwards the Otters carefully washed their faces and took it in turns to lie on their backs in the bow of the boat with their eyes blissfully shut, while one of their number groomed them thoroughly (plate 56).

Chandpai village marked the end of the jungle. Thereafter we were in largely cultivated country, with wide expanses of paddyfields and occasional villages sheltering beneath graceful Coconut and Betel Palms. The familiar Black Kites, House Crows and Pied Mynas swarmed around every village and Cattle Egrets stalked the paddies or rode on the backs of the slow-moving domestic buffaloes. Shipping became more frequent, including now many ocean-going freighters from other countries. All were heading for the inland ports of Mungla or Khulna. As we moved farther inland we passed more and more floating islands of Water Hyacinth, gay with delicate mauve blossoms and often with Whiskered Terns riding on them.

We reached the crowded harbour at Khulna by sundown. As far as the eye could reach, ships of every shape and size were anchored, among which dozens of small sailing boats, barges and canoes were passing back and forth. The barges were loaded with sisal, jute, bamboos, Golpatta fronds, fruit, pottery, fish meal or the twisted branches of Sundri trees for firewood, which were still weeping their blood-red sap into the muddy water. The shores were crowded with an indescribable shanty-

57 *Above* In the Sylhet forests Barking Deer, or Muntjak, were the favourite prey of Leopards. *Below* The Five-striped Palm Squirrel was the most numerous of the many squirrel species in Pakistan.

town of wooden buildings on stilts, with split bamboo or cor-
rugated-iron roofs. All was noise and animation, which contrasted sharply with the peace of the jungle which we had left
behind us. Rather sadly we set foot on paved streets again and
went in search of officialdom and news of the helicopter.

The helicopter venture next day was not an unqualified
success. We had hoped for a machine large enough to carry at
least two photographers, but there was room for only one.
Moreover the cabin 'bubble' was of green perspex and neither
a window nor a door could be opened in flight to permit an
uninterrupted view. We agreed that George Shannon should be
given the task of overcoming these difficulties as best he could.
He climbed aboard, armed with his cinema camera and a hand
camera for stills. In order to overcome the vibration, his cinema
camera was screwed to a gyroscopic mount, a device which
had proved invaluable when used in a helicopter in Jordan.

The young Squadron Leader piloting the helicopter was a
keen *shikari* and entered into the unusual assignment with great
enthusiasm. In the course of an exciting flight back over the
Sunderbans, he did everything in his power to enable George to
get the shots he wanted, hedge-hopping over the cultivated
approaches, rising and diving over the jungle and at one point
skimming the tree-tops and almost landing in order to examine
a Crocodile on a mud-bank. George used his cameras very ably
and found later that although reflections on the perspex dome
had spoilt some shots, the green tint had only slightly affected
the colours of the film.

58 *Above* Black-breasted Kalij Pheasants were seen at dawn on the Sylhet
jungle tracks. *Below* Throughout the wet areas of Pakistan the Pond Heron,
or Paddybird, was common.

Immediately after the return of the helicopter, George and Eric had to leave the expedition and begin their journey home, by way of Dacca. The rest of us were to go that night by river on the famous *Rocket* steamer; but as the time of our arrival in Dacca was uncertain, George and Eric took a plane to make sure of catching their connection to Karachi and London. These two stalwart companions had accompanied me on every expedition I had ever organised and I knew I should miss them badly during our forthcoming explorations in Sylhet. We loaded them into a Jeep and gave them a warm send-off.

With the remainder of the day to spare, Edmund and I drove out of Khulna to see the countryside, which was intensively farmed. Among new bird species were Singing Bush Larks, a Bluethroat, a very fine Pied Harrier and, very surprisingly in an area of open paddyfields, a Wryneck. Grey and Small Indian Mongooses were very numerous, foraging busily along the ditches with complete disregard for passers-by.

It was in Khulna that we first heard the rumour that a Sumatran, or Two-horned Rhinoceros had been shot in the Chittagong Hill Tracts. The total world population of this species probably does not exceed one hundred, in scattered localities in Burma, Malaya, Sumatra and North Borneo. I was later able to obtain further information about this scandalous affair through Jerry Wood-Anderson. For some time it had been known that a few of these extremely rare animals existed in the jungle on the Burmese side of the frontier not far from Cox's Bazaar. One of them had apparently entered the territory of East Pakistan and had at once been shot. Its carcass had been taken in triumph to Chittagong, where it was sold in small pieces as an aphrodisiac for a total of Rs 15,000 (about £1,150).

We are still seeking confirmation, but if the story is true it is a sad blow to the international efforts which are being made to save this unique species and a further indication of the need to introduce effective conservation in the Chittagong Hill Tracts.

I had to give another Press conference before we sailed that evening. The editor of the local newspaper had already published a very well written account of our work elsewhere in Pakistan and I was glad to give him the opportunity to scoop the Dacca papers with a report on our findings in the Sunderbans.

The *Rocket* was a grand old paddle boat, which had plied between Khulna and Dacca for many years. The lounge and impeccably neat cabins were almost Victorian in their lavish use of mahogany and lace curtains. The food was excellent. We had most of the first-class accommodation to ourselves, but the lower deck was crammed to overflowing with a picturesque crowd of merchants and others, each carrying enormous bundles.

Sharp at eight o'clock, amid much shouting and ringing of bells, the great paddles began thrashing the water and we cast off, promptly colliding broadside with a sickening crash into a steamer which had crept up in the darkness on the port side. However, only the housing of the paddle was damaged and after the captains had exchanged insults through loud-hailers we edged our way out into the moving shipping. Our search-light was kept swinging from side to side as a warning to the host of suicidally minded canoeists who were zigzagging in the darkness among the larger vessels.

All through the night and the following day we continued our journey up the wide river through verdant country, stopping occasionally at picturesque little ports to unload merchandise, or pick up passengers. At Chandpur, which was crowded with extremely beautiful sailing barges with multi-coloured sails, I watched the muscular, bare-footed coolies unloading crates of machinery. According to the stencilled legends on the lids, each crate weighed 180 lb. A total of twenty of these were carried at a trot on the heads of the perspiring men, up a steep gang-plank and into a warehouse. I wondered what our dockers back home would say about such a feat.

When we turned into the main channel of the Ganges I was reminded of its tremendous size. Although we were now two and a half days' sailing from the open sea, the river was still nearly eight miles wide—and this was the rainless season.

We reached Narayanganj, the port of Dacca, as night fell and arrived at our hotel in time for dinner. Here Christopher Savage awaited us for the last lap of the expedition. He brought with him a bundle of mail from England and for the next twenty minutes there was complete silence as we devoured the contents of our letters from home. Then, after showers, haircuts and other manifestations of a return to civilisation, we assembled for dinner, looking for all our darkly tanned faces, just like tourists in our freshly pressed lounge suits and clean white shirts. The riches of Sylhet lay ahead of us and we knew they were going to be quite different from anything we had yet seen.

10

The Jungle of Sylhet

Arrangements for our visit to Sylhet had been carefully rehearsed by Karim. By ten o'clock next morning we were already on our way, with stores replenished and not a moment lost. He had been up most of the night and we were filled with admiration for his devotion to our needs.

We flew as far as Sylhet airport, where Jeeps were waiting to take us to Moulvi Bazaar and then on to our destination, which was a Tourist Department rest-house in the hills at Akbarpur. In the distance we could see the long, richly forested range of the Khasi Jaintia mountains, which divide Sylhet from Indian territory. It was some little time before we could leave the airport, because an important Minister had been on our plane and out of courtesy we waited until the speeches of welcome to him were completed. A large crowd had been brought in by a fleet of thirty buses and it took us half an hour to squeeze past them on the way to Moulvi Bazaar. A monumental traffic jam blocked the town and we had time to get out and buy fresh fruit before the frantic police had broken the tangle. Thereafter we had an uninterrupted run until we came to a ferry across a wide river, where we were surprised to see Gangetic Dolphins so far from the coast. The ferry was of very ancient construction and leaking. We were not surprised to learn that it sank in mid-stream a week later.

We were the first guests to be lodged at the rest-house and the staff had completed the plumbing only that morning. It was spacious and comfortable, with a deep veranda on the second floor, overlooking a wide tract of scrub jungle. The trees had been clear-felled around the house, leaving a rather ugly bare patch which was to be turned into a garden. In a dell behind the house was a concrete training college belonging to the Department of Education.

We soon explored the woods surrounding the rest-house and found them full of vegetation and bird species different from those we had previously seen. Sylhet Division adjoins the frontier with Assam and many of the birds here have Himalayan affinities, or are typical of the high rain forests of Assam. Within the first hour we had identified three new species of flycatchers and no fewer than five different Bulbuls—the Black, the Red-whiskered, the Red-vented, the Black-headed and the Black-crested Yellow. Pigeons and doves of many species and a host of unidentifiable warblers kept us in a state of great confusion for a while. That evening, while we were changing for dinner, a wild chorus of screeching broke out in the scrub below the rest-house as a pack of Jackals set out on their night's hunting. It was an inspiring welcome to our new study area.

The best was, however, to come. Early next morning we drove through extensive tea gardens to the Kalinga (Tarap Hill) Forest Reserve, where we found ourselves for the first time in typical rain forest. This was the type of country I remembered so well in Assam and Burma during the Second World War—huge, soaring trees and forty-foot clumps of bamboo rising from vivid green undergrowth and blanketed by impenetrable flowering vines. This was the kind of jungle in which the British Army had fought during the Burma campaign. I remembered driving through Sylhet on my way to Assam, more than twenty-five years ago. In those days the forest had stretched without interruption from Sylhet almost to the Chinese border. I had felt puzzled and disoriented by the change in the landscape during our journey to Akbarpur and had found nothing familiar in the miles of paddyfields through which we had passed. Here at Kalinga at last was what I had been seeking.

Botanists classify the forest type found in Sylhet as tropical semi-evergreen. This can be more clearly defined as closed high forest, with a mixture of evergreen and deciduous trees, with dense undergrowth and a copious growth of climbers and epiphytes. The mean annual temperature here approaches 80°F, with high humidity. This forest type zone extends at altitudes of from 200 to 2,500 feet from eastern India to Assam and the Manipur Hills, southward through Mymensingh and the Chittagong Hill Tracts to the Burmese Arakan.

When we stopped at the forest rest-house for refreshments, I questioned the District Forest Officer about the changes which had taken place. To my astonishment, I learned that almost all the primary forests of Sylhet had now disappeared. Huge areas had been cleared for growing rice and to make room for the rapidly expanding human population. More forest had gone for the extension of tea estates, or for plantations of commercial timber such as Teak. Now, he said, only about ten square miles of untouched primary forest remained and this was the tract through which we had just driven. It formed part of the Tarap Hill Forest Reserve and would shortly be felled and replaced by a monoculture of Teak. I was appalled by this information and said I would continue the discussion when we had completed our examination of the area.

We spent two days studying the precious remnant of the forest which had once been the glory of Sylhet. By common consent we regarded this as the most fascinating period of the whole expedition, for the region was alive with unusual wildlife and vegetation. It appeared to be acting as a kind of vacuum, into which flowed mammals and birds which elsewhere had been deprived of their natural habitats, for their concentration was very dense.

The following morning we approached the forest at dawn and I asked our drivers to go very slowly and quietly. This precaution was richly repaid when we turned a corner and found two spectacular Black-breasted Kalij Pheasants feeding on the sandy track. Although less brightly coloured than some of Pakistan's five magnificent pheasants (all of which are now rarities), the Kalij is a very striking bird, with an upstanding tuft of feathers on the crown, a dark purple body, a crimson face and a brightly chequered black and white rump. We later saw five others and I managed to photograph them; in the pale dawn light the pictures were inevitably of poor quality, though valuable records (plate 58).

At the far side of the forest we put up a large Wild Boar, which raced away with an angry snort and its tail held vertically in alarm. Shortly afterwards a woodsman stepped out from the trees and signalled us to stop. After a brief conversation with Siddiqi he motioned to us to follow him. Siddiqi explained that

59 *Above* The demand for skins of the beautifully marked Clouded Leopard has reduced it to extreme rarity. *Below* The Crested Indian Porcupine is a powerful animal well able to defend itself.

a Tiger had killed a Wild Boar that morning and that we were to be shown its tracks. We followed in single file down a slope through the trees, across a clearing and into dense undergrowth where, sure enough, very fresh pug-marks of a large Tiger were imprinted in the mud. While I was kneeling to photograph them, the woodsman said nervously that the Tiger was almost certainly lying close by in the thicket, watching us. Although we had all by now become a bit blasé about Tigers, I fancy there was a certain repressed urgency about our return to the safety of the road, for we were unarmed. Another Tiger had recently mauled a tea picker on an adjacent estate and had been shot. These were, however, probably not resident animals but vagrants from across the borders of Tripura or Assam.

There were many Langur and Assamese Macaque Monkeys in the forest. Macaques are rather ugly animals, with frowning expressions and red behinds. These tended to keep to the edges of cultivation near the villages. The Langurs, which are supremely graceful creatures with endearing little faces and very long tails, preferred the seclusion of the jungle, where they could find plenty of tender shoots and fruit. Their agility was extraordinary and they thought nothing of leaping thirty feet from branch to branch. They had a great fondness for the fruit of the Balu tree *Dillenia pentagyna* and of the *Michania* vine. To climb the soft billows of delicate tendrils of this vine would be like trying to climb soapsuds, even to so lightweight an animal. To reach the fruit, the Langurs leaped into an adjacent clump of bamboos, selected the tallest frond, and climbed to the top,

60 *Above* Elephants proved to be ideal for exploring the difficult wetlands areas at Hail and Hakaluki. *Below* President Ayub Khan and the author at the conclusion of the expedition.

their weight bowing the frond down over the vine. Holding on with their hind feet and tightly wrapped tails, they then reached down and plucked the fruit with their delicate black fingers. We never tired of watching them.

The local squirrels were numerous and difficult to identify. The typical Orange-bellied Himalayan Squirrel was easy enough, but we saw others with red, black or brindled coats which might have been colour morphs of this species or of the Hoary-bellied Himalayan Squirrel. Indian Tree Shrews, which, though classified as primates, are remarkably squirrel-like, were also seen and we had one imperfect sighting of a suspected Malayan Giant Squirrel.

Driving back that afternoon we heard a Barking Deer calling. They were locally plentiful (plate 57). Instantly Edmund jumped from the Jeep and set up his recording gear. Kneeling in the grass at the side of the track, earphones firmly clamped to his head, he focused the microphone on the distant barking and switched on the recorder. When the barking stopped, he immediately switched on the speaker and played back the tape. The deer answered, coming closer and closer, until it was right up to the edge of the jungle. We sat silently in our Jeeps, fascinated. This was sound recording the way I liked to see it used and my mind flashed back to a sunlit wood in the Mátra Mountains in Hungary, where we had played back the recording of a River Warbler and brought the frenzied little singer down to within a few feet of the microphone seeking the rival to its territory.

Perhaps the most important discovery we made during our stay in Sylhet fell to John Buxton. At dawn that morning he had driven over to have breakfast with one of the tea planters, who had an estate at Duracherra, before joining us in the forest. On the way he had clearly seen a large, puma-like animal with a long tail and rich golden fur. Without doubt this was a Golden Cat, one of the rarest and most beautiful animals of the much persecuted cat family. It has a vestigial range extending through Assam, Sikkim and Nepal; though very few of them now survive, its occurrence on the border between Sylhet and Assam would not be out of place. It was, however, one more proof of the extreme importance of this area to the conservation of wildlife.

We were invited that day to take tea with Dr and Mrs McKay in their very comfortable bungalow on one of the tea estates. They were both very keen naturalists and Mrs McKay had quite a little menagerie of pets, including a Mongoose, a fine Porcupine and many birds. The Porcupine was cautiously allowed out of its enclosure so that we could examine it while it trotted around the garden. These are difficult and very destructive animals, which can dig their way out of almost any enclosure; but our hostess had succeeded in keeping hers in perfect condition in a concrete and wire pen, back to which it was safely guided.

On the veranda we enjoyed a typical Scottish tea, complete with home-made muffins and strawberry jam, to the accompaniment of a running commentary by a talkative Hill Myna and the chirruping of Blossom-headed Parakeets in an aviary. In a tree in the garden a pair of wild Spotted Owlets watched us intently with big yellow eyes (plate 22). The garden was a riot of colour and included several of the more beautiful flowering trees of south-east Asia.

On our way back to Akbarpur we added an important new bird to our list, a chestnut-coloured Rufous Woodpecker. Like the unique Ruddy Kingfisher, it is the only species of a numerous family of birds with boldly coloured plumage patterns to have plumage giving the effect of a single colour.

At dinner that night the news leaked out that it was my birthday. Our cook, always anxious to please, made some highly decorated pancakes to mark the occasion and placed candles in bottles on the table, apologising for the fact that he had not known in time to make me a birthday cake. I was feeling rather unwell and had a slight fever caused by the poisonous bites of Hemp Moths and my neck had broken out in an unsightly, painful rash. I was therefore much cheered by the cook's gesture. I was even more pleased when presently a boy came in with a present from the staff. I unwrapped the crumpled brown-paper bag which he placed carefully on my plate. Inside was a live Jungle Nightjar, which the boys had picked up on the veranda. The bird was unharmed and after taking its picture by electronic flashlight, I let it fly off into the night (plate 48).

We spent two days studying the major wetlands areas in Sylhet. These were vitally important to the tens of thousands of ducks and geese which migrated there each winter when the lakes in Tibet froze over. The first of these was Hail *haor*. A *haor* in Bengali means a low-lying, perennially flooded area; the open water areas and marshes are called *bheels* (equivalent to the *jheels* of West Pakistan).

We explored Hail in flat-bottomed and far from leak-proof punts, each carrying two passengers and a bare-footed local fisherman who wielded the punt pole. After a spell in the jungle it was a pleasant change to be back among water birds again, under a wide open sky, though after seven hours' sitting on wet bamboo matting we were all stiff and glad to be back on land.

The spectacle which greeted us once we had penetrated the thousands of acres of floating Lotus and Water Hyacinth beds was extremely exciting. From horizon to horizon the sky was full of wheeling ducks and their clamorous voices could be clearly heard for half a mile. As we drew nearer, we could see that the majority were Lesser Whistling Teal, which we estimated to number at least twenty thousand birds. Among them were about a thousand Large Whistling Teal and a few parties of Common Teal, Pintail, Gadwall, Garganey, Pochard and Cotton Teal. How many birds were beyond our view we could only guess. Christopher, to whom the sight of so many of his favourite birds was a powerful stimulant, assured us that it was too early in the winter for us to see the tremendous numbers which would presently assemble on the *bheels*.

We edged our punts slowly forward through a maze of picturesque fish traps which extended for hundreds of yards in all directions, until we were a mile out from the shore and nearing the centre of the area. As soon as we ceased to move, ducks came showering out of the sky, to settle in thousands among the floating vegetation around us, until the water was a solid brown carpet of moving birds. The high chirruping cries of the Lesser Whistling Teal were almost deafening, as flock after flock added to the congregation.

Surfeited by the spectacle and after taking our fill of pictures we made our way to a low island, where we had lunch while Eastern Sky Larks sang gaily overhead. Ducks still streamed around us, little disturbed by our presence, and fat

Purple Gallinules hooted and went about their business in the reeds which surrounded us.

A troupe of Manipuri dancers was to entertain us that evening and we had to be back in time for an early dinner, so we regretfully left the *haor* and drove back to our rest-house.

The dancers were extremely good, though the troupe had only recently been formed. I had seen a less sophisticated group dancing in Manipur State during the war and remembered the strange rhythm of the traditional *dhole, murli* and harmonium which accompanied them. The hall was crowded with an appreciative audience, which included a number of planters and their wives. During the performance Christopher passed me a note saying that I was expected to make a speech afterwards and I presently found myself on the stage, surrounded by the colourfully clad dancers. As some of the girls were remarkably pretty I found this no hardship. I urged them not to let the native traditions of the area disappear under the impact of the brave new world and took the opportunity also to talk about Sylhet's riches in wildlife, which I recommended them to preserve. On behalf of my colleagues I then presented the troupe with a handsome contribution towards the cost of their elaborate new costumes, a gesture which was received with rapturous applause.

Afterwards we went to the Planters Club for drinks and had some useful discussions about the local status of wildlife. Everyone told the same story: wild animals and their habitats were disappearing and what had once been a sportsman's paradise would soon be one unbroken area of cultivation. The Leopards and other cats, the monkeys and the Barking Deer were regarded as troublesome pests and would soon all be destroyed.

Rice, tea, jute and commercial timber were what counted now and with a human population already exceeding 1,400 to the square mile in some areas there was no room for animals. The natural treasures of Sylhet seemed doomed. With a density of human population which was one of the highest in the world, the whole of East Pakistan was bursting at the seams. Its largely agrarian people could now expand only into the undeveloped parts of the Chittagong Hill Tracts (with further inevitable losses of vegetation and wildlife), or by translocation into the desert areas of West Pakistan, which might be brought into cultivation by the new Mangla and Tarbela dam projects.

Driving back to the rest-house I vowed that somehow we would save the Kalinga forest and some of the marshes, so that at least the small remnants of unspoilt wilderness could provide sanctuary for the surviving wildlife.

Our visit to Hakaluki *haor* on the following day was even more remarkable than our trip to Hail. To begin with, we used elephants to get there and this was a new experience (plate 60).

We approached the *haor* by way of Azimganj Bazaar, where our host, Mr Najmul Islam, Chairman of the Sujanagar Union Council, had made remarkably generous arrangements, which included not only the provision of elephants, but boats and boatmen for the day. I never ceased to marvel at the spontaneous generosity of the many Pakistani people we met on our travels. It was a great compliment to the work of the World Wildlife Fund.

The four elephants, accompanied by a rather frisky young one, were lined up waiting for us, surrounded by about a hundred interested villagers. As our Jeeps came to a halt, the elephants curled back their trunks and trumpeted a ceremonial greeting.

There is no dignified manner of climbing on to an elephant, unless perhaps one is a circus performer. When I was invited to mount, I stepped on to the kneeling hind leg as I had seen *mahouts* do, and scrambled up with as much elegance as its immense behind permitted, hitching myself forward until I had one foot behind each of its ears. The *mahout* sat astride its neck and Karim climbed up behind me. The others mounted their elephants in similar fashion and we ambled off at the long, swinging pace which makes elephant riding such a comfortable form of locomotion.

Out over the wide paddyfields we plodded, following the narrow earth bunds which had been built up for eighteen inches around each plot to retain the life-giving water for the tender rice. Although my mount's huge feet were much wider than the top of the bund, they were planted with perfect precision every time and each right-angle corner was negotiated at the same even pace. When presently we came to the first of several deep canals, the elephants descended the steep banks carefully, testing the ground delicately with the tips of their trunks at each step. The water was deep enough to wet my boots and I had to grasp the rope securing the pad on which we rode to prevent myself from sliding off as we climbed the opposite bank.

We reached the shore of Hakaluki *haor* and dismounted to take to the boats which were waiting. Our thoughtful host had provided cane chairs and this time we sat in comfort. The boatmen poled us out through the reed-beds, where glossy Drongos were gracefully swooping after the dragonflies. A Kingfisher alighted on a reed by my boat, holding a gleaming fish which it battered to death against the stem before throwing up its head and swallowing it with a flourish.

The marsh, which contained a number of extensive *bheels*, covered an even larger area than Hail. We had time to see only part of it, but again were amazed by the great numbers of wildfowl. Those whose numbers we could estimate amounted to about fifteen thousand, but a sweep of the horizon suggested that there must have been about seventy thousand ducks throughout the marshes. Again Lesser Whistling Teal predominated, with a total of 7,500. There were about 6,000 Pintails, 800 Large Whistling Teal, 400 Common Teal and smaller numbers of Garganey, Pochard, Ferruginous Ducks, Tufted, Gadwall, Shoveler, Spotbills and Cotton Teal.

The marshes also contained countless waders, among which Pheasant-tailed Jacanas were conspicuous by their numbers and noisy behaviour; having all moulted their long tails, they looked quite unlike those we had seen in summer plumage. Many harriers and eagles of several species were flying over the reed-beds, attracted by the unlimited prey below. Notable among the birds of prey was our first Steppe Eagle, a species regarded by some authorities as possibly conspecific with the Tawny.

The netting and shooting of ducks was practised here on a large scale, though special arrangements had been made to suspend these activities for two weeks before our visit, so that the birds were not disturbed. The *bheels* provided an important source of fish to the surrounding towns and villages, being drained periodically and in rotation for the collection of their contents. Fish nets on long poles extended for hundreds of yards along the edges of the reed-beds and we had to weave our way among them during our explorations.

Like Hail, Hakaluki obviously represented an important centre for wildlife and its importance to migratory ducks increased year by year as the reclamation of swamps for agriculture progressed. Ducks in large numbers were an economic problem in a region where rice was king; but they were also important both as food for the local population and for sport. Fishing, too, had considerable economic value to the community. Properly managed, the *haors* could serve all these purposes on the basis of a sustained yield, providing stocks were maintained and limits were imposed. At present there were no controls and the whole area was subjected to constant disturbance by fishermen and hunters. In spite of the temporary ban on shooting, we found a couple of men blazing away at the Whistling Teal, though Karim soon apprehended them.

After completing our examination we decided to recommend that at least one-fifth of the areas of Hakaluki and Hail should be set aside as wildlife reserves under carefully devised and supervised management plans. These would include adequate safeguards for hunting and fishing, quotas being fixed in relation to fluctuations in availability. The erection of nest boxes for tree-nesting ducks such as the two species of Whistling Teal, the Cotton Teal and the rare Nukhta Duck and the suspension of reed-cutting during the breeding season, would quickly stimulate nesting, which at present was at a negligible level.

On our way back to Azimganj we were able to see how elephants were employed to control the irrigation of the paddy-fields. With a minimum of quietly spoken commands from their *mahouts* and with infinite skill, they lifted the heavy sluice-gates and dropped them neatly back between the retaining posts of the next channel to be blocked off. In spite of the slippery, forty-five degree mud-banks on which they were standing they balanced their loads perfectly in their trunks.

The baby elephant which had accompanied us was not yet trained to the dignified pace of its elders. Its mother, on which I was riding, had several times to call it back in line with a deep, rumbling command. Once, when we were walking a narrow bund through ripening rice, the young elephant began snatching trunkfuls of the succulent crop as it ambled along. Obviously this was something the older beasts had been trained never to do and its mother let out a shrill cry of protest. As the baby did not stop, its mother reached forward and seized its ear in her mouth, almost toppling it over, and administered a heavy whack with her trunk. Thereafter the baby trotted in front of her with perfect decorum.

We spent our last day in the forest again and it was just as exciting as the first. Again we saw the Kalij Pheasants at dawn. This time, however, we penetrated a little way into the jungle on either side of the track. John and I selected a glade where Langurs were feeding in the tree tops and sat on a log to enjoy the pageant.

Soon after the disturbance of our entry had been accepted, we were rewarded by seeing a pair of the most colourful rare birds of East Pakistan. I first caught sight of a gleam of scarlet among the leaves and then, out into full sunlight, came a dove-sized bird with a flaming scarlet head and breast, black and white wings and a large, orange and white tail. It was a Red-headed Trogon, followed quickly by its mate. I had seen trogons in tropical South America and Africa and all were very colourful birds, but with the exception of the long-tailed Quetzal of Guatemala, this was certainly the most striking species of a remarkable family.

The monkeys above us were puzzling. They were certainly not Capped Langurs, being darker and smaller, though of similar form. Instead of having black faces they had white lips and distinctive fluffy, whitish eye-rings. Moreover their underparts were also white. Not until we examined John's films the following year did we realise they were undoubtedly Dusky Leaf Monkeys *Presbytis obscurus*. This species, closely related to the Langurs, is a typical inhabitant of Malaya. Another very similar animal, Phayre's Leaf Monkey *Presbytis phayrei* occurs in Burma, but this lacks the white marking on the face. The apparently thriving colony of Dusky Leaf Monkeys at Kalinga was therefore an astonishing discovery, extending the known range of the species by some 750 miles.

John followed the monkeys across the road and into the forest on the other side, where he made some very fine film shots of them. I remained in the glade, knowing that I should see more by keeping still than by moving about. Presently I was taken again to be part of the scenery by the birds which were flitting about among the vegetation and they ignored me. Several times a Black-naped Monarch Flycatcher, ultramarine-blue with a black-tufted crown, came within six feet of me, followed by a pair of lemon-yellow Grey-headed Flycatchers. A Crow Pheasant peered at me from the undergrowth, shaking its orange wings and big black tail. Deciding that I was harmless, it came out into the open and began scratching about among the fallen leaves like a barnyard fowl, clucking reflectively to itself. A Purple Sunbird and a diminutive Scarlet-backed Flowerpecker hovered over the *Michania* vine flowers, where presently a Gold-fronted Chloropsis with an emerald-green back and a shining purple and yellow throat, burst into a cascade of melodious song. Around me and wherever we went in the forest there was a steady, subdued clatter of falling dead leaves from the Teak trees, as dry and brittle as tinder, so that it was impossible to walk anywhere without making a loud crunching noise. For twenty minutes I could hear a large animal of some kind moving slowly in the undergrowth behind me and as the cautious footsteps on the dead leaves drew nearer and the intervals between them longer, I thought it wise to move in case I was being stalked by a Leopard. We had been warned that there were many of them in the forest and that they were more dangerous than Tigers.

Near the entrance to the forest stood an immense Wild Fig tree, which was a great attraction to the various pigeons. I climbed up the hillside, which had been clear-felled, to a good vantage point overlooking the tree. Through my binoculars I watched the comings and goings of the birds which were feeding on the abundant fruit. I counted eighty Thick-billed Green Pigeons, beautiful grey-green birds with vinous wings strongly marked with yellow. There were also fifteen Lineated Barbets and a dozen Blue-throated Barbets, all gorging themselves on the fruit as though their lives depended on the maximum consumption in the shortest possible time. Those which had fed until they could hold no more sat with gaping bills until they could summon the energy to fly, most of the pigeons merely gliding on stiff wings to the forest below. A very magnificent Large Yellow-naped Woodpecker sat sunning itself on the topmost twig of the tree, its green and plum-coloured wings spread and its saffron-yellow crest erected like a shining crown.

During my watch a Shikra hawk (a close relative of the Goshawk) alighted in the tree. I was surprised to see that the feeding birds paid no attention whatever to the arrival of a predator. The hawk sat watching them for a while and then, without warning, suddenly dropped a few feet to a branch below, from which it seized a fat Lineated Barbet in its yellow talons. With a roar of wings, every bird in the tree fled instantly. The hawk calmly plucked and ate the Barbet, whose green feathers drifted in a long, sad stream to the ground below. Within a few minutes of the hawk's departure the tree was again laden with feeding birds. Such was life and death in the jungle.

As the sun began to descend, I leaned back against a stump and lit my pipe. From my high vantage point the whole panorama of the jungle canopy was spread out like a sea below me, with the almost fluorescent whitish froth of the *Michania* vine flowers shining here and there like spindrift on the green waves. The feathery tops of the bamboo clumps made little pale green islands among the dark evergreens; patches of scarlet marked the clustered trumpets of flowering climbers. After the humidity of the enclosed valley the air was sweet and cool. Behind me the tall, flowering grasses made a gently swaying harp for the breeze and their sharp scent was like the bouquet of young wine.

To-day was our last day in the jungle. At midnight we were to take the train from Srimangal to Dacca, where I had appointments with Ali Asghar, Chief Secretary of the East Pakistan Government and with Nooruddin Ahmad, Chief Conservator of Forests, who was deeply interested in our work. I had also promised to visit the Madhurpur National Park, in Mymensingh District. All these were important assignments. And after that there would be another round of meetings, Press conferences and interviews in Karachi before we returned to England.

For two months we had been exploring deserts, mountains, swamps and jungles and had seen a greater variety of wildlife than most people could see in a lifetime. My companions had worked like Trojans, with a devotion which had been beyond praise. Our notebooks were crammed with information which would require months of careful analysis before our reports could be prepared. We had taken more than three thousand photographs and ten thousand feet of cinema film, which would involve hundreds of hours of work in the darkroom and at the editing table.

Throughout the expedition the support we had received from officials and private individuals in Pakistan had been more than generous. Our work had aroused the enthusiastic backing of the Press and broadcasters; public opinion was now actively roused in support of wildlife conservation. I felt confident that with President Ayub Khan's obvious interest in our work, the recommendations which we had prepared would bear fruit and that effective measures to save the endangered animals of Pakistan would be introduced. Time was not, however, on the side of the animals and every week that passed brought a further diminution of their habitats. If only we had come to Pakistan ten years earlier! Yet had we done so, perhaps we would have been too late to save the Coto Doñana in Spain, or to create the wildlife reserves which had resulted from our work in Jordan. One could stick a pin almost anywhere in the map of the world and find conservation problems of equal urgency and I felt a sudden sense of desperation at the magnitude of the tasks as yet untouched.

Governments and rich men thought nothing of spending millions on the preservation of man-made treasures such as great works of art, cathedrals or places of historic interest, yet money to save unique animals from extinction—the irreplaceable natural treasures of the world—was pitifully hard to find. The World Wildlife Fund already had more than two hundred fully documented and urgent survival projects which could not be implemented for lack of money. But there was never a shortage of funds for land clearance, that time-worn euphemism for total destruction of nature. In 1967 thirty million dollars' worth of defoliants were dropped on the green jungles of Viet Nam in order to convert them to lifeless desert. Just ten per cent of this sum would have enabled the World Wildlife Fund to complete its outstanding projects and to have saved many doomed animal species from extinction.

The world's awareness of its imbalance of priorities was awakening, it was true, but slowly, and when two-thirds of the world was hungry the preservation of beauty had low priority in man's conscience. I thought of the worried, indignant expressions on the faces of the young Pakistani students at the University of the Punjab when I had described what was happening to the wildlife of their country. Already few of them would be able to see the great majority of the major animal species of their native land except those languishing behind bars. Would the children of these students forgive this generation if it said it had been too busy with human needs and ambitions to spare a thought for saving the beauties of the environment which it passed on to them?

However, the problem was not as simple as this, nor was it caused merely by ignorance or thoughtlessness. Nothing could halt the demand for more land for the swelling tide of the world's human population. By the year 2000—barely thirty years from now—the present three and a half billion population would rise to seven billion. Already for every day that passed there were nearly 200,000 additional mouths to feed. Pakistan and India between them were now faced with feeding 650 millions from their limited land resources, plus what they could get from more fortunate countries. How much of the subcontinent could they afford to reserve for wildlife under such a pressure? I recalled the grave words of Dr B. R. Sen, Director-General of the United Nations Food and Agriculture Organisation: 'The next thirty-five years will be a most critical period in man's history. Either we take the fullest measures to raise productivity and to stabilise population growth, or we will face disaster of an unprecedented magnitude.' But to feed empty bellies was not enough! Man did not live by bread alone—the quality of his environment also needed to be preserved if he was to find spiritual fulfilment and was not to become a mere robot in a concrete and steel megalopolis.

The cry of an eagle overhead recalled me to my surroundings. It was a long, wailing cry, which seemed to echo my thoughts. A cry from the wild. An appeal that man should leave just a little of the wilderness and the vanishing jungle to shelter the creatures which shared his planet with him.

APPENDIX A

Observations concerning mammals in Pakistan

Unconfirmed records are shown in square brackets

Insectivora

Long-eared Hedgehog *Hemiechinus auritus collaris*. Occurs throughout W. Pakistan.

Afghan Hedgehog *Hemiechinus megalotis*. Occurs in highlands of Baluchistan and Waziristan.

Brandt's Greater Gypsy Hedgehog *Paraechinus hypomelas hypomelas*. Occurs in Baluchistan, from Mekran coast to Waziristan.

Brandt's Lesser Gypsy Hedgehog *Paraechinus hypomelas blanfordi*. Occurs along banks of Indus from central Sind to Salt Range: plate 12a.

Pale Hedgehog *Paraechinus micropus micropus*. Occurs in southern Sind and Lasbela.

Chiroptera

Anderson's Desert Fruit Bat *Rousettus arabicus*. Locally common near Karachi.

Indian Flying Fox *Pteropus giganteus*. Large colony seen at Lahore; common in many parts of E. Pakistan: plate 21a.

Lesser Rat-tailed Bat *Rhinopoma hardwickei hardwickei*. Common around Karachi and in Bahawalpur.

Great Horseshoe Bat *Rhinolophus ferrumequinum tragates*. Seen only at Gupis (Gilgit Agency).

Indian Pygmy Pipistrelle *Pipistrellus mimus mimus*. Seen Bahawalpur.

Kelaart's Yellow-vested Pipistrelle *Pipistrellus ceylonicus subcanus*. Common in plains around Karachi and in Sind.

Tube-nosed Bat *Murina huttoni tubinaris*. Seen Gilgit and Gupis.

Primates

Indian Tree Shrew *Anathana ellioti*. Several seen in Sylhet Division.

Slow Loris *Nycticebus coucang bengalensis*. Occurs in Pakistan only in Chittagong Hill Tracts: plate 53a.

Eastern Rhesus Macaque *Macaca mulatta mulatta*. Fairly common in Chittagong Hill Tracts in spite of numbers taken for medical research purposes.

Himalayan Rhesus Macaque *Macaca mulatta villosa*. Occurs in western Himalayas of Pakistan.

Assamese Macaque *Macaca assamensis*. Common in Sylhet and Sunderbans.

Common Langur *Presbytis entellus*. Himalayan race occurs in the Khagan Valley.

Capped Langur *Presbytis pileatus pileatus*. Occurs in Pakistan only in Sylhet Division.

Southern Capped Langur *Presbytis pileatus durga*. Occurs in Pakistan only in the Chittagong Hill Tracts.

Dusky Leaf Monkey *Presbytis obscurus*. A colony found at Kalinga (Sylhet). Previously thought to be restricted to Malaya.

Hoolock Gibbon *Hylobates hoolock*. Occurs in Pakistan only in the Chittagong Hill Tracts.

Pholidota

Indian Pangolin *Manis crassicaudata*. Occurs in Bahawalpur, Sind, Salt Range and Baluchistan.

Lagomorpha

[Assam Rabbit *Caprolagus hispidus*. Occurs in Assam–Sylhet border region. Two probable sightings in Sylhet.]

Cape Hare *Lepus capensis tibetanus*. Occurs in Gilgit, Baltistan and Kashmir.

Indian Hare *Lepus nigricollis dayanus*. Common throughout Indus Valley and southern Baluchistan.

Rodentia

Five-striped Palm Squirrel *Funambulus pennanti*. Common between Kirthar Range, Bahawalpur and Salt Range: plate 57*b*.

[Malayan Giant Squirrel *Ratufa bicolor*. A slightly doubtful sighting in north-east Sylhet Division.]

Orange-bellied Himalayan Squirrel *Dreomys lokriah*. Seen in north-east Sylhet Division.

Hoary-bellied Himalayan Squirrel *Dreomys pygerythrus*. Seen in Sylhet and Chittagong Hill Tracts.

Red Flying Squirrel *Petaurista petaurista albiventer*. Occurs in Gilgit Agency.

[Woolly Flying Squirrel *Eupetaurus cinereus*. Occurs in Gilgit, Hazara, Dhir, Swat and Chitral. A slightly doubtful sighting in Naltar.]

Smaller Kashmir Flying Squirrel *Hylopetes fimbriatus fimbriatus*. Occurs in Gilgit Agency.

[Grey Hamster *Cricetulus migratorius fulvus*. One seen in Gilgit Agency.]

Little Hairy-footed Gerbil *Gerbillus gleadowi*. Plentiful in Sind.

Indian Gerbil *Tatera indica indica*. Occurs in Sind, W. Punjab and Baluchistan. Seen Cholistan.

Desert Jird *Meriones hurrianae*. Common in dry regions of Sind.

Little Sand Jird *Meriones crassus swinhoei*. Seen captive; status not ascertained: plate 41*b*.

Western Greater Metad *Millardia meltada pallidor*. Common in abandoned cultivation throughout Sind and Bahawalpur.

Lesser Metad *Millardia gleadowi*. Occurs in Sind and W. Punjab.

House Rat *Rattus rattus*. Abundant in W. and E. Pakistan.

Turkestan Rat *Rattus rattoides turkestanicus*. One found drowned in Gilgit.

Short-tailed Mole Rat *Nesokia indica scullyi*. Occurs in Gilgit. *N. i. indica* is abundant in some regions of W. Pakistan.

Bird-foot Pygmy Jerboa *Salpingotus michaelis*. Seen captive; status not ascertained.

Crested Indian Porcupine *Hystrix indica indica*. Numerous throughout Pakistan: plate 59*b*.

Crestless Indian Porcupine *Hystrix hodgsoni hodgsoni*. Seen Sylhet.

[Brush-tailed Porcupine *Atherurus macrourus assamensis*. Seen in Chittagong Hill Tracts.]

Cetacea

[Gangetic Dolphin *Platanista gangetica*. Unconfirmed sightings in freshwater areas of Indus Delta and Sunderbans and in Sylhet.]

Plumbeous Dolphin *Sousa plumbea*. Fairly numerous in Indus Delta.

[Common Dolphin *Delphinus delphis*. Unconfirmed sightings at mouth of Indus and mouth of Pusur River (E. Pakistan).]

Little Indian Porpoise *Neomeris phocaenoides*. Recently killed specimen seen in Sunderbans.

Carnivora

Wolf *Canis lupus*. Desert race *C. l. pallipes* seen at Kharrar *jheel*; Himalayan race *C. l. chanco* numerous in Gilgit Agency.

Jackal *Canis aureus*. Western race *C. a. aureus* fairly common in W. Pakistan; eastern race *C. a. indicus* common in Sylhet and probably elsewhere in E. Pakistan.

Hill Fox *Vulpes vulpes montana*. Occurs in northern valleys of Gilgit, Chitral and Kashmir.

Desert Fox *Vulpes vulpes griffithi*. Occurs in southern parts of Gilgit, where it is probably sympatric with *V. v. montana*.

White-footed Fox *Vulpes vulpes pusilla*. Seen Salt Range and Indus Delta. May hybridise with *V. v. montana* where their ranges overlap.

Himalayan Black Bear *Selanarctos thibetanus laniger*. Occurs in high forests of
Gilgit Agency and northern mountains of W. Pakistan southward to
the Murree Hills. *S. t. gedrosianus* occurs in Baluchistan, Mekran and
Kharan.

Brown Bear *Ursus arctos isabellinus*. Occurs in very small numbers, usually
above the tree line, in Gilgit Agency, Chitral, Baltistan and Kashmir.

Alpine Weasel *Mustela altaica temon*. Fairly common in parts of Gilgit Agency,
Hunza, Chitral and Karakoram Range.

Stone Marten *Martes foina intermedia*. Occurs throughout Gilgit Agency,
northern regions of W. Pakistan and Baluchistan above 5,000 feet.

Ratel (Honey Badger) *Mellivora capensis indica*. Occurs in Sind, Bahawalpur
and southern Baluchistan.

Common Otter *Lutra lutra kutab*. Occurs in Gilgit, Swat, Dhir, Chitral and
Kashmir.

Indian Smooth Otter *Lutra perspicillata sindica*. Severely persecuted by skin
traders and becoming rare, particularly in W. Pakistan: plate 56.

Small Indian Civet *Viverricula indica bengalensis*. Fairly common around
cultivation and villages in Sind and W. Punjab. *V. i. thaii* occurs in E.
Pakistan.

Palm Civet *Paradoxurus hermaphroditus pallasi*. Seen in Chittagong Hill Tracts
and Sunderbans. Status not ascertained.

Small Indian Mongoose *Herpestes auropunctatus*. Western race *H. a. pallipes*
seen Masan and Indus Delta; eastern race *H. a. auropunctatus* seen Sylhet.

Indian Mongoose *Herpestes edwardsi*. Desert race *H. e. ferrugineus* seen in
Cholistan; eastern race *H. e. nyula* common in E. Pakistan.

Striped Hyena *Hyaena hyaena*. Occurs throughout open country in W. and E.
Pakistan.

Desert Cat *Felis libyca*. Fairly plentiful in drier parts of W. Pakistan.

Jungle Cat *Felis chaus prateri*. Fairly plentiful in parts of W. Pakistan; status
not ascertained in E. Pakistan.

Leopard Cat *Felis bengalensis trevelyani*. Occurs in Gilgit, Swat, Chitral,
Kashmir, Murree Hills; *F. b. bengalensis* occurs in E. Pakistan.

Indian Caracal *Felis caracal schmitzi*. Becoming rare, though still fair numbers
in Baluchistan and Thar Desert regions: plate 20.

Lynx *Felis lynx isabellina*. A few still occur in Gilgit, Chitral, Baltistan, Hunza
and Kashmir.

Marbled Cat *Felis marmorata*. Now very rare in Pakistan. Seen in southern
Chittagong Hill Tracts in 1968. Occurs in Assam, Burma, Nepal and
Sikkim.

Golden Cat *Felis temminckii*. Now extremely rare. Seen in Sylhet. A few still occur in Chittagong Hill Tracts, Nepal, Sikkim and Assam.

Fishing Cat *Felis viverrina*. Becoming rare. Occurs in Indus Valley south of Larkana and in Indus Delta and Sunderbans.

Clouded Leopard *Neofelis nebulosa macrosceloides*. Declining rapidly. Occurs in Pakistan only in Chittagong Hill Tracts and near Assam–Tripura borders: plate 59*a*.

Tiger *Panthera tigris*. Rapidly declining. A few still remain in Chittagong Hill Tracts; vagrants occur in Sylhet Division; between 50–100 remain in Sunderbans: plates 46*b*, 51*a*.

Leopard *Panthera pardus*. Evidence of presence in Gilgit, Masan and Salt Range (*P. p. saxicola*); in Sylhet and Chittagong Hill Tracts (*P. p. fusca*); and Kirthar Range (*P. p. sindica*): plate 51*b*.

Snow Leopard *Panthera uncia*. Severely exploited by skin traders and hunters; declining rapidly. Occurs in small numbers in Gilgit, Hunza, Chitral, Baltistan and Kashmir.

[Asiatic Cheetah *Acionyx jubatus venaticus*. Two reported shot in Mekran area in 1967. Though generally regarded as extinct, this species may still be surviving, though unlikely to recover.]

Proboscidea

Indian Elephant *Elephas maximus*. Becoming scarce. A few remain in the Chittagong Hill Tracts and along the Assam–Tripura borders.

Perissodactyla

[Indian Wild Ass *Equus hemionus khur*. Between 20–30 reported to occur regularly in Great Rann of Kutch, where several have been shot recently. Main population is in Indian Little Rann.]

[Two-horned Rhinoceros *Didermocerus sumatrensis*. One shot in Chittagong Hill Tracts in 1967, a vagrant from Burma.]

Artiodactyla

Wild Boar *Sus scrofa cristatus*. Abundant and increasing everywhere.

Musk Deer *Moschus moschiferus moschiferus*. Severely persecuted for its musk pods. Occurs in small numbers in Gilgit, northern Hazara, Baltistan and Kashmir.

Barking Deer (Muntjac) *Muntiacus muntjak*. Fairly plentiful in Sylhet Division, Mymensingh and Chittagong Hill Tracts. Also occurs in parts of Swat, Hazara, Dhir and Kashmir: plate 57*a*.

Chital (Axis Deer) *Axis axis*. Population drastically reduced. Still plentiful only in Sunderbans; a few in Mymensingh and Chittagong Hill Tracts: plate 50*a*.

Hog Deer *Axis porcinus*. Fairly common in Sind; a few occur in Indus Delta and northern parts of Sunderbans. Status elsewhere not ascertained.

Sambur *Cervus unicolor equinus*. A few occur in Chittagong Hill Tracts and Sylhet; status elsewhere not ascertained: plate 50*b*.

Nilgai *Boselaphus tragocamelus*. Nearing extinction in a wild state in Pakistan, though vagrants from India occur in Soleimanke, Bahawalpur and extreme north-west of East Pakistan.

Gaur *Bos gaurus*. In Pakistan now probably survives only in southern Chittagong Hill Tracts, where several were seen in 1968.

Gayal *Bos gaurus frontalis*. Occurs in wild state in Chittagong Hill Tracts, where three were seen: plate 8*b*.

Blackbuck *Antilope cervicapra*. Nearing extinction in Pakistan. Only one seen, near Fort Abbas; a herd of twelve was reported here in 1968.

Chinkara (Indian Gazelle) *Gazella gazella*. Now very scarce. Largest remaining numbers in Iran–Baluchistan border region and Mekran; a few remain in Bahawalpur, Salt Range and Kirthar Range: plate 11*b*.

Serow *Capricornis sumatraensis*. Rare in Pakistan. Seen in the southern Chittagong Hill Tracts in 1968. Occurs in Assam and Burma.

Persian Wild Goat (Sind Ibex) *Capra hircus blythi*. Still plentiful in Kirthar Range, though declining. Also occurs in Baluchistan south of Quetta Division: plate 37*b*.

Himalayan Ibex *Capra ibex sibirica*. Population in Gilgit Agency reduced to about 3,000 and declining. Also occurs in Chitral, Baltistan, Hunza and Kashmir.

Astor Markhor *Capra falconeri falconeri*. Population in Gilgit Agency down to about 1,000 and declining. Also occurs in Baltistan: plate 32*a*.

Shapu *Ovis orientalis vignei*. Reduced to about 500 in Gilgit Agency. Also occurs in Chitral, Baltistan and Kashmir: plate 32*b*.

Punjab Urial *Ovis orientalis punjabiensis*. Now occurs only in Salt Range, where about 500 are secure in Kalabagh Reserve: plates 8*a*, 11*a*.

Baluchistan Urial *Ovis orientalis blanfordi*. Declining, though still in fair numbers. Occurs in Kirthar Range and extends to southern Iran.

Marco Polo's Sheep *Ovis ammon polii*. A few still occur in Hunza and Karakoram Range, though severely hunted. Breeding area in Russian Pamirs is relatively secure.

List of amphibians and reptiles observed in Pakistan

Marsh Crocodile *Crocodilus palustris*: plate 49*a*

Estuarine Crocodile *Crocodilus porosus*

Gharial *Gavialis gangeticus*: plate 49*b*

Grey Indian Monitor *Varanus bengalensis*

Ocellated Water Monitor *Varanus salvator*

Tricolor Caspian Monitor *Varanus griseus caspicus*: plate 14*b*

Eastern Yellow Desert Monitor *Varanus griseus konieczuyi*

Ruddy Snub-nosed Monitor *Varanus flavescens*

Blue-throated Rock Agama *Agama nupta*

Blue-fronted Sand Agama *Agama agilis*

Spiny-tailed Ground Agama *Uromastix hardwickei*

Bloodsucker Tree Agama *Calotes versicolor*: plate 21*b*

Saffron-bellied Wall Gecko *Hemidactylus flaviviridis*

Leopard Gecko *Eublepharis fasciolatus*: plate 3*a*

Merton's Tokay *Gecko gecko azhari*: plate 29*a*

Blue-tailed Sand Lizard *Acanthodactylus cantoris*

Jerdon's Little Lacertid *Ophisops jerdoni*

Common Sand Fish *Ophiomorus raithmai*

Five-lined Grass Skink *Mayuba dissimilis*

Chequered Keelback *Fowlea piscator*

Indian Sand Boa *Eryx johni*

Cliff Racer *Coluber rhodorhachis*

Common Racer *Coluber ventromaculatus*

Common Krait *Bungarus caeruleus*

Black Cobra *Naja naja naja*: plate 3*b*

Monocled Cobra *Naja naja kuthia*

Gama Cat Snake *Boiga trigonata trigonata*

Macmahon's Sand Viper *Eristicophis macmahoni*

Russell's Viper *Vipera russelli*: plate 14*a*

Indian Diadem Rat Snake *Spalerosophis diadema diadema*

Royal Sand Rat Snake *Spalerosophis arenarius*

Rock Python *Python molurus*: plate 29*b*

Reticulated Python *Python reticulatus*: plate 23*a and b*

Banded Sea Snake *Hydrophis mammalaris*

Beaked Deep Sea Snake *Enhydrina schistoza*: plate 55*b*

Flap-shelled Spotted Turtle *Lissemys punctata punctata*

Sacred Black Mud Turtle *Trionyx nigricans*

Roof Turtle *Machuga tecta tecta*

Indian Star Tortoise *Testudo elegans elegans*

Four-toed Tortoise *Testudo horsfieldis horsfieldis*

Skittering Frog *Rana cyanophlyctis*

Streaked Cricket Frog *Rana limnocharis*

Indian Tiger Bull Frog *Rana tigrina*

Indus Valley Toad *Bufo andersoni*

South Asian Garden Toad *Bufo melanostictus*

List of birds observed in Pakistan

This list refers to the 423 species identified in West or East Pakistan from mid-October to mid-December 1966 and 1967. Subspecific scientific names are given where a known race was involved (frequently different races occur in the two Provinces). In the space available it is possible to give only the broadest indications as to status, which in some instances is still a matter of conjecture. The following codes are used: R=resident breeding species; these are often restricted to very small areas within the Province. w=winter visitor, usually referring to regular migrants. v=vagrants or occasional visitors. x= rare species. ?=doubtful status. Square brackets indicate slightly doubtful identification. Full details as to numbers and localities are given in the expedition reports. Nomenclature follows Ripley's *A Synopsis of the Birds of India and Pakistan*.

	W.Pak.	*E.Pak.*
Great Crested Grebe *Podiceps cristatus*	w	w
Black-necked Grebe *Podiceps caspicus*	w	?
Little Grebe *Podiceps ruficollis*	R	R
White Pelican *Pelecanus onocrotalus*	w	?
Spot-bill Pelican *Pelecanus philippensis*	w	w
Cormorant *Phalacrocorax carbo*: plate 42c	R	R
Little Cormorant *Phalacrocorax niger*: plate 4a	R	R
Darter *Anhinga rufa*: plate 42a	R	R
Grey Heron *Ardea cinerea*	R	R
Purple Heron *Ardea purpurea*	R	R
Little Green Heron *Butorides striatus javanicus*: plate 50b	R	R
Pond Heron *Ardeola grayii*: plate 58b	R	R
Chinese Pond Heron *Ardeola bacchus*	—	v
Cattle Egret *Bulbulcus ibis coromandus*	R	R
Great White Egret *Egretta alba modesta*: plate 4a	R	R
Intermediate Egret *Egretta intermedia palleuca*	—	R
Little Egret *Egretta garzetta*: plate 4a	R	R

	W.Pak.	E.Pak.
Indian Reef Heron *Egretta gularis*: plate 40a	R	—
Night Heron *Nycticorax nycticorax*	R	R
Little Bittern *Ixobrychus minutus*	R	V
Chestnut Bittern *Ixobrychus cinnamomeus*	RX	R
Painted Stork *Ibis leucocephalus*: plate 44	RX	R
Black-necked Stork *Xenorhynchus asiaticus*	RX	R
Adjutant *Leptoptilos dubius*: plate 50a	V	R
Lesser Adjutant *Leptoptilos javanicus*	?	R
White Ibis *Threskiornis melanocephala*	R	R
Glossy Ibis *Plegadis falcinellus*	V	R
Spoonbill *Platalea leucorodia major*	R	RX
Flamingo *Phoenicopterus ruber*	R	V
[Forest Bean Goose *Anser fabilis middendorffi*	—	w]
Grey Lag Goose *Anser anser rubirostris*	w	w
Bar-headed Goose *Anser indicus*	w	w
Lesser Whistling Teal *Dendrocygna javanica*	V	R
Large Whistling Teal *Dendrocygna bicolor*	—	R
Ruddy Shelduck *Tadorna ferruginea*	w	w
Shelduck *Tadorna tadorna*	w	V
Pintail *Anas acuta*	w	w
Teal *Anas crecca*	w	w
Spotbill Duck *Anas poecilorhyncha*	R	R
Mallard *Anas platyrhynchos*	w	w
Gadwall *Anas strepera*	w	w
Wigeon *Anas penelope*	w	w
Garganey *Anas querquedula*	w	w
Shoveler *Anas clypeata*	w	w
Pochard *Aythya ferina*	w	w
Ferruginous Duck *Aythya nyroca*	w	w
Tufted Duck *Aythya fuligula*	w	w
Cotton Teal *Nettapus coromandelianus*	R	w
White-headed Duck *Oxyura leucocephala*	wx	—
Black-winged Kite *Elanus caeruleus vociferus*	R	R
Honey Buzzard *Pernis ptilorhynchus ruficollis*: plate 19a	R	R
Black Kite *Milvus migrans*: plate 2b	R	R
Black-eared Kite *Milvus migrans lineatus*	w	—
Brahminy Kite *Haliastur indus*: plate 5b	R	R
Goshawk *Accipiter gentilis schvedowi*: plate 13a	V	—

	W.Pak.	E.Pak.
Shikra *Accipiter badius*	R	R
Sparrow Hawk *Accipiter nisus*	V	W
Long-legged Buzzard *Buteo rufinus*	W	—
White-eyed Buzzard *Butastur teesa*: plate 2*a*	R	R
Bonelli's Eagle *Nisaetus fasciatus*	R	R?
Golden Eagle *Aquila chrysaetos hodgsoni*	R	—
Imperial Eagle *Aquila heliaca*	W	W
Tawny Eagle *Aquila rapax vindhiana*: plate 1	R	R
Steppe Eagle *Aquila nipalensis*	R?	W
Greater Spotted Eagle *Aquila clanga*	R	W
Lesser Spotted Eagle *Aquila pomarina hasitata*	V?	R
White-bellied Sea Eagle *Haliaeetus leucogaster*: plate 47	—	R
Pallas's Fishing Eagle *Haliaeetus leucoryphus*: plate 19*b*	R	R
Grey-headed Fishing Eagle *Icthyophaga ichthyaetus*	—	R
Black Vulture *Torgos calvus*	R	R
Griffon Vulture *Gyps fulvus*	R	V
Himalayan Griffon Vulture *Gyps himalayensis*	R	—
Long-billed Vulture *Gyps indicus jonesi*	R	R
White-backed Vulture *Gyps bengalensis*: plates 17*a*, 18	R	R
Egyptian Vulture *Neophron percnopterus*	R	?
Bearded Vulture (Lammergeier) *Gypaetus barbatus aureus*: plate 35*a*	R	—
Pallid Harrier *Circus macrourus*	W	W
Montagu's Harrier *Circus pygargus*	W	W
Pied Harrier *Circus melanoleucos*	—	W
Marsh Harrier *Circus aeruginosus*	W	W
Crested Serpent Eagle *Spilornis cheela*: plate 48*a*	V	R
Osprey *Pandion haliaetus*	W	W
Laggar *Falco biarmicus jugger*: plate 5*a*	R	R
Peregrine *Falco peregrinus japonensis*	W	W
Red-capped Falcon *Falco peregrinus babylonicus*	R	—
Shahin *Falco peregrinus peregrinator*	R	R
Hobby *Falco subbuteo subbuteo*	WX	W
Oriental Hobby *Falco severus rufipedoides*	R	W
Red-headed Merlin *Falco chicquera*	R	R
Kestrel *Falco tinnunculus*	R	W
Seesee Partridge *Ammoperdix griseogularis*	R	W
Himalayan Snow Cock *Tetraogallus himalayensis*	R	—
Chukor Partridge *Alectoris graeca*	R	—

	W.Pak.	E.Pak.
Black Partridge *Francolinus francolinus*	R	R
Grey Partridge *Francolinus pondicerianus mecranensis*	R	—
Swamp Partridge *Francolinus gularis*	—	R
Western Tragopan *Tragopan melanocephalus*	RX	—
Monal (Impeyan) Pheasant *Lophophorus impejanus*: plate 26*a*	RX	—
Black-breasted Kalij *Lophura leucomelana lathami*: plate 58*a*	—	R
Red Jungle Fowl *Gallus gallus*: plate 53*b*	R	R
Peafowl *Pavo cristatus*	R	R
Common Crane *Grus grus*	W	W?
Sarus Crane *Grus antigone*	?	RX
Water Rail *Rallus aquaticus korejewi*	V	W
Little Crake *Porzana parva*	V	—
Ruddy Crake *Amaurornis fuscus bakeri*	R	R
White-breasted Waterhen *Amaurornis phoenicurus chinensis*	R	R
Moorhen *Gallinula chloropus indica*	R	R
Purple Gallinule *Porphyrio porphyrio*	R	R
Coot *Fulica atra*	R	R
Great Indian Bustard *Choriotis nigriceps*	VX	—
Houbara Bustard *Chlamydotis undulata macqueenii*	W	—
Pheasant-tailed Jacana *Hydrophasianus chirurgus*	R	R
Bronze-winged Jacana *Metopidius indicus*	RX	R
Oystercatcher *Haematopus ostralegus*	W	R
Lapwing *Vanellus vanellus*	W	W
Red-wattled Lapwing *Vanellus indicus*: plate 24*b*	R	R
Yellow-wattled Lapwing *Vanellus malabaricus*	V	R
Grey Plover *Pluvialis squatarola*	W	W
Large Sand Plover *Charadrius leschenaultii*: plate 41*a*	W	W
Little Ringed Plover *Charadrius dubius*	R	R
Kentish Plover *Charadrius alexandrinus*	R	W
Lesser Sand Plover *Charadrius mongolus atrifrons*: plate 41*a*	W	W
Whimbrel *Numenius phaeopus*	W	W
Curlew *Numenius arquata*: plate 37*a*	W	W
Bar-tailed Godwit *Limosa lapponica*	W	—
Spotted Redshank *Tringa erythropus*	W	W
Redshank *Tringa totanus*	W	W
Marsh Sandpiper *Tringa stagnatilis*	W	W
Greenshank *Tringa nebularia*	W	W
Green Sandpiper *Tringa ochropus*	W	W

	W.Pak.	E.Pak.
Wood Sandpiper *Tringa glareola*	w	w
Terek Sandpiper *Tringa terek*: plate 37*b*	w	w
Common Sandpiper *Tringa hypoleucos*	w	w
Solitary Snipe *Capella solitaria*	w	v
Pintail Snipe *Capella stenura*	?	w
Great Snipe *Capella media*	—	vx
Fantail Snipe *Capella gallinago*	w	w
Jack Snipe *Capella minima*	w	w
Eastern Knot *Calidris tenuirostris*	w	w
Sanderling *Calidris albus*	w	w
Little Stint *Calidris minutus*	w	w
Temminck's Stint *Calidris temminckii*	w	w
Dunlin *Calidris alpina*: plate 37*b*	w	w
Ruff *Philomachus pugnax*	w	w
Black-winged Stilt *Himantopus himantopus*	R	R
Avocet *Recurvirostra avosetta*	w	w?
Crab Plover *Dromas ardeola*	wx	—
Stone Curlew *Burhinus oedicnemus*	R	R
Great Stone Plover *Esacus magnirostris recurvirostris*	w	R
Indian Courser *Cursorius coromandelicus*	R	R
Herring Gull *Larus argentatus heuglini*	w	w
Lesser Black-backed Gull *Larus fuscus*	w	v
Great Black-headed Gull *Larus ichthyaetus*	w	w
Brown-headed Gull *Larus brunnicephalus*: plate 43*a*	w	w
Black-headed Gull *Larus ridibundus*	w	w
Slender-billed Gull *Larus genei*	R	—
Whiskered Tern *Chlidonias hybrida indica*	R	w
Gull-billed Tern *Gelochelidon nilotica*	R	R
Caspian Tern *Hydroprogne caspia*	w	w
Indian River Tern *Sterna aurantia*	R	R
Black-bellied Tern *Sterna acuticauda*	R	R
Little Tern *Sterna albifrons*	R	R
Lesser Crested Tern *Sterna bengalensis*: plate 43*b*	R	R
Indian Sandgrouse *Pterocles exustus erlangeri*	R	—
Imperial Sandgrouse *Pterocles orientalis*: plate 4*b*	R	—
Close-barred Sandgrouse *Pterocles indicus*	R	v
Thick-billed Green Pigeon *Treron curvirostra nipalensis*	—	R?
Orange-breasted Green Pigeon *Treron bicincta*	—	R

	W.Pak.	E.Pak.
Green Pigeon *Treron phoenicoptera*	V?	R
Green Imperial Pigeon *Ducula aenea sylvatica*	—	R
Blue Rock Pigeon *Columba livia*	R	R
Wood Pigeon *Columba palumbus casiotis*	RX	—
Purple Wood Pigeon *Columba punicea*	—	R
Turtle Dove *Streptopelia turtur*	VX	—
Rufous Turtle Dove *Streptopelia orientalis*	V	R
Collared Dove *Streptopelia decaocto*	R	R
Red Turtle Dove *Streptopelia tranquebarica*	V	R
Spotted Dove *Streptopelia chinensis tigrina*	—	R
Little Brown Dove *Streptopelia senegalensis cambayensis*	R	R?
Emerald Dove *Chalcophaps indica*	—	R
Large Indian Parakeet *Psittacula eupatria nipalensis*	R	R
Rose-ringed Parakeet *Psittacula krameri borealis*: plate 6a	R	R
Red-breasted Parakeet *Psittacula alexandri fasciata*	—	R
Eastern Blossom-headed Parakeet *Psittacula roseata*	—	R
Pied Crested Cuckoo *Clamator jacobinus serratus*	—	V?
Common Hawk-Cuckoo *Cuculus varius*	—	R
Koel *Eudynamys scolopacea*	R	R
Large Green-billed Malkoha *Rhopodytes tristis*: plate 55a	—	R
Crow-Pheasant *Centropus sinensis*	R	R
Lesser Coucal *Centropus toulou bengalensis*	—	R
Barn Owl *Tyto alba stertens*	R	R
Collared Scops Owl *Otus bakkamoena*	R	R
Turkestan Eagle Owl *Bubo bubo turcomanus*	RX	—
Brown Fish Owl *Bubo zeylonensis leschenaulti*	R	R
Barred Owlet *Glaucidium cuculoides rufescens*	—	R
Spotted Owlet *Athene brama indica*: plate 22a	R	R
Short-eared Owl *Asio flammeus*	V	W
Indian Jungle Nightjar *Caprimulgus indicus*: plate 48b	W	R
Hume's Nightjar *Caprimulgus europaeus unwini*	R	—
Long-tailed Nightjar *Caprimulgus macrurus*	R	R
Indian Nightjar *Caprimulgus asiaticus*	R	R
Franklin's Nightjar *Caprimulgus affinis*	R	R
Alpine Swift *Apus melba*	W	W
House Swift *Apus affinis*	R	R
Palm Swift *Cypsiurus parvus infumatus*	—	R
Red-headed Trogon *Harpactes erythrocephalus*	—	RX

	W.Pak.	E.Pak.
Lesser Pied Kingfisher *Cyrule rudis leucomelanura*	R	R
Common Kingfisher *Alcedo atthis*	R	R
Blue-eared Kingfisher *Alcedo meninting coltarti*	—	R
Brown-winged Kingfisher *Pelargopsis amauroptera*: plate 25b	—	R
Stork-billed Kingfisher *Pelargopsis capensis*: plate 54b	—	R
Ruddy Kingfisher *Halcyon coromanda*	—	R
White-breasted Kingfisher *Halcyon smyrnensis*	R	R
Black-capped Kingfisher *Halcyon pileata*: plate 54a	—	R
White-collared Kingfisher *Halcyon chloris humii*: plate 25a	—	R
Chestnut-headed Bee-eater *Merops leschenaulti*	—	R
Blue-tailed Bee-eater *Merops philippinus*	R	R
Green Bee-eater *Merops orientalis*: plate 6b	R	R
Indian Roller *Coracias benghalensis*	R	R
Hoopoe *Upupa epops*	R	R
Indian Pied Hornbill *Anthracoceros malabaricus*: plate 24a	—	R
Lineated Barbet *Megalaima lineata hodgsoni*	—	R
Blue-throated Barbet *Megalaima asiatica*	—	R
Crimson-breasted Barbet *Megalaima haemacephala indica*	R	R
Wryneck *Jynx torquilla chinensis*	R	W
Speckled Piculet *Picumnus innominatur malayorum*	—	R
Rufous Woodpecker *Micropternus brachyurus phaioceps*	—	R
Scaly-bellied Green Woodpecker *Picus squamatus squamatus*	R	—
Large Yellow-naped Woodpecker *Picus flacinucha flacinucha*	—	R
Lesser Golden-backed Woodpecker *Dinopium benghalense*	R	R
Sind Pied Woodpecker *Dendrocopos assimilis*	R	—
Himalayan Pied Woodpecker *Dendrocopos himalayensis albescens*	R	—
Brown-fronted Pied Woodpecker *Dendrocopos auriceps auriceps*	R	—
Fulvous-breasted Pied Woodpecker *Dendrocopos macei macei*	R	R
Yellow-fronted Pied Woodpecker		
Dendrocopos mahrattensis mahrattensis	R	R
Pygmy Woodpecker *Dendrocopos nanus nanus*	R	R
Large Golden-backed Woodpecker		
Chrysocolaptes lucidus guttacristatus	—	R
Singing Bush Lark *Mirafra javanica*	R	R
Red-winged Bush Lark *Mirafra erythroptera*	R	V
Ashy-crowned Finch-lark *Eremopterix grisea*	R	R
Black-crowned Finch-Lark *Eremopterix nigriceps affinis*	R	—
Desert Lark *Ammonanes deserti phoenicuroides*	R	—

	W.Pak.	E.Pak.
Hoopoe Lark *Alaemon alaudipes doriae*	R	—
Short-toed Lark *Calandrella cinerea*	W	W
Sand Lark *Calandrella raytal*	R	R
Horned Lark *Eremophila alpestris albigula*	R	—
Crested Lark *Galerida cristata*	R	—
Sky Lark *Alauda arvensis dulcivox*	W	—
Eastern Sky Lark *Alauda gulgula*	R	R
Collared Sand Martin *Riparia riparia diluta*	R	R
Plain Sand Martin *Riparia paludicola chinensis*	R	R
Crag Martin *Hirundo rupestris*	W	—
Pale Crag Martin *Hirundo obsoleta pallida*	W	—
Swallow *Hirundo rustica*	W	W
Wire-tailed Swallow *Hirundo smithii filifera*	W	R
Striated (Red-rumped) Swallow *Hirundo daurica japonica*	—	W
House Martin *Delichon urbica*	W	W
Great Grey Shrike *Lanius excubitor*	R	V?
Bay-backed Shrike *Lanius vittatus*	R	R?
Isabelline Shrike *Lanius collurio isabellinus*	W	—
Grey-backed (Tibetan) Shrike *Lanius tephronotus*	—	W
Rufous-backed Shrike *Lanius schach erythronotus*	R	—
Black-headed Shrike *Lanius schach tricolor*: plate 16a	—	R?
Brown Shrike *Lanius cristatus cristatus*	—	W
Golden Oriole *Oriolus oriolus*	R?	V
Black-naped Oriole *Oriolus chinensis diffusus*	—	R
Black-headed Oriole *Oriolus xanthornus xanthornus*	—	R
Black Drongo *Dicrurus adsimilis albirictus*	R	R
Grey Drongo *Dicrurus leucophaeus hopwoodi*	—	R
White-bellied Drongo *Dicrurus caerulescens caerulescens*	—	R?
Bronzed Drongo *Dicrurus aeneus aeneus*	—	R
Greater Racket-tailed Drongo *Dicrurus paradiseus grandis*	—	R
Ashy Swallow-Shrike *Artamus fuscus*	—	R
Glossy Stare *Aplonis panayensis affinis*	—	R
Grey-headed Myna *Sturnus malabaricus malabaricus*	—	R
Rosy Pastor *Sturnus roseus*	W	—
Common Starling *Sturnus vulgaris*	R	—
Pied Myna *Sturnus contra*	—	R
Common Myna *Acridotheres tristis*: plate 16b	R	R
Bank Myna *Acridotheres ginginianus*	R	R

	W.Pak.	E.Pak.
Jungle Myna *Acridotheres fuscus*	R	R
Yellow-billed Blue Magpie *Kitta flavirostris cucullatus*	R	—
Magpie *Pica pica bactriana*	R	—
Indian Tree Pie *Dendrocitta vagabunda*	R	R
Himalayan Tree Pie *Dendrocitta formosae*	R	—
Nutcracker *Nucifraga caryocatactes multipunctata*	R	—
Yellow-billed Chough *Pyrrhocorax graculus digitatus*	R	—
Red-billed Chough *Pyrrhocorax pyrrhocorax centralis*	R	—
House Crow *Corvus splendens*: plate 17b	R	R
Jungle Crow *Corvus macrorhynchos*: plate 17b	R	R
[Carrion Crow *Corvus corone orientalis*	w?	—]
Raven *Corvus corax*	R	—
Pied Flycatcher-Shrike *Hemipus picatus*	—	R
Common Wood Shrike *Tephrodornis pondicerianus*	R	R
Large Cuckoo-Shrike *Coracina novaehollandiae*	—	R
Smaller Grey Cuckoo-Shrike *Coracina melaschistos melaschistos*	R	W
Scarlet Minivet *Pericrocotus flammeus*	—	R
Short-billed Minivet *Pericrocotus brevirostris*	W	R
Small Minivet *Pericrocotus cinnamomeus*	R	R
Common Iora *Aegithina tiphia*	?	R
Gold-fronted Chloropsis *Chloropsis aurifrons*	—	R
Gold-mantled Chloropsis *Chloropsis cochinchinensis*	—	R
Black-headed Bulbul *Pycnonotus atriceps cinereoventris*	—	R
Black-headed Yellow Bulbul *Pycnonotus melanicterus flaviventris*	—	R
Red-whiskered Bulbul *Pycnonotus jocosus*	—	R
White-cheeked Bulbul *Pycnonotus leucogenys*	R	—
Red-vented Bulbul *Pycnonotus cafer*	R	R
White-throated Bulbul *Criniger flaveolus flaveolus*	—	R
Black Bulbul *Hypsipetes madagascariensis*	R	R
Spotted Babbler *Pellorneum ruficeps*	—	R
[Slaty-headed Scimitar Babbler *Pomatorhinus schisticeps*	—	R]
Rufous-bellied Babbler *Dumetia hyperythra*	—	R
Common Babbler *Turdoides caudatus*	R	R?
Striated Babbler *Turdoides earlei*	R	R
Jungle Babbler *Turdoides striatus*	R	R
[Black-gorgeted Laughing Thrush *Garrulax pectoralis melanotis*	—	R]
Variegated Laughing Thrush *Garrulax variegatum simile*	R	—
Streaked Laughing Thrush *Garrulax lineatus*	R	—

	W.Pak.	E.Pak.
Quaker Babbler *Alcippe poioicephala fusca*	—	R
Sooty Flycatcher *Muscicapa sibirica gulmergi*	R	W
Red-breasted Flycatcher *Muscicapa parva*	W	W
Little Pied Flycatcher *Muscicapa westermanni*	—	W
Verditer Flycatcher *Muscicapa thalassina*	—	W
Grey-headed Flycatcher *Culicicapa ceylonensis*	R	R
White-browed Fantail Flycatcher *Rhipidura aureola*	R	R
White-spotted Fantail Flycatcher *Rhipidura albogularis*	W	—
Paradise Flycatcher *Terpsiphone paradisi*	R	R
Black-naped Flycatcher *Monarcha azurea*	—	R
Streaked Fantail Warbler *Cisticola juncidis cursitans*	R	R
Franklin's Longtail Warbler *Prinia hodgsonii rufula*	R	R
Rufous-fronted Longtail Warbler *Prinia buchanani*	R	—
Streaked Longtail Warbler *Prinia gracilis*	R	R
Plain Longtail Warbler *Prinia subflava*	R	R
Ashy Longtail Warbler *Prinia socialis inglisi*	R	R
Yellow-bellied Longtail Warbler *Prinia flaviventris sindiana*	R	R
Longtailed Grass Warbler *Prinia burnesii*	R	R
Streaked Scrub Warbler *Scotocerca inquieta striata*	R	—
Tailor Bird *Orthotomus sutorius*	R	R
Striated Marsh Warbler *Megalurus palustris toklao*	?	R
Indian Great Reed Warbler *Acrocephalus stentoreus*	R	W
Paddyfield Warbler *Acrocephalus agricola*	W	W
Lesser Whitethroat *Sylvia curruca*	R	—
Chiffchaff *Phylloscopus collybita*	R	W
Yellow-browed Leaf Warbler *Phylloscopus inornatus*	W	W
Greenish Leaf Warbler *Phylloscopus trochiloides*	—	W
Blyth's Leaf Warbler *Phylloscopus reguloides*	—	W
Grey-headed Flycatcher-Warbler *Seicercus xanthoschistos albo-superciliaris*	—	W
Yellow-bellied Flycatcher-Warbler *Abroscopus superciliaris*	—	R
Stoliczka's Tit-Warbler *Leptopoecile sophiae sophiae*	R	—
Bluethroat *Erithacus svecicus*	R	W
Magpie-Robin *Copsychus saularis*	R	R
Shama *Copsychus malabaricus indicus*	—	R
Blue-headed Redstart *Phoenicurus caeruleocephalus*	R	—
Black Redstart *Phoenicurus ochruros*	R	W
Güldenstädt's Redstart *Phoenicurus erythrogaster grandis*	R	W

	W.Pak.	E.Pak.
Plumbeous Redstart *Phyacornis fuliginosus*	R	W
Little Forktail *Enicurus scouleri*	R	R
Black-backed Forktail *Enicurus immaculatus*	—	R
Stonechat *Saxicola torquata*	W	W
Pied Bush Chat *Saxicola caprata*	R	R
Isabelline Wheatear *Oenanthe isabellina*	R	—
Red-tailed Chat *Oenanthe xanthoprymna kingi*	W	—
Desert Chat *Oenanthe deserti deserti*	R	—
Pied Chat *Oenanthe picata*	W	—
Hume's Chat *Oenanthe alboniger*	R	—
White-capped Redstart *Chaimarrornis leucocephalus*	R	W ?
Indian Robin *Saxicoloides fulicata*	R	R
Rock Thrush *Monticola saxatilis*	W	—
Blue Rock Thrush *Monticola solitarius*	R	W
[Malabar Whistling Thrush *Myiophoneus horsfieldii*	VX	—]
Blue Whistling Thrush *Myiophoneus caeruleus temminckii*	R	R
Orange-headed Ground Thrush *Zoothera citrina*	R	R
Tickell's Thrush *Turdus unicolor*	R	W
Dusky Thrush *Turdus obscurus*	—	W
Black-throated Thrush *Turdus ruficollis atrogularis*	W	W
Mistle Thrush *Turdus viscivorus bonapartei*	R	—
Wren *Troglodytes troglodytes neglectus*	R	—
Brown Dipper *Cinclus pallasii tenuirostris*	R	W
Rufous-breasted Accentor *Prunella strophiata jerdoni*	R	—
Grey Tit *Parus major*	R	R
Crested Black Tit *Parus melanolophus*	R	—
Rufous-bellied Crested Tit *Parus rubidiventris rufonuchalis*	R	—
Chestnut-bellied Nuthatch *Sitta castanea*	R	R
White-cheeked Nuthatch *Sitta leucopsis leucopsis*	R	—
[Velvet-fronted Nuthatch *Sitta frontalis*	—	R]
Wall Creeper *Tichodroma muraria nepalensis*: plate 26*b*	R	—
Himalayan Tree Creeper *Certhia himalayana*	R	W
Hodgson's Tree Pipit *Anthus hodgsoni hodgsoni*	—	W
Tree Pipit *Anthus trivialis*	W	W
Paddyfield (Richard's) Pipit *Anthus novaeseelandiae*	W	R
Tawny Pipit *Anthus campestris campestris*	W	W
Hodgson's Pipit *Anthus pelopus*	R	W
Water Pipit *Anthus spinoletta coutelli*	W	W

	W.Pak.	E.Pak.
Yellow Wagtail *Motacilla flava*	W	W
Yellow-headed Wagtail *Motacilla citreola*	W	W
Grey Wagtail *Motacilla caspica caspica*	R	W
White Wagtail *Motacilla alba*	R	W
Large Pied Wagtail *Motacilla maderaspatensis*	R	W
Plain-coloured Flowerpecker *Dicaeum concolor olivaceum*	—	R
Scarlet-backed Flowerpecker *Dicaeum cruentatum cruentatum*	—	R
Purple Sunbird *Nectarinia asiatica*	R	R
Yellow-backed Sunbird *Aethopyga siparaja*	—	R
Little Spiderhunter *Aracnothera longirostris longirostris*	—	R
Streaked Spiderhunter *Aracnothera magna magna*	—	R
White-eye *Zosterops palpebrosa palpebrosa*	R	R
House Sparrow *Passer domesticus indicus*	R	R
Tree Sparrow *Passer montanus*	R	R
Sind Jungle Sparrow *Passer pyrrhonotus*	R	—
Cinnamon Tree Sparrow *Passer rutilans cinnamomeus*	R	V
Baya *Ploceus philippinus*	R	R
Streaked Weaver *Ploceus manyar*	R	R
Silverbill *Lonchura malabarica malabarica*	R	R
Black-headed Munia *Lonchura malacca atricapilla*	—	R
Chaffinch *Fringilla coelebs*	VX	—
White-winged Grosbeak *Mycerobas carnipes carnipes*	R	—
Goldfinch *Carduelis carduelis caniceps*	R	—
Hodgson's Mountain Finch *Leucosticte nemoricola altaica*	W	—
Mongolian Trumpeter Finch *Rhodopechys mongolica*	W	—
Common Rosefinch *Carpodacus erythrinus*	R	W
Pine Bunting *Emberiza leucophalos*	W	—
Black-headed Bunting *Emberiza melanocephala*	W	—
White-capped Bunting *Emberiza stewarti*	W	—
Rock Bunting *Emberiza cia*	R	—

Notes on Photography
by Eric Hosking

It has been my privilege to direct the photography on many of Guy Mount-fort's expeditions to various parts of the world. While I have always thoroughly enjoyed the experience, the nature of our work in Pakistan imposed severe limitations on photography. As a perfectionist I prefer to work from a hide and to portray wildlife in detail and at close quarters. This involves remaining in one place for long periods, so that the subject can become accustomed to the presence of a hide. On the Pakistan expeditions this was impossible, because our primary object was to cover as much ground as possible in making a general reconnaissance of the deserts, jungles, mountains and swamps of a very large country.

Thus, our work was essentially mobile and therefore very frustrating to the photographers. We had to seize every opportunity to obtain pictures without ever being able to do full justice to our subjects and certainly without ever erecting a hide. Instead of careful portraiture, therefore, we were usually snap-shooting with telephoto lenses, ranging from 135mm to 1,000mm. Lenses of up to 400mm were used on hand-held cameras mounted on shoulder braces with pistol grips; for greater magnifications a tripod was, of course, essential.

Much of our work was done from moving boats—steamboats, motor launches, or even canoes. This involved additional hazards from vibration, smoke, or heat-haze radiated from metal decks. Jungle photography introduced quite different problems. Inside the jungle, light values were often negligible and high-speed films were necessary. Little animal life is visible during the heat of day and most photography therefore has to be done at dawn or dusk when the animals come out to feed. Jungle tracks and margins are the best places to see birds, but here difficulty is experienced with the brilliance of the sunlight on the foliage and with the harsh contrast of black shadows. Some of the most beautifully coloured small birds, such as the sun-birds and flowerpeckers of Pakistan, dart in and out of the foliage so rapidly that photography is exceptionally difficult. Even birds which habitually hunt for food in the open, such as the kingfishers, usually perch in deep shade between sallies in the sunlight.

Dust was a constant problem when we were working in the deserts or on mountain trails. Plastic bags were used to cover our equipment, but it was necessary to clean all optical apparatus every night very thoroughly. This had to include the working parts of cinema cameras and sound-recording gear also.

Zeiss electronic flash equipment was used for some nocturnal subjects, such as gecko lizards and beetles. Night photography with the aid of static, electronically-fired floodlights was tried with the Tiger, but, as Guy Mount-fort has described in the book, we failed: we did, however, learn the useful lesson that the copious dew which falls in the jungle at night requires the electric connections to be very carefully covered—to say nothing of the need to keep the photographer dry! We are indebted to George Schaller and Peter Jackson for making good our failure with the Tiger. Where we were unable to obtain pictures of one or two other important animals in the wild we have included in this book portraits of them taken in captivity, for example of the Caracal.

Zeiss Contarex cameras with quick-change magazine backs were used for taking all the pictures. Black and white exposures were made on Kodak Panatomic X films wherever possible; but where rapid exposures had to be made of birds in flight, or when working at dusk, this film was replaced by Tri X. For colour, Kodachrome II was our favourite stock. When this had to be replaced with something faster to stop rapid movement we used High Speed Ektachrome. To indicate the variety of lenses, apertures and shutter speeds used, some examples of the technical details are given below:

Colour

Plate 5a Laggar Falcon. Kodachrome II: 300mm: Kilfitt lens: f/5.6: 1/500 second.

   5b Brahminy Kite. High Speed Ektachrome: 400mm: Novaflex lens: f/5.6: 1/500 second: taken from moving boat.

   8a Urial. High Speed Ektachrome: 1/1000mm: M.T.O. Mirror lens: f/10: 1/500 second: distance, quarter of a mile.

   8b Gayal. High Speed Ektachrome: 250mm: Olympia Sonnar lens: f/4: 1/1000 second.

   27b Shishak River. Kodachrome II: 50mm: Zeiss Planar lens: f/8: 1/125 second.

   53a Slow Loris. Kodachrome II: 125mm: Sonnar Lens: f/8: 1/250 second.

Black and White

Plate 2*b* Black Kite. Tri X: 400mm: Novaflex lens: f/5.6: 1/1000 second.

9*a* Sadiqgarh Palace. Panatomic X: 50mm: Zeiss Planar lens: f/11: 1/125 second.

12*a* Hedgehog. Panatomic X: 135mm: Sonnar lens: f/8: 1/125 second.

13*a* Goshawk. Panatomic X: 85mm: Sonnar lens: f/5.6: 1/125 second: captive bird used for falconry.

18 Vulture in flight. Tri X: 400mm: Novaflex lens: f/5.6: 1/1000 second: soaring over carcass of Buffalo.

29*a* Gecko. Panatomic X: 85mm: Sonnar Lens: f/8: taken with Ikotron electronic flash unit at five feet.

22*a* Spotted Owlets. Tri X: 1000mm: M.T.O. Mirror lens: f/10: 1/250 second: taken after sunset.

37*a* & *b* Curlews, and Dunlin and Terek Sandpiper in flight. Tri X: 500mm: M.T.O. Mirror lens: f/8: 1/1000 second: taken from moving boat.

47 White-bellied Sea Eagle. Tri X: 400mm: Novaflex lens: f/11: 1/1000 second.

Selected Bibliography

Ali, Salim (1941) *The Book of Indian Birds*: Bombay. A very good pocket guide to the more common species.

(1941) *The Birds of Bahawalpur*: Journ. Bombay Nat. Hist. Soc 42: 704–47.

(1949) *Indian Hill Birds*: Bombay. Valuable when visiting the Himalayas.

(1962) *Birds of Sikkim*: London.

Ayub Khan, President Mohammad (1967) *Friends Not Masters*. Lahore. A revealing and most instructive autobiography.

Baker, Stuart (1932–5) *The Nidification of Birds of the Indian Empire*: London.

Bates, R. S. P. & Lowther, E. H. N. (1952) *Breeding Birds of Kashmir*: London. Excellently illustrated.

Burton, Maurice (1962) *Systematic Dictionary of Mammals*: London.

Champion, H. (1938) *A Preliminary Survey of Forest Types in India and Burma*: Ind. For. Sec. (N.S.) 1.

Corbett, J. (1957) *Man-eaters of India*: London.

Delacour, Jean T. (1964) *The Pheasants of the World*: London.

Denis, Armand (1964) *Cats of the World*: London.

Ellerman, J. R. & Morrison-Scott, T. C. S. (1961) *Checklist of Palaearctic and Indian Mammals 1758 to 1946*: London.

Feldman, Herbert (1958) *Pakistan, Land and People*: London.

Finns, Frank (1929) *Sterndale's Mammalia of India*. London.

Gee, E. P. (1961) *Wildlife Sanctuaries of India*: New Delhi.

(1964) *The Wildlife of India*: London. Authoritative and beautifully illustrated.

Glenister, A. G. (1951) *The Birds of the Malay Peninsula, Singapore and Penang*: London.

Hollom, P. A. D. (1960) *The Popular Handbook of Rarer British Birds*: London. Includes many Asiatic species.

Khan, Tahawar Ali (1961) *The Maneaters of the Sunderbans*: Lahore.

Knight, E. F. (1919) *Where Three Empires Meet*: London. Early adventures in the Gilgit region.

Longstaff, Tom (1950) *This My Journey*: London. Life in Gilgit at the turn of the century.

Malayan Natural History Society (1968) *An Introduction to the Mammals of Singapore and Malaya*. Kuala Lumpur.

Merrill, E. D. (1954) *Plant Life of the Pacific World*: New York.

Morris, Desmond (1965) *The Mammals*: London. The best comprehensive work, well illustrated.

Mountfort, Guy (1958) *Portrait of a Wilderness*: London.
  (1962) *Portrait of a River*: London.
  (1965) *Portrait of a Desert*: London.
  (1967) *Saving the Wildlife of Pakistan*: Pakistan Quarterly 14 (4).
  (1968) *Pakistan Protects its Wildlife*: Geog. Mag. XI (15): 1255–67.

Peterson, R., Mountfort, G. & Hollom, P. A. D. (1967) *A Field Guide to the Birds of Britain and Europe*: London. Many European species occur in Pakistan.

Pope, C. H. (1963) *The Giant Snakes*: London.

Prater, S. H. (1965) *The Book of Indian Animals*: Bombay. Excellent descriptive text and pictures.

Quereshy, I. H. (1956) *The Pakistani Way of Life*: London.

Rashid, Haroun er (1967) *Systematic List of the Birds of East Pakistan*: Dacca. A useful, up-to-date checklist.

Richards, P. W. (1957) *Tropical Rain Forest*: Cambridge.

Ripley, S. Dillon (1961) *A Synopsis of the Birds of India and Pakistan*: Madras. The leading work on distribution and nomenclature. Essential for ornithologists.
  and the Editors of Life (1964). *The Land and Wild Life of Tropical Asia*: New York.

Schaller, George B. (1965) *My Year with the Tigers*: Life 58 (25): 60–66.
  (1967) *The Deer and the Tiger*: Chicago. A fascinating study, well illustrated.

Seshadri, B. (1968) *The Indian Tiger fights for Survival*: Animals 10 (9): 414–19.

Siddiqi, M. S. U. (1961) *Checklist of Mammals of Pakistan*: Biologia 7 (1 & 2): 93–225. Lahore.

Simon, Noel (1966) *Red Data Book, Vol. 1—Mammalia*. I.U.C.N. Survival Service Commission: Lausanne. Gives latest status of all endangered mammal species.

Smythies, B. E. (1953) *The Birds of Burma*: London.

Stamp, L. Dudley (1952) *Asia, a Regional and Economic Geography*: London.

Taber, Richard *et al* (1967) *Mammals of the Lyallpur Region, West Pakistan*: Lyallpur.

Vaurie, Charles (1959) *The Birds of the Palaearctic Fauna*: London.

Vincent, Jack (1966) *Red Data Book, Vol. 2—Aves*. I.U.C.N. Survival Service Commission: Lausanne. Gives latest status of all endangered bird species.

Waite, W. H. (1951) *The Birds of the Punjab Salt Range*. Journ. Bombay Nat. Hist. Soc. 48: 93–117.

Wheeler, Sir Mortimer (1950) *Five Thousand Years of Pakistan*: London.

Whistler, Hugh (1949) *A Popular Handbook of Indian Birds*: Edinburgh. Still a classic, though out of date.

Index

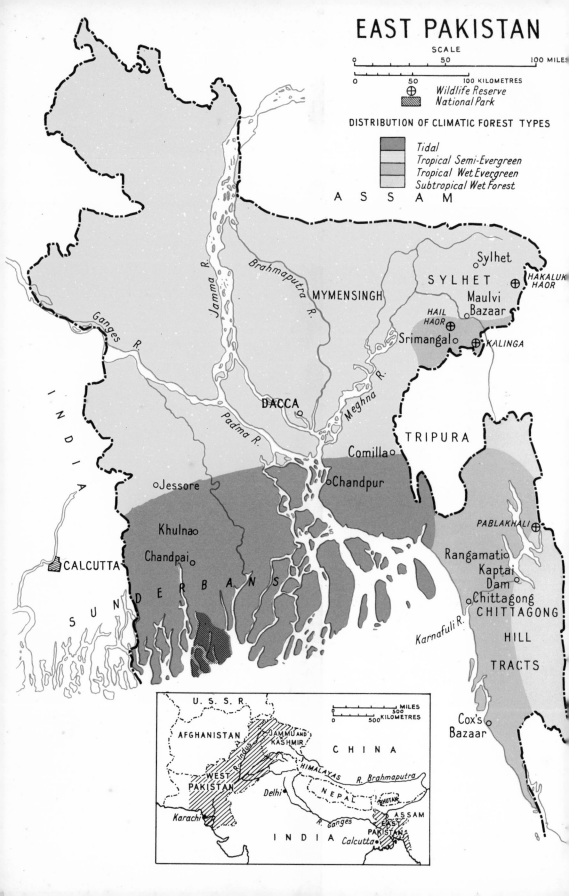

EAST PAKISTAN

SCALE

50   100 MILES

50   100 KILOMETRES

⊕ Wildlife Reserve
▨ National Park

DISTRIBUTION OF CLIMATIC FOREST TYPES

Tidal
Tropical Semi-Evergreen
Tropical Wet Evergreen
Subtropical Wet Forest

A S S A M

○ Sylhet

SYLHET   ⊕ HAKALUK
                      HAOR

Maulvi
Bazaar

HAIL   ⊕
HAOR
○ Srimangal   ⊕ ← KALINGA

MYMENSINGH

Brahmaputra R.

Jamma R.

Ganges R.

Meghna R.

DACCA ○

Padma R.

TRIPURA

Comilla ○

○ Jessore

○ Chandpur

Khulna ○

Chandpai ○

▨ CALCUTTA

S U N D E R B A N S

PABLAKHALI ⊕

Rangamati ○
Kaptai
Dam ○
Chittagong ○

CHITTAGONG

HILL

TRACTS

Karnafuli R.

Cox's
Bazaar ○

I
N
D
I
A

Inset map

U. S. S. R.

MILES
500
0   500 KILOMETRES

AFGHANISTAN

JAMMU AND
KASHMIR

C H I N A

R. Indus

WEST
PAKISTAN

HIMALAYAS

R. Brahmaputra

Delhi ○

NEPAL

BHUTAN

ASSAM

Karachi ○

R. Ganges

EAST
PAKISTAN

I N D I A   Calcutta ○